New Media and Politics

New Media and Politics

edited by

Barrie Axford and Richard Huggins

SAGE Publications
London • Thousand Oaks • New Delhi

First published 2001

SAGE Publications Ltd
6 Bonhill Street
London EC2A 4PU

SAGE Publications Inc
2455 Teller Road
Thousand Oaks, California 91320

SAGE Publications India Pvt Ltd
32, M-Block Market
Greater Kailash – I
New Delhi 110 048

British Library Cataloguing in Publication data

A catalogue record for this book is
available from the British Library

ISBN 0 7619 6199 2
ISBN 0 7619 6200 X (pbk)

Library of Congress catalog card number available

Typeset by Photoprint, Torquay, Devon
Printed and bound in Great Britain by Athenaeum Press,
Gateshead

Contents

Contents

Preface

This book takes as its central theme the putative transformation of some of the cardinal features of political modernity under the impact of new media and in the context of what some commentators choose to call media cultures. These features include received models of liberal democracy and of the public sphere, definitions of political space and identities and the nature of citizenship. The book also addresses the extent of change in the conduct of political leadership, in the routines of governance and in the functioning of political parties. It also takes up the vexed question of the role of the political audience in politics that are, as Manuel Castells says, increasingly 'framed by and in the idiom of electronically based media' (1996: 74).

A politics framed by media would have profound consequences for the characteristics, organization and goals of political processes, actors and institutions. However, none of the contributions to this book assume a neat and accomplished transformation of modern politics, even where they note significant changes wrought by innovations in media technologies and formats. Rather, there is a properly questioning stance on the idea of transformation and on the role of 'new' media in effecting change. In part this is due to the problems involved in pinning down the concept of 'new' media. As a rule of thumb, all forms of computer-mediated communications are included, but these technologies are often grafted on to older media formats (talk-shows, phone-ins) to produce hybrid forms. In addition, it is difficult, but also misguided, to assess the impact of new, or any media, in isolation from other variables. We may all live in thoroughly mediatized cultures, and this influences cultural production and identity formation. At the same time, it is impossible to understand the dynamic of media cultures without reference to consumerism and the now global culture of neo-liberalism. In turn, the creation of a truly global cultural economy is increasingly reliant upon the ubiquity of information and communications technologies.

Because of these complexities, there is a lot to be said for staying close to the manifold changes in political communications that have taken place in recent decades and which have, at the very least, contributed to a professionalization of political marketing, and transformed the conduct of leadership. Some chapters in this book adopt such an approach, while others are rather more exercised by the characteristics of mediatized cultures, where that refers to major shifts in cultural production, consumption and exchange. Mediatized cultures are characterized by promotional discourses, the aestheticization of social and political life and by the dominance of image. Engaging with such notions edges debate towards the idea of postmodern discourses and postmodern politics and some contributors do entertain this kind of shift.

But even if the thesis of transformation – postmodern or not – is accepted, interpretations of the process and of the outcomes often spring from strong and opposing normative positions. Such positions can be presented in simple, though compelling, pictures of a world on the brink of ruin, where politics is reduced to a media-brokered spectacle, or else conveniently summarized in compelling, but probably misleading, notions about the 'packaging' or 'Americanization' of politics and political discourses. On the other hand, the vision of cyber-enthusiasts may be equally blinkered, or as naive, replacing obsessive hand-wringing with reflex hand-clapping.

Although none of the contributions to this book fall into either of these categories, they show a properly critical and, where appropriate, a committed engagement with the issues. Detailed empirical observation is offered, along with critical judgements about the quality of the politics under construction. When we first conceived the idea for the book, we were anxious to extend the discussion beyond the usual critique of electoral communications and campaign politics that have both informed, but limited, the study of political communication over the years. In addition we looked to canvass informed and critical research and opinion across the discipline of political science and communications research. In both these aims we have been successful and the resulting contributions offer a wide-ranging, lively and diverse set of observations on the important and complex issues under discussion. As befits a theme of this sort, there is a good deal of productive synergy between chapters, since it is neither possible nor helpful to try to seal off areas of debate into discrete chapters. Themes like democracy, publicness and citizenship run through many of the chapters, even where the evidence used and the perspectives employed are different.

We have been fortunate enough to traffic some of the ideas in this book at various seminars and conferences in Europe and North America, as well as in the UK. Among these we should mention the IAMCR conference on 'Media and Politics' in Brussels in 1997, organized by Jan Servaes, the 'Images of Politics' conference in Amsterdam, in 1998 and the 'Regulating the Internet' conference in

Seattle, April 2000, organized by the University of Washington. In particular, we would like to express our thanks to Giorgio Sola and Agostino Massa at the University of Genoa for providing a congenial venue for various papers and for their wonderful hospitality.

Barrie Axford and Richard Huggins
Oxford

Contributors

Barrie Axford is Professor of Politics at Oxford Brookes University.

Stephen Coleman is Research Director of the Hansard Society for Parliamentary Government.

Peter Dahlgren is Professor of Communications at the University of Lund.

Ivan Horrocks is a Lecturer in the Scarman Centre for the Study of Public Order, University of Leicester.

Richard Huggins is Senior Lecturer in Politics at Oxford Brookes University.

Kathleen Hall Jamieson is Dean of the Annenberg School for Communication and Director of the Annenberg Public Policy Center of the University of Pennsylvania.

Sandra Moog is a PhD candidate in Sociology at the University of California, Berkeley.

Ken Newton is Professor of comparative politics at the University of Southampton and Executive Director of the European Consortium for Political Research.

Sinikka Sassi is Senior Lecturer in the Department of Communication at the University of Helsinki.

Jeff Sluyter-Beltrao is a PhD candidate in Political Science at the University of California, Berkeley.

John Street is Reader in the Department of Politics at the University of East Anglia.

Jennifer Stromer-Galley is Assistant Professor at the Annenberg School for Communication.

Dominic Wring is Lecturer in Communications at Loughborough University.

1   The Transformation of Politics or Anti-Politics?

Barrie Axford

Transforming politics?

At the start of a new millennium the language of transformation, sometimes glossed as crisis, is rife. Of course change – whether growth or entropy – comes with the territory, but periodically the spectre or promise of foundational shifts in the organizational principles and modalities of social life diverts us. So it is with politics, where visions of a world in flux or in the throes of epochal change appear in accounts that privilege the ideological completion of Westernized modernity (Fukuyama, 1992) and in those that traffic more visceral and morally taxing predictions about the global future (Barber, 1996; Beck, 2000; Gray, 1998; Virilio and Lotinger, 1997). Even in the rude domain of usual politics, the theme of transformation has achieved a kind of *faux* chic through the modernization rhetoric of the New Labour government in the UK, which recognizes, and is keen to embrace, the juggernauts of global and technological change (Giddens, 1998; Hay, 1999).

Thus, it is fashionable, if no longer prescient, to claim that modern politics in the West is being transformed. The usual suspects in this putative transformation include the faltering of the universalist project in an era of ontological uncertainties, globalization in various guises, the withering of social class and, most germane to this book, the framing qualities of the eponymous 'new' media. Framing, of which more later, allows actors to simplify their environments by 'encoding objects, situations, events, experiences and sequences of action' (Snow and Benford, 1992: 137). For Paul Virilio, machines, including the hardware and cultural software of media technologies, actually constitute our environments, while for Manuel Castells (1996) all politics now subsists within the frame of electronic media. These are robust claims, but the trouble is, that while the relationships between contributory forces is likely to be synergistic and any model of change multidimensional, too often there is an essentialist quality about explanatory accounts that privilege one domain over others.

However, there is no need to resort to a unidimensional, much less a determinist, position on the impact of new media, or anything else, on politics to support the claim that some of the key modalities of modern politics are being challenged, even superseded (Giddens, 1998; Krieger, 1999). These changes include an 'unbundling' (Ruggie, 1992) of the territorial basis of modern politics, the deconstruction of the institutional and ideological foundations of mass politics and the rise of a more fragmented 'modular' politics based on communal sentiments as well as less grounded identities. A crucial element in these seminal changes is the extent to which cultural factors and aesthetics have assumed a growing significance, not only in matters of political display, but as registers of power and interest. There is no neat 'logic' about any of this and ample room for retrenchment as well as for renewal. Whatever the outcome of the 'battle for the future', as Best and Kellner (1997: 1) have it, the contest is being fought out on different terrains – material, ideological, spatial, technological and, of course, cultural. It is appropriate to see in this contest the emergence of a postmodern politics that is nowhere complete, but which has already altered the 'onto-political' certainties that underlie modern politics (Connolly, 1992). It is also apparent that the evidence for such a claim is contested.

In a multidimensional account there is no room for technological determinism, in part because no technology impacts unmediated upon societies and cultures, and in part because there is no 'logic' or essence to particular technologies that can be abstracted from their use by actors. Changes in the temper of political life and in the conduct of politics are being effected through transformative practice, rather than simply imposed through the power of exogenous constraints – technological or otherwise – over action and identity. The idea of transformative practice qualifies any assumed 'logic' of new media, because while all politics now subsists within the space or frame of electronic media (Castells, 1996) this does not negate the claim that agents are active in the construction of their own worlds. These sentiments impart a rather optimistic gloss to the accusation that changes in media technologies and formats have led to a 'know-nothing populism' (Diamond and Silverman, 1995: 14) or are immanently 'anti-political', whether in a Baudrillardian sense, or through damage to the canons of the liberal-territorialist paradigm and the etiquette of democratic politics. For all that, in a book of this sort, a healthy pluralism must rule. Some other contributors to this volume are less convinced of the emergence of a new era in politics, while others are more agnostic, or less optimistic, about the framing role played by new media and their impact upon the character of political life.

The language of transformation clearly pervades much of the current analysis of the 'new' communications environment. As Jay Blumler has opined, almost everything to do with political communication is in flux today, from media technologies and strategies of persuasion, to owner-ship and the nature of the audience (1999: 241). For students of political communication in its widest sense, the intriguing question has always been how to unwrap the interaction between various media and the changing modalities of politics. Are communications media simply conduits for other social forces and trends, or do they possess a 'logic', a power, that is itself constitutive of thought, identity and action? Too often a number of key questions are elided. First, do changes *in* media technologies and formats imply or even precipitate the transformation *of* politics? As a corollary, are some zones or sites of political experience and action more sensitive and vulnerable to mediated communication than others? Second, in what ways do both old and new media enhance or negate the dynamic effects of other independent or intervening variables, and how do all these factors affect agency? Third, at what point in the construction of discourses on the media and politics does analysis tip over into normative engagement or mere polemic, and where, if at all, is this legitimate? Running through these issues is an intriguing double dialectic, comprising the ways in which new media can reshape older genres to create a different 'logic' of mediation (Bolter and Grusin, 1998) and the extent to which this logic of mediation re-shapes the fabric of politics.

Discourses of change

It is obvious that issues of this complexity will be subject to different social constructions and world-views. Frequently, discussions about the relationships between the 'new' media and politics display an Orwellian regard for the subtle distinctions of Newspeak. Phrases like 'media culture', 'promotional culture', 'commercial populism', 'techno-politics', 'postmodern politics' and, of course, the 'framing' of politics by media are either expressions of approbation or abuse, depending on the context in which they are used and the intellectual provenance or normative stance of the researcher. The room for labelling certain mediations – talk show radio, most forms of political advertising and the prime-ministerial Web site at No. 10 Downing Street come to mind – as 'anti-political', and therefore good or bad by definition, is perhaps too obvious to merit extended consideration. Of course, such labelling is itself a convenient way of making sense of the world, but the political world thus painted is made up of only black or white. Because of this, there is little room for any fluid or perspectival take on complex reality. The upshot is a significant failure of imagination, locking definitions of politics and descriptions of appropriate arenas for political discourse and action into a conceptual and a moralistic strait-jacket. None of this is surprising and it is seldom completely reprehensible, but it does show that, as fields of meaning, discourses provide quite different contexts for experience, thought and, in some cases, action.

I want to distinguish a number of discourses evident in the treatment of the new media and politics, while noting that they are far more nuanced than I am able to convey here. They differ broadly in terms of whether change is seen as transformative or not, or as having transformative potential, and in the normative judgements attached both to the process and to the outcomes of change. In turn, those who identify major political and social transformation sometimes differ on the causes and the direction of change. Among those who witness radical shifts in the modalities of politics, three broad positions can be discerned. The first, which I will simplify as *techno-progressive*, credits the new, and especially digital, media with a restructuration of political spaces and identities. Tim Luke opines that 'territorial matter . . . is being eclipsed by telemetrical data' (1998: 3), adding that 'in boosting human actions into the digital domain, new modes of identity and community, territory and sovereignty, culture and society are emerging' (1998: 4; see also O'Tuathail, 1998). Michael Shapiro (1995) cautions that the neo-Tocquevillian paradigm for acceptable definitions of political community and forms of civic association is being altered by the respatializing of interest and affect consequent upon the emergence of network spaces.

In both accounts, the charge carried by new forms of electronic mediation is to problematize what constitutes a political sphere or a cultural order and who are to be allotted roles as legitimate and competent actors within them (Axford, 2000). Such radicalism is the occasion for all sorts of excursions and alarums on the part of those exercised by the frailties of usual politics, but anxious about the direction of change. In a recent contribution, James Slevin (2000) addresses the vexed issue of the social effects of Internet technologies and offers a mite of comfort for those who see virtual worlds as destructive of civility and other qualities of community (In addition see Castells, 1996; Tarrow, 1996). His structurationist cast on mediated experience has Internet technology as the gateway to new forms of social intercourse, new patterns of interdependency and new opportunities for political renewal. The contrary case is put with equal or greater vigour.

As I have indicated, these, and others like them, are complex and multi-layered accounts of a contested political reality and of the consequences for experience that follow from particular forms of mediation. In its own way, each suggests that while the dominant liberal-territorialist model of politics and political community looks increasingly threadbare, there are major practical and conceptual difficulties with grafting new modalities on to the shards of an older paradigm. One of the many problems is that cyberspace and the recently modal culture of cyber-politics are considered by many to be liminal zones where only the counter-cultures of libertarianism and anarchism can flourish (Negroponte, 1996; Rheingold, 1994). Such a climate can be seen as hostile to the basic presuppositions of liberal democracy and the routines of democratic governance.

The second strand of transformationalist thinking evinces a generally negative critique of new media (the spread of which is often related to the commercialization of the world economy and the commodification of culture) and in some cases a vein of *retro-nostalgia* for an imagined political past. In referring to them as retro-nostalgic, I do not mean to dismiss thoughtful positions that identify the role of key global processes and new technologies in transforming political communications and how we define ourselves in relation to the world. However, for some observers, the transformation of politics through new media technologies and formats is treated uncontentiously as a form of 'democratic illness' (Balandier, 1992). The thrust of George Balandier's argument, and that of many others (see, for example, Franklin, 1994 and 1997), is that the 'logic' in, or the cynical misuse of, new media by politicians have suborned more authentic forms of politics and political discourse. The curiously retro quality of such positions derives from their tendency to impart iconic status to institutions and practices said to embody, or to have once embodied, the virtues of a relatively unmediated or more benignly mediated past. In this *gestalt*, the representative and educative functions of programmatic and mass political parties, the mythology of a deliberative politics effected through the 'macro' public sphere and the knock-about of the hustings and the pieties of public service broadcasting (PSB) have all become almost fashion items in the selective reinvention of democratic elitism as an ideal form of governance (Boggs and Dirmann 1999; Robins and Webster, 1999).

Apart from the nostalgic quality of these discourses, a sentiment hard to sustain when set against much of the historical record, another, more visceral, factor may be at work. It is what Arthur Koestler once referred to as 'Ahor' or the Ancient Horror experienced by the legislators, interlocutors, peer-reviewers and gatekeepers of good taste – indeed by most experts in classifying and mediating experience – when confronted by the uncontrollable, the populist and, as Tom Wolfe would say, the downright low rent (Wolfe, 1970). The fear of flying immanent in the possible removal of, or disillusion with, authoritative sources, is as obvious as the experience itself must be discommoding (Fiske, 1995).

In a recent piece on democracy and digital media, Ben Barber rehearses the familiar refrain that the logic of new digital media is to disadvantage thicker and more deliberative forms of discourse and civic association (1998). Because new media specialize in niche marketing and segmentation of the demos, they exacerbate wider social trends to anomie and isolation. Moreover, Barber says that unlike the more holistic 'old' media, segmented 'new' media lack public spaces at which we can all 'commune, grieve and celebrate' (1998: 7). Leaving aside for the moment the tricky question of intimacy and the fact that there are many kinds of discourse on the Web, it is hard to see when and where the model of a robust dialogical and deliberative politics has ever mapped neatly on to the terrain of usual politics. Both the theory and practice of democratic elitism look to amorphize identities and broker experience in pursuit of those biddable common denominators translatable into winning coalitions. As for the defence of 'old' media implied in the notion that national broadcasting (as opposed to 'new' forms of narrow-casting) subvents a healthy and inclusive public sphere, during the golden age of national broadcasting in the UK the model of British culture on offer was insular, elitist and insufferably smug.

Other visions of a dystopian future are available, couched at different levels of generality. Herb Schiller's sustained critique of global monoculture (1976, 1995) is perhaps the best known of those accounts that echo the cultural pessimism of the early Frankfurt School (see also Herman and McChesney, 1997). It trades heavily on the thesis that transnational media systems are the primary carriers of a commercialized – read Americanized – consumer culture. With varying degrees of material determinism, similar arguments endorse the thesis that homogenization of cultural experience proceeds through consumption (Howes, 1996; Ritzer, 1993; Ritzer and Liska, 1997). As Sandra Moog and Jeff Sluyter-Beltrao remind us in Chapter 2 of this book, changes in political communication across the world have to be seen within the larger context of global economic changes, namely the processes of liberalization and deregulation. But, as their detailed, comparative argument suggests, while it is necessary to acknowledge the apparent global 'logic' of commercialization, this logic is still context dependent, mediated by local traditions and susceptible to counter-cultural incursions. For some brands of cultural anthropologists and for most students of audience research (Friedman, 1994; Hannerz, 1996; Martin-Barbero, 1993), the notion that the global marketing and distribution of material and symbolic cultural goods may not produce cultural homogenization is a staple; for others, it remains exotic fare (Tomlinson, 1999).

The cultural convergence thesis relies on the pervasive power of market forces and the ideology of the market to effect what Schiller calls the 'corporate envelopment of public expression' (1989: 94). In like vein, Andrew Wernick (1991) argues that promotional texts, whether verbal, written or visual, are transforming both political communications and political culture, as the ideology of the market seeps in to every facet of social existence. Even the Internet, self-styled bastion of libertarian and anarchistic impulses, is susceptible to the power of commercialization (Sassen, 1999) through the global deregulation of provision and access and the rapid growth of e-commerce. In addition, older media genres, like talk radio, are re-branded to catch the demotic flavour of the times and have become vehicles for a commodified media–spectator relationship (Boggs, 1997; Munson, 1993), unless, perchance, they inhabit the pages of a Garrison Keillor story.

Much of this debate echoes previous incursions on the dangers to rationality and discursiveness carried through 'new' media genres, regardless of the technologies and media formats in question (Habermas, 1991). Jurgen Habermas, less infected with the *geistgesicht* of some of his Frankfurt mentors, is still deeply suspicious of technologies that, in his estimation, destroy communicative interaction and thus the discursive basis for an open and democratic society. His argument leaves very little room for the thesis that new forms of electronic communication and innovative uses of older media formats can provide new public spaces and new locations for civic discourse (Keane, 1995). In part, perhaps altogether, this debate is coloured by the tendency to uncouple and juxtapose the categories of informed citizen and avid consumer, and to treat audiences as mere consumers, victims of promotional culture. The considerable weight of evidence that now points to the interpretative capacity of diverse audiences and the savvy manner in which they attach meanings to, but also distance themselves from, promotional messages is often unremarked. Of course, conferring what amounts to a radical chic on the ability of audiences, including political audiences, to understand that the production of cultural norms may be for profit or political gain can still leave them without the means and perhaps the desire to affect the process. The danger of turning victims into heroes is well illustrated in Nancy Fraser's otherwise admirable take on the role of 'subaltern counter cultures' (1993: 124) as 'parallel discursive arenas where members of subordinated social groups invent and circulate counter-discourses, which in turn permit them to formulate oppositional interpretations of their identities, interests, and needs' (1993: 123). She argues that a growing number of competing publics can only improve the quality of democratic discourse, but all that it may achieve is to increase the number of players and to glamorize the status of victims.

When push comes to shove, it may be that ambivalence is the only emotionally and intellectually sustainable response when faced with the special pleading and closet elitism of some PSB modernists on the one hand, and the commercial populism of the multi-media conglomerates on the other. Best and Kellner (1997) offer a cautious endorsement of an 'affirmative' postmodern politics to combat both the essentialism of modernist narratives and the nihilism that lurks on the wilder shores of postmodernism. Their support for this notional 'third way' is tempered because the required synthesis of modern and postmodern, macro and micro perspectives and universality and particularity is a hard trick to conjure. At the moment the promise of e-politics, including new ways of structuring public talk through electronic media, for the most part is unrealized.

And if all politics now takes place within the space or frame of electronic media, can a politics thus configured supply sufficient resources and outlets for discursiveness, or, to paraphrase Hannah Arendt (1998), anything that even resembles public spaces of appearance, where speech and action are instantiated and narrative enacts a world that is made and remade reflexively? Even a committed transformationalist, such as Manuel Castells, is riven by doubts about the democratic propriety of informationalized politics (1996, 1997). If electronic media have become the privileged space of politics, in an era still attached to the forms and norms of the modern age there is bound to be dislocation, manipulation and possibly chaos. Castells notes the room for a regenerated and decentralized politics as well as the potential for electronic communication both to enhance political participation and confound the particular mobilization of bias implicit in all forms of brokered politics. At the same time, he says, because most forms of cultural reproduction are closely tied to the activities and styles of the powerful culture industries (Axford and Huggins, 1997) there is no doubt that politics will be conditioned by the demands of image making and breaking, of product placement, niche marketing and the routine use of negative research (Hall Jamieson, 1992).

On no less plangent a theme, Ulrich Beck sees the mass media as fundamental to the progress of a reflexive second modernity, where media act as the prime sites for the social definition of risk and thus contribute to the production and reproduction of attentive and active publics (1999, 2000). They also exacerbate the secular trend towards individualization, and on this Beck too is ambivalent. He rejects the notion that, as a result, society is losing its capacity for political action arising out of collective self-definitions, but is wary of the inescapable burden that personal autonomy places upon selves cut adrift from collective consciousness and collective security. This may be just designer anxiety, but a politics framed by media is often seen as both the leitmotif of reflexive modernization and as signifying or threatening the end of 'real' politics. Exciting pictures of Basque activists scaling the Millennium Dome in Greenwich, London may contribute to an 'innovative and variegated type of politics' (Falk, 1997: 18, 1999) but only because as a spectacle their antics are suitable for the sign-off slot at the end of prime-time news. Full of energy and eclat, this sort of media event may still constitute a withdrawal of energy from traditional domains of citizen action and produce no substantive gain for its perpetrators.

As a final, though hardly residual, category of discourse, it is relevant to mention those who are sceptical about the transformative power of new media. Sceptics are not exercised by the same intensity of vision that informs the views of the techno-progressives and the retro-nostalgics. Nor are they overly troubled by the world-historical weight attached to the notion of transformation. In fact sceptics tend to view new media as instrumentalities for the more-or-less efficient delivery of usual politics. Sceptics may cavil at changes they describe as being more-or-less desirable, but the key point for them is that 'new' media possess no independent logic, no immanent dynamic, that displaces established practice. Rather, while some limited process of change and adjustment may be taking place, the modalities remain pretty much intact, and in good time normal service may be resumed. Such caution is often welcome after the heat of commitment. Writing in this volume (Chapter 9), Dominic Wring and Ivan Horrocks offer the salutary message that, in the UK at any rate, the demeanour of the party system and the resilience of political parties as collective actors are affected only marginally by information and communications technologies (ICTs). On a related theme, Rachel Gibson and Steven Ward, perhaps unwittingly, underline the importance of agency when they cite evidence for the selective take-up of ICTs by political parties more concerned to improve internal communications than deliberation by the grass-roots (1999). And if I read Michael Schudson (1998) correctly, he too questions the idea that digital technologies can transform democracy, by breathing life into the ideal of the informed and active citizen, largely on the grounds that this model is only one of the strains of citizenship available to students of democracy and actual members of the polis. In Wring and Horrocks's account of wired political parties, the usefully sceptical thread that runs through the piece is the scurrilous idea that the impact of new media is less pronounced than much virtual hype contends because there is no such beast as 'new' media anyway, and therefore no disjunction between different forms of mediation, only a pragmatic accommodation to changing circumstances. In Chapter 7 of this book, Ken Newton carefully unravels the ways in which new and old media have affected key aspects of governance, including government secrecy, policy content and the role of parliament. He argues that new media systems have had a substantial impact on the structure of central government in Britain and that the impetus towards political marketing has produced a 'bland populism' that is not altogether unhealthy. Overall, it is wise to avoid sweeping generalizations about how new media have transformed government.

In the rest of this chapter I will examine the concept of 'new' media and suggest that, while there is no clear disjunction between 'old' and 'new' media, there are important features of new media that are contributing to the transformation of modern politics. Chief among these are the qualities of interactivity, immediacy and resistance to hierarchical mediation (Barber, 1998: 3), and the fact that the mediatization of political discourses is itself a part of the cultural shift in politics. I will then put the case for significant changes in the modalities of politics and political discourses before ending with some reflections on whether these changes can be read as a debilitating anti-politics.

What's new about new media?

Neophilia is not just excessive zeal for novelty but a reluctance to acknowledge that what is hailed as new is often just a variation on older forms and practices. Even where change promises to be disjunctive, the impact may be dissipated or redirected because actors are still wedded to older practices and the values that inform them. On the other hand, it is very easy to treat the relations between actors and cultural hardware and software as being technologically determined, and one need not be a diehard cyber-enthusiast to depict new digital technologies as catalysts for massive social change. On the borders of possibility, Web technologies could enable wholesale 'cybersecession' (Luke, 1998: 8) from the face-to-face trammels and joys of everyday life – in banks, in schools, in leisure pursuits, in shopping, in routine dealings with the state and in both casual and impassioned intimacy with each other.

Leaving aside for the moment the slew of concerns that attend such a vision, there remains the nagging doubt that we may well be overstating the impact of new media, or else overestimating how much of it is really new. New media often use 'old' technologies, and those who are

technological innovators are imbued with the values of previous generations. In other words, the unremitting presentism of new digital technologies always runs up against the ruttedness of pre-existing identities and
world-views. By the same token, succeeding generations are unlikely to
experience new technologies as in any way discommoding because they
are woven into the fabric of everyday living.

The information revolution has spawned a second and now a third
generation of media technologies of which the most potent to date is the
soft technology of the Internet. It is certainly appropriate to assess the
impact of network technologies as corrosive of structures and identities
'sustained by spatial containment, anchored by physical sites and repro-
duced by shared interactions in some particular built environment'
(Luke, 1998: 23). But the fact is that while the Net is already undergoing
significant changes through the spread of e-commerce and the promise
of convergence between old and new media, it is still primarily a text-
based medium. As such it remains very much a part of word-based
culture; but for how much longer?

Convergence between old media, telecomms and information technology sectors has become much less of a shibboleth since the mega-mergers
of Time–Warner and AOL, and Vodaphone and Mannesmann. These
mergers will turn the Net from a carrier of text, music and simple,
largely static, images into a medium dominated by the moving image, as
the giant multi-media companies shift content to the Net. If all this
sounds like an epitaph for text-based cultures and dialogical interaction,
we can draw little comfort from the knowledge that modernizing
processes involving changes in technology have always played a cardinal
role in the destruction of collective memories (Halbwachs, 1950; Virilio,
1991). At the same time, evidence cited by Richard Huggins in Chapter
6 of this book suggests that an altogether more nuanced reading of the
impact of fast media on consciousness is necessary. Far from losing
touch with spoken and written texts, the youthful political audience that
is the subject of his investigation are at home in both cultures. They even
expressed some nostalgia for forms of political communication – particularly advertising and news – that are text based and unencumbered
by images or the special talents of the creative director. As Huggins
notes, it is hard to tell if this betokens a preference for telling it like it is
through the use of plain English, or a vein of affectation on the part of a
constituency tied to literary culture only by the thin thread of tabloid
journalism.

John Thompson (1995) provides a useful way of categorizing different
forms of mediated communication and a means of distinguishing the
qualities of action and interaction created by different media genres. In

pristine form, dialogical communication requires face-to-face inter-action, and to that extent it is unmediated. In contemporary politics across much of the globe this mode of communication scarcely figures in the interaction between governors and governed. Mediated interaction, which is Thompson's second category, is a property of both old and new media. It involves the use of a mode of communication – a letter, a fax, the telegraph, the telephone and, of course, the computer – and an associated technical medium – paper, electrical cables, satellite technol-ogy, and so on – to enable communications between actors separated in space and time. All mediated communication is essentially dialogical. The third category, which Thompson calls 'quasi-mediated interaction', refers to the media of mass communication – newspapers, radio and television. This mode of communication is (or, rather, was) strictly monological and not, for the most part, directed at clearly identified others.

In each of these modes of communication the clear distinction between old and new media is often difficult to sustain, but each carries a pronounced normative burden. Unmediated communication or face-to-face communication has the ring of authenticity about it, reflecting a powerful mythology in which immediacy implies intimacy. While some elements of mediated interaction, such as letters, are deemed to promote both dialogue and intimacy, others, notably e-mail, are often treated as destructive of intimacy and community (Slevin, 2000). Yet the great selling point of computer-mediated communication (new media) lies precisely in its claim to erase signs of mediation by supplying immediacy, often by disguising the user interface in a 'fusion of art and technology' (Johnson, 1997). Through virtual reality, photo-realistic graphics and synthetic animation it can also conjure alternative realities, although these avatars are still rare in the political world. Such attributes attract praise and calumny in almost equal measure. But calumny also attaches to the ways in which the media of mass communication (old media) have been used (remediated) in the construction of a heavily marketed politics, reliant upon promotional texts of one sort of another and the slick management of visibility (Hall Jamieson, 1992; Scammell, 1999; Thompson, 1995). Here too the imbrication of old media technology and new media formats combine to subvent or subvert democracy, depending on where you stand (Davis and Owen, 1999).

What does all this suggest? First, that as Bolter and Grusin (1998) claim, 'remediation' – the process whereby new media refashion prior media forms – is a feature of all processes of mediation. Second, to adopt Foucault, that technologies and forms of mediation have 'no essence' or at most an 'essence that was fabricated in a piecemeal fashion from alien forms' and through practice (1977: 142). Such arguments qualify the temptation to turn the undoubted attributes of new (or any) media into an undiluted logic that simply spills over into the reform or transformation of political modalities. Third, the relationships between media technologies and politics are shaped not just by what is communicated, but how it is communicated, which, confusingly, throws the onus back upon the qualities of the medium and any implied logic it possesses. However – and here it gets complicated – the uses and perceived effects of both message and medium are also contingent on prevailing definitions of politics, the parameters within which any given politics functions and the perspectives and expectations of practitioners.

On this, Ben Barber is helpful (1998: 5–7). Writing about the relationships between digital technologies and democracy he notes that it is conventional to construe the latter in quite different ways: as indirect and 'thin', as direct and plebiscitary or as deliberative and 'thick'. Because of this it is of little use to applaud or decry the impact of new media *tout court*. Rather, we should acknowledge that while digital technologies may be suitable for enhancing democracy in one of its guises, they can be harmful for others. These distinctions could be taken as qualifying the claim (Davis and Owen, 1999; Graber, 1996) that new media are quantitatively and qualitatively different from old media. However, this would be too dismissive and insufficiently sensitive to those attributes of new technologies that have the potential to transform media practices and to contribute to a re-imagining and a restructuration of political modalities. But it is not enough just to intone the lexicon of technology change. Students of political communication must pay due attention to the contexts in which new technologies are applied, to the perspectives and resources of agents and, of course, to the different forms of both 'old' and 'new' media and how they remediate each other.

Let us return to the qualities of 'new' media, in order to explore their impact further. We can distinguish old from new media in a number of ways that I will call systemic, technological and aesthetic differences and – a loaded term – differences in 'logic'. Systemic differences refer to the different organizational principles of old and new media orders. The old media order was based primarily on national systems of broadcasting and national print mediums; a high incidence of state ownership, funding and regulation; the limited availability of broadcast spectrums; and the centrality of the public service ethos. By contrast, the new media order is distinguished by transnational and global communication and also by a good deal of local variation; by privatization and the deregulation of technical and legal barriers on ownership, content, programming and production; by spectrum abundance; and by commercialization of both mission and outputs. These are substantial differences. Yet remnants of the old media order have been remediated by the technologies of the new, to spawn, among other things, electronic newspapers and round-the-clock news programmes, and segments of the new media order still wish to clothe themselves in the legitimating guise of the public service ethic (Axford and Huggins, 1996).

At least some of these systemic changes have been driven by technological innovations, as well as by the deregulatory and border-destroying force of global neo-liberalism. As a result, the limited volume of broadcast space has been replaced by almost limitless availability, through the digital encoding of sound, text and images, the use of fibre optic lines, breakthroughs in switching technologies and a massive expansion in the availability of frequencies for transmission. In addition, satellite and cable technologies have made transnational broadcasting routine. Whether all this delivers a greater diversity of content and output, as opposed to an endless recycling of staple product packaged to fit market segments, is open to question. Of course, equally open to question is the whole idea of product being 'packaged' at all in what are by now thoroughly mediatized cultures.

Whatever doubts persist about the life-enhancing qualities of new technologies, there is no doubt that they have facilitated various new media of political communication. These include telephone polling and database marketing, direct-mail videos and electronic town meetings, as well as e-mail and Web-based bulletin boards and portals. These media have become the very stuff of political marketing in general and campaign politics in particular (O'Shaughnessy, 2000; Scammell, 1999). In this volume (Chapter 8), Jennifer Stromer-Galley and Kathleen Hall Jamieson visit the intriguing, but little canvassed, matter of the impact of new media on the style and functions of political leadership. They note that leaders are practised in the management of their own image and visibility and more able to set the national agenda than they once could. However, new communications technologies are having a pronounced effect on the very definition and conduct of leadership and on the experience of followers – *qua* supporters and citizens. Here too it may be hard to avoid the vagaries of Newspeak, since it is possible to interpret the predilection of some 'modernizing' leaders to speak directly to citizens over the heads of narrow interests, party ideologues and hacks as a hankering for a plebiscitary form of leadership, or as an experiment in new kinds of public talk and practical citizenship (Hall, 1998).

The aesthetic differences between old and new media reside in those qualities of the latter which promote immediacy and interactivity, greater scope for reflexivity and the dominance of images over text. Digitalized media are fast media. The concepts of e-democracy or government-on-line imply direct links between the man and woman in the cyber-café and the incumbent in the Oval Office or the Elysée Palace. On a less elevated plane they also suggest that municipal plans for pedestrian zones or the extension of CCTV surveillance become items in a continuing and transparent dialogue between governors and governed. Cutting out the middleman or the intermediary organization has considerable appeal and some obvious cost savings, whether buying a motor car or cutting straight to the chase when canvassing public officials. The truth is that such communications are seldom unmediated, even where they are fast. Electronic referendums are always mediated in some fashion, usually through assiduous agenda setting by interested parties and through framing of the questions used or the alternatives on offer. In talk-show radio, admittedly a new version of an old medium, the scope for mediation is vast, from the screening of the switchboard operators to the desire of the host to use the programme for self-presentation and to boost audience figures in a chosen market segment. Fast news, whether delivered by CNN, C-Span or BBC News 24, speeds up the news cycle and – on the face of it – makes attempts at news management less effective, but increases the element of hyper-reflexivity in the relationships between the story and any stakeholders in it, the broadcasters and the audience.

Of course, it could be argued that the opportunities for mediation, and thus for manipulation, are no more pronounced than under any other media regime. Which leaves the attribute of speed itself and its consequences for political life. For users of digital media, immediacy of interaction and response are seminal virtues. However, critics are often anxious about the 'reductive simplicity' (Barber, 1998: 7) of media whose primary attribute is speed. In large measure such concerns turn on what is seen as the unconscionable dumbing down of complex issues and the restrictions on proper deliberation that may follow from the application of digital technologies to the routines of democracy. Not all types of democracy of course, because Barber's strictures cast doubts only on the debased quality of the strong or deliberative variant, rather than the representative or plebiscitary models. In quotidian reality, the dominant liberal-democratic paradigm of representative democracy has seen both direct participatory and deliberative structures attached to it in an attempt to marry the goals of individuality and community, representation and harmony. Such *de facto* accommodations direct attention to the ways in which different forms of public talk are structured and to the functions – extant or implied – of various discursive procedures and devices. Such devices include the strategic monitoring of public opinion through the use of focus groups, the 'People's Panels' beloved of New Labour in the UK; plebiscitary mechanisms, which may or may not smack of a 'listening dictatorship'; and a raft of measures designed to promote open government (Axford and Huggins, 2000; Donovan, 1998; DETR, 1998).

Each of these instrumentalities makes routine use of new media technologies and forms, but they are conceived with different aims in mind and have unintended as well as intended consequences. For example, deliberative forums often run the danger of being exercises in group therapy unless they are tied to practical considerations and outputs. As exercises in communicative rationality they may be useful for promoting a rather abstract form of political competence. But the quality of participation they permit is a function of the degree to which they promote purposive rationality by getting citizens involved in the policy process on hard issues. In a democracy, the introduction of deliberative procedures 'from above' should always raise questions about the motivations of policy makers. Growing them 'from below' triggers the perennial issue of where and how such 'counterpublics' (Benhabib, 1996) can subsist in a political landscape often made up of insiders and outsiders. The health of a democratic system is often judged by how pluralistic it is and how open and agonistic are its politics. New media keep a rather greater distance from mainstream politicians and institutions than traditional media and this may be a signal democratic virtue to set against their failings. Even in the age of electronic news gathering and relentless exposure of private as well as public personas, many old media practices – 'sources close to the prime minister', unattributable briefings, lobby privileges, and so on – still abide, along with a tendency to narrow discussion of reported issues to the agenda set in Westminster and Whitehall, or the White House and Capitol Hill, where the arts of spin, of prebuttal and rebuttal are legion.

The interactive qualities of new media could well vitiate the conventional distinctions between insiders and outsiders, making them harder to justify and sustain, as well as supplying resources at relatively low cost to outsider groups. However, some cautionary studies on the continued use of gendered language in cyberspace and on the qualitative experiences of African-Americans on-line may well qualify the potential for informed and interactive participation through the Web (Herring, 1996; Lekhti, 2000). Inevitably, the evidence is partial and confusing. Data on the effectiveness of the Internet as a medium for political communication and interaction for African-Americans and other marginal groups is damning, largely because it tends to assess the impact of the Internet on 'traditional' forms of political activity, rather than as a gateway to new and unconventional forms of sociality and consciousness-raising.

The image of new media as being counter-cultural, populist and distanced from the political mainstream is not, or need not be, entirely romantic or dystopian. Yet a thorough assessment of its contribution to participatory opinion formation and civic competence (Slevin, 1999: 78) remains difficult because of the relative lack of evidence and the leap of imagination required to overcome modal definitions of politics and political discourse and the rules and resources that constrain inter-activity and the 'repertoires of possibility' available on the Net (Bordieu, 1993).

Admittedly these repertoires include the opportunities to practise rather voyeuristic and anodyne forms of sexual gratification by using Web-Cam, but they also admit the life-enhancing prospect of 'directing' the camera angles at a Six Nations rugby match or a European Champions League soccer final. Furthermore, unlike mass media, the Internet and some remediated 'old' media are dialogical. Internet technologies permit a range of one-to-one, but also many-to-many encounters, as sustained or as fleeting as cost, circumstance and preference allow. The fact that much of this intercourse takes place in private, as it were, with a modem and a screen mediating thoughts that are profound and trivial, for some, robs Net exchanges of their sensual qualities and moral weight. For the political realm, the message here is obvious. Politics is not and should not be a solitary activity, and virtual networks are not real communities, any more than electronic voting is an expression of a true *demos*. In Barber's terms, I suppose that networks are just 'thin' contexts for identity formation, allegiance and action, unless we are talking about the powerful instrumentalities of global companies, which, through strategic networking, show a single face to the world, or some diasporas and social movements whose identity and commitment transcend mere connection. In other words, the prospects are remote for a functioning civil society being constructed out of the many cases of diffusion, political exchange, gossip-swops, issue networks and wired movements that now populate cyberspace and occasionally infiltrate the worlds of usual politics.

Writing about different forms of transnational collective action, Sidney Tarrow (1996) worries lest the burgeoning amount of e-politics and discourse on the Net are proving so seductive because of their capacity to reduce transaction costs and afford an easy visibility that they blind participants and the rest of us to the real social costs incurred. These costs are that virtual networks cannot deliver the same 'crystallization of mutual trust and collective identity' (1996: 14) as the interpersonal ties and common ground evident in 'real world communities' (Barber, 1998: 9). Such anxieties add to the fund of contested observation and anecdote on the decline of civic association and the consequences of this trend for democracy (Norris, 1996; Putnam, 1995). Robert Putnam's strictures on the debilitating effects of media culture on civic engagement and the public sphere are among the best known of these accounts, although the bulk of his criticism is reserved for the culturally and morally enervating effects of commercialized television. Yet recent research in the UK (Norris *et al.*, 1999) suggests that we should be wary about claiming that media consumption has a debilitating effect upon levels of political knowledge and political participation. Regular attention to news media seems to mobilize some forms of civic engagement, like voting, rather than the opposite.

Being home alone with the Net attracts the same sort of criticism, primarily because the experience is seen as asocial, instrumental and narcissistic. And, in truth, the libertarian and individualist slant of much early cyber-ideology underwrites the suspicion that the Net is primarily a medium through which people construct and reconstruct their individuality, rather than a vehicle to foster civic association and communities of affect. Except that for many Netizens these are just what it affords. Virtual networks are not quite as ecumenical as they at first appear, because, mythology and rhetoric apart, they are seldom free of the problems that characterize phenomenal bodies – notably insider–outsider and powerful and powerless. At the same time, they enable diasporic public spheres (Appadurai, 1996); subvent ethnicity by e-mail (Rex, 1998: 83); sustain the activities of a tranche of INGOs (International Non-Governmental Organizations) and social movements – witness the J18 and Seattle demonstrations against the governance of the world economy – and provide a degree of information and support for a host of people ill served by the public services in the 'real' civic spaces where they live out their lives. In Chapter 4 of this book, Sinikka Sassi offers a glimpse into the regenerative impact of virtual networks, which have provided a forum for the discussion of community problems and, in some parts of the world, a model of governance untainted by ethnic divisions and particular histories. She also reminds us of the need to understand electronic media as part of the cultural shift in the tenor of life in posthistorical societies, echoing Castells's (1996) argument that electronic media now encompass all expressions of culture.

Yet the idea of virtual communities sits a mite uneasily with received models of 'thick' identity and cultures (Axford, 2000). Thick cultures are held to provide the basis for cohesive and stable communities; they are elemental and binding. If nothing else, this unease demonstrates the continued power of the territorial narrative and the appeal of 'real' places. So it requires a substantial leap of faith, or else a lot of evidence, to see the MUDs and bulletin boards of the Web as training grounds for new kinds of sociality and new normative structures, providing their own version of security in a fast world (Turkle, 1996). The emergence of thin networks and protean identities on the Net is bound to be dis-commoding for any politics configured by the notions of bounded space and ontological unity. But, as Ulf Hannerz says (1996: 98), 'what is personal, primary and has the feeling of intimacy is not always restricted in space'.

The contingent qualities of global risk society (Beck, 1999) certainly increase the scope for uncertainty and anomie, but also the prospects for greater reflexivity between actors and the conditions for action (Beck et al., 1994). How far evidence of greater reflexivity in the relationships between actors and action is available to corroborate Beck's ideas about a fructive 'sub-politics' at both national and transnational levels is moot. No doubt the potential for expanding the boundaries of the political and the room for individual emancipation and self-realization is tempered, and in some cases lost altogether, by inequalities or inefficiencies in access to technical resources and skills. Optimism is also qualified by the uncomfortable fact that the excess of contingency does not always produce benign and emancipatory politics, but an atavistic rant at the world as it has become. Even if the threat of techno-sophisticated racists and ethnic purists may still be something of a limiting case, 'techno-populism' (Lipow and Seyd, 1995) of the sort harnessed by Silvio Berlusconi and Pat Buchanan is now a feature of most election cam-paigns and involves a technically adroit exploitation of new and old media resources by more or less cynical politicians and their professional cohorts. In this version of media influence, reflexivity begets only hyper-reflexivity in a world synched into fast entertainment, fast food and fast politics.

For all that, the room for what Pierre Taguieff (1996) calls 'media-constructed saviours' to market an electronic plebiscitary enterprise successfully must turn on the extent to which citizens have been reduced to consumers – and pretty gullible ones at that – and politics consumed as a 'mere spectacle'. Which charge rehearses the complaint that new media have contributed to a trivialization of politics, even where they have not managed to undermine its foundational principles. The charge of trivializing political discourse laments the extent to which the aes-thetics of visual and commercial media – in the form of entertainment and production values – now invest most types of political communica-tion. Such claims are a convenient way of demonizing opponents. For example, shortly after the 1997 general election in the UK, the Con-servative opposition felt constrained to remind New Labour that a government is not an advertising agency. Rank hypocrisy aside, the remark touches a sensitive chord because of Labour's penchant for a bespoke politics in which image making and breaking, the strategic monitoring of public opinion, a nice line in political display and a *faux* populist disregard for the mediating institutions of party and parliament are key ingredients in its modernized politics.

One of the more trenchant and sustained criticisms of the qualities of new media is that they elevate images over text and thus privilege instant gratification above reflection, inviting viewers to apportion praise or blame as a function of the aesthetic appeal of the pictures on display. Digital technologies are held to enhance the prospects for some form of videocracy because of the ubiquity and quality of the images that they produce. In the pathological version of a digitalized politics anything is possible, even the virtual ideal candidate, morphed from the information stored in databases and tested before a battery of focus groups. Lara Croft is a sex goddess and there are virtual pop-stars; why not a digital political equivalent? Of course, producing the ideal, or at least sellable, policies on the same basis might prove a shade more difficult, as most current evidence shows. Much of the concern with the power of images is that as 'circulating fictions' they hide a more fundamental truth, or make interpretation of messy reality too simple by half. Despite the evidence from audience research, the citizen–consumer is often depicted as terminally vulnerable to these diversions, only too willing, or else unable, to resist the visual blandishments of product presentation or the beautiful–terrible lure in some 'killer' picture – of famine, of troops in the streets, of Diana's funeral, or the wife of a prime minister with a new baby. This is the debased image of the citizen in a mediatized politics. In Chapter 5 of this book, Stephen Coleman is also exercised by the debased quality of civility and of citizenship in many contemporary societies. However, he does not take refuge in nostalgia, but looks to new, digital media as the means whereby a more robust and practical citizenship can be built, not least because the relationships between representatives and citizens can be made more routine, transparent and accountable. He even suggests that digital media may constitute a 'Fifth Estate'.

Apart from addressing only one aspect of the impact of new media, the thesis that visual cultures and digital technologies greatly increase the chances of political manipulation and demagoguery, repeats a cardinal sin of retro-nostalgia and flirts with an ersatz determinism. The sin is to believe that advances in technology outstrip consciousness in such a way that individuals are left well nigh defenceless when faced with the 'giddy proliferation of communications' (Vattimo, 1988: 78). In large measure this seems to be a conceit of the chattering classes and of those – critics of talk-show populism are a case in point – who wish to disparage a whole medium because they object to the ideological tenor of particular manifestations. Short shrift is given to agency in this version, largely because agency is characterized as audience and audiences are either intellectually supine and or easily mobilized as bit players in spectacles contrived by commercial interests and fast media. Determinism is apparent in the willingness to impart an ineluctable logic to the impact of new media.

As to the latter, it is true that in all forms of mediated communication the means of communication shape the communication itself and the manner in which it is experienced. Television, as John Tomlinson says, is a highly mediated experience (1999: 155). Being a visual medium, it is technically determined of course, but also carries a complex set of semiotic codes, conventions, formats and production values with which viewers engage. Digitalized media, as we have seen, also possess certain attributes, chief among which are immediacy and individualization. But there is no single communicative logic at work here, and certainly not one that need produce atomized rootless selves rather than reflexive individuals, or which, *ipso facto*, is 'corrupting of democracy' (Barber, 1998: 15).

As part of Chapter 3 on changes to democracy, Peter Dahlgren offers a much more nuanced reading of the implied logic of new media. He argues – *pace* Castells and others – that new media are transforming politics because political life has become so extensively situated within the domain of media. In other words, politics is increasingly organized as a media phenomenon. It is possible to interpret this idea as meaning no more than that journalists, programmers, Internet Service Providers and politicians are engaged in a self-referential dance and that the public – various publics – are mere gazers at the spectacle. Of course, to some extent this is precisely the burden and the danger of a politics conducted in the frame of media, but Dahlgren offers a more challenging and, to some extent, daunting interpretation. His argument is that politics has embraced the logic of media and in the process transformed itself. This does not mean that all politics is constrained by media, or that a politics so configured is anodyne, morally weightless and devoid of the exercise of political agency, even where that has to be seen as the agency of diverse audiences. However, it does redress the view – equally without merit – that media practices are somehow just tacked on to the world of politics, their real function being only to represent an external reality. The idea of the logic of media is better understood in terms of the extent to which most forms of political expression are mediated by electronic communications. As Castells argues (1996: 374–5), the forces involved must be understood as cultural forces, because culture is made up of processes of communications and electronically based communications systems now encompass all expressions of culture. In other words, mediatized cultures provide some of the key conditions (note, only *some*) that are reconstituting political space, identities and imagined worlds. What sort of changes are in train?

What sort of transformation?

The mediatization of politics so described is part of what has become known as the cultural shift in politics and, more contentiously, a feature of the reworking of modern politics. In the concluding chapter to this book, John Street argues persuasively that politics should be understood as a form of popular culture, because politics communicates through the techniques and rhetorics of a variety of mass (and, it should be said, new and 'remediated') media forms. Politics seen as a form of 'artistic expression' appears novel, even quirky, but Street does not claim that what results is obviously a 'new' sort of politics, rather, that judgements about politics and political players are now aesthetic judgements. In itself the aestheticization of political judgement poses critical questions about the nature of and claims to political authenticity and credibility, and so speaks to a redefinition of political value. The recognition that such judgements now inform all politics does not rob it of ethical considerations, despite the tendency to invest talk-show democracy and designer election campaigns with varying degrees of censure.

Street stops short of labelling these changes postmodern, but media cultures (and the global cultures with which they are imbricated) reveal key elements of the postmodern. Chief among these are 'increased cultural fragmentation, changes in the experience of time and space and new modes of experience, subjectivity and culture' (Kellner, 1999: 2). Along with rapid changes in the organization of socio-economic systems due to the powerful ideologies and practices of neo-liberalism and post-Fordism, the application of new media technologies and formats affords a glimpse into a postmodern type of social formation and, arguably, a postmodern politics as well. As we have noted, it is possible to interpret these changes in radically different ways, but taken together they constitute a major assault on the ontological certainties of social, political and, of course, aesthetic modernity.

In politics, which is the main concern of this book, the potential for change is enormous, not to say epochal. Of course the realities are somewhat less dramatic and certainly messier, because everywhere post-modern characters still perform their roles in modernist plays. Let us briefly rehearse the script and some of the important changes to it. The aim of modern politics was to subject all forms of authority to the discipline of reason, by way of a public sphere that was inclusive and deliberative. The pursuit of universal goals, such as freedom, justice and equality were integral to the project. These philosophical and practical goals, that also served to free the individual actor from the trammels of the past, were given expression through a cluster of institutions and a body of philosophical thought. The institutions were industrialism, market capitalism and the paradigm political form of the territorial nation-state. The philosophical corpus celebrated the concept of social progress achieved through scientific rationality and driven by the capacities of the individual actor and his capacity for rational thought and action.

The Enlightenment creed so formulated remains at the core of the modernist project. In reality the history of modernity has been anything but a linear progress to societies based on rationality, self-development and individual autonomy. Liberal theories of government, based on individual rights and ideals promoting the consent of the governed, have had to come to terms with the phenomenon of mass politics, brokered by organized political parties and the mass media, and increasingly regulated by the bureaucratic and coercive structures of the nation-state. Interestingly, it is this latter version of political modernity that is said to be under most threat from the forces of globalization, mediatization and the fragmented identities of late or postmodernity. The historical account is also sullied by the frequent and bloody denial that individuals possess status and inalienable rights as a function of their very humanity.

Postmodernism evinces a philosophical critique of the foundationalist principles of Enlightenment (modernist) thought. As an aesthetic strategy it looks to relativize scientific discourse and the notion of whole identities, instead privileging the affective and existential qualities of life. As a condition, postmodernity also denotes an epochal cultural shift seen in many features of the external world, including the organization and conduct of politics. Modern politics is about the representation of fixed identities, primarily through mass political parties, forms of functional representation and parliamentary institutions. Governance takes place within bounded states and societies and only occasionally as a function of their interaction.

By contrast, a postmodern politics is much less centred, less easily contained and brokered. It is a micro-politics based on the cultural manufacture of identities – which themselves are no more than convenient summaries of difference – rather than a macro-politics based upon fixed identities having an ontological status because they reflect the social divisions that made the modern world. It is easy to see how a politics thus configured might cause unease. Pathological strains of identity politics or the politics of difference may result in a rabid

pluralism, discriminating of neither demand nor method. The legitimation of difference, while apparently liberating, may do nothing to
increase the actual power of marginal groups. It may also undermine the
very reflexivity that an excess of postmodern contingency is said to
promote, pushing whole categories of people downward into a rights-
sanctioned dependency or a mindless kicking against the pricks, rather
than upward into roles as competent self-analysts and social critics
(Axford, 1995). Postmodern politics is also much less constrained by the
legal and imagined boundaries of modern politics and manifestations of
this are not hard to find. They include expressions of lifestyle and
identity politics, social movements and groups that have politicized
issues left off the agenda by the scions of usual politics and all those sites
at which different forms of subjectivity and cultural reproduction have
intruded upon conventional political consciousness and action. Even in
the realm of usual politics, the framing of politics by media is modal,
evidence of the extent to which matters of culture and subjectivity have
altered the identity as well as the routines of institutions and actors like
political parties and parliaments. It is important that these latter changes
are read as more than the application of smart techniques and technologies to election campaigns or recruitment drives, as is the temptation in
some treatments of the differences between modern and postmodern
electioneering (see Scammell, 1999, for an extended discussion).

At this point it is worth recalling that modern and postmodern politics
are entwined, both part of a tortuous dialectic being played out in a
globalizing world. Appadurai's allusive discussion of various global
'scapes' (1990, 1996) captures the indeterminateness, the uncertainty
and the fragmentation of this hybrid politics. He argues that mediascapes are those aspects of cultural flow that produce and disseminate
information and value, providing 'image-centred, narrative-based strips
of reality from which imagined worlds are built' (Appadurai, 1990: 56).
In one guise, transnational mediascapes are clear intimations of a
borderless world and of a borderless politics conducted across it because
they enlarge the repertoire of opportunities for established players and
for marginal and other outsider groups. In another guise, they provide a
twist to the familiar politics of regulation, wherein national actors and
international regimes struggle to codify the technoscapes created by
global corporations and to police the wilder shores of political
activism.

Although the impact of postmodern politics is sometimes inchoate,
postmodern discourses are not easily accommodated by or assimilated
into existing paradigms of politics. To that extent, the overall temper of
the times is discommoding the *onto*-political certainties of modern
politics to effect a profound, though contested, reworking of political

reality. This reworking is apparent in a number of trends: (1) the deterritorialization of social relations and governance; (2) the decentralization and fragmentation of the nation-state; (3) the transnationalization of what was once called domestic politics; (4) the blurring of private and public domains of life; (5) the privatization of various functions of governance; (6) the significance of culture, subjectivity and identity in shaping meaning and definitions of interest; (7) the consequent proliferation of political identities and actors; and (8) the modal significance of information and communications technologies and media formats in the constitution of political life. (For an extended discussion of some of these features, see Kenis and Schneider, 1991.)

In the global system these changes are precipitating a new kind of transnational politics with a morphology built out of the growing density and reach of networks of actors and flows of information, images, capital, goods and services. In domestic politics (now something of an oxymoron) they are realizing a different modality, which can be understood as a form of postmodern populism (Axford and Huggins, 1997, 2000). This displays many of the features of a media-saturated politics, including promotional discourses, new and electronically mediated ways of structuring public opinion and a rich vein of political action 'from below'. Despite the provenance of the expression it does not – need not – imply that this is a politics devoid of agency or one in which various publics are rendered supine or have no discursive spaces in which to commune and deliberate.

Anti-politics?

All the indicators of transformation set out above are matters of practical and moral weight and some of them have world-historical significance. In different ways each is taken up in the chapters that follow, with the role of new media providing the cohering theme. Contributors take substantially different positions on the nature and direction of change and on its impact on the quality of political and especially democratic life. Each author recognizes that politics has become thoroughly mediatized and conducted in the space or frame of media. To that extent they endorse Manuel Castells's claim that mediatization has 'profound consequences for the characteristics, organization and even the goals of the political process' (1996: 476). Generally, contributors express ambivalence about the opportunities afforded by such developments and they are ambivalent too in their judgements on the propriety of some media-induced changes. Crucially, not one of them treats the changes as superficial or as in some way 'external' to a 'real' politics that can be resuscitated simply by breathing life into the discourses and routines of usual politics, or through being sufficiently strict about the commercial impulses of new, and not so new, media. At the same time, their critical insights usually stop short of either whole-hearted endorsement or ritual denunciation of the impacts of new media.

Of course, judgements about the anti-political flavour or logic of mediatized politics must, in part, abjure the weight of empirical evidence, since they cleave to normative prescriptions about the proper tenor and scope of politics and about its ends. At the same time, many of the issues raised in this book have been subject to only limited empirical investigation. Ten years on and students of political communication, smart technologies and democratic renewal will have a greater stock of more reliable data to assess – or just more ammunition to expend in the pursuit of knocking copy. To close on an Orwellian note: the concept of anti-politics invites reproof, reeking as it does of despondency, hopelessness and manipulation. On the other hand it may signify a break with past definitions of politics and the extent to which they legitimated only certain types of discourse and particular sorts of action. In this garb, instead of anti-politics, read new politics. These two possibilities express the threat and the promise of the new millennium.

References

Appadurai, A. (1990) 'Disjuncture and difference in the global cultural economy', in M. Featherstone (ed.), *Global Culture: Nationalism, Globalization and Modernity*. London: Sage.

Appadurai, A. (1996) *Modernity at Large: Cultural Dimensions of Globalization*. Minneapolis: University of Minnesota Press.

Arendt, H. (1998) *The Human Condition*. Chicago: Chicago University Press.

Axford, B. (1995) *The Global System: Economics, Politics and Culture*. Cambridge: Polity.

Axford, B. (2000) 'Enacting globalization: transnational networks and the deterritorialization of social relationships in the global system', *Protosociology: Towards a Sociology of Borderlines*, Special Project Issue: 115–43.

Axford, B. and Huggins, R. (1996) 'Media without boundaries: fear and loathing on the road to eurotrash or transformation in the European cultural economy?', *Innovation*, 9 (2): 175–84.

Axford, B. and Huggins, R. (1997) 'Anti-politics or the triumph of postmodern populism in promotional cultures?', *Javnost: The Public*, 4 (3): 5–27.

Axford, B. and Huggins, R. (2000) 'Public opinion and postmodern populism: a crisis of democracy or the transformation of democratic governance?', in S. Splichal (ed.), *Democracy and Public Opinion: Vox Populi – Vox Dei?*. Cresskill, NJ: Hampton Press. pp. 193–213.

Balandier, G. (1992) *Le Pouvoir Sur Scenes*. Paris: Balland.

Barber, B. (1996) *Jihad vs McWorld*. New York: Ballentine.

Barber, B. (1998) 'Democracy and digital media: which technology and which democracy?', presented at the conference on 'Media in Transition', MIT. http://media-transition.mit.edu/conferences/democracy/barber.html

Beck, U. (1999) *World Risk Society*. Cambridge: Polity.

Beck, U. (2000) *What is Globalization?* Cambridge: Polity.

Beck, U., Giddens, A. and Lash, S. (1994) *Reflexive Modernization: Politics, Tradition and Aesthetics in the Modern Social Order*. Cambridge: Polity.

Benhabib, S. (1996) *Democracy and Difference*. Princeton, NJ: Princeton University Press.

Best, S. and Kellner, D. (1997) *The Postmodern Turn*. New York: Guildford Press.

Blumler, J. (1999) 'Political communication systems all change: a response to Kees Brant', *European Journal of Communication*, 14 (2): 241–9.

Boggs, C. and Dirmann, T. (1999) 'The myth of electronic populism: talk radio and the decline of the public sphere', *Democracy and Nature*, 5 (1): 65–94.

Boggs, K. (1997) 'The great retreat: decline of the public sphere in late twentieth-century America', *Theory and Society*, 26 (2): 141–80.

Bolter, J. and Grusin, R. (1998) 'Remediation and the cultural politics of new media', unpublished.

Bordieu, P. (1993) *The Field of Cultural Production: Essays on Art and Literature*. Cambridge: Polity.

Castells, M. (1996) *The Rise of the Network Society*. Oxford: Blackwell.

Castells, M. (1997) *The Power of Identity*. Oxford: Blackwell.

Connolly, W. (1992) *Identity and Difference: Democratic Negotiations of Political Paradox*. Ithaca, NY: Cornell University Press.

DETR (1998) *Modernising Local Government: Local Democracy and Community Leadership*. London: DETR.

Davis, R. and Owen, D. (1999) *New Media and American Politics*. London: Routledge.

Diamond, E. and Silverman, R. (1995) *White House to Your House*. Cambridge, MA: MIT Press.

Donovan, M. (1998) 'Political leadership in Italy: towards a plebiscitary democracy?', *Modern Italy*, 3 (2): 281–93.

Falk, R. (1997) 'Resisting "globalization from above" through "globalization from below" ', *New Political Economy*, 2 (3): 17–24.

Falk, R. (1999) *Predatory Globalization: A Critique*. Cambridge: Polity.

Fiske, J. (1995) *Media Matters: Everyday Culture and Political Change*. Minneapolis: University of Minnesota Press.

Foucault, M. (1977) 'Language and counter-memory, practice', in D.F. Bouchard (ed.), *Selected Essays and Interviews*. Ithaca, NY: Cornell University Press.

Franklin, B. (1994) *Packaging Politics: Political Communications in Britain's Media Democracy*. London: Edward Arnold.

Franklin, B. (1997) *Newszak and News Media*. London: Arnold.

Fraser, N. (1987) 'Rethinking the public sphere: a contribution to the critique of actually existing democracy', in C. Calhoun (ed.), *Habermas and the Public Sphere* Cambridge, MA: MIT Press.

Friedman, J. (1994) *Cultural Identity and Global Processes*. London: Sage.

Fukuyama, F. (1992) *The End of History and the Last Man*. London: Hamish Hamilton.

Gibson, R. and Ward, S. (1999) 'Party democracy online: UK parties and new ICTs', *iCS*, 2 (3): 97–121.

Giddens, A. (1998) *The Third Way: The Renewal of Social Democracy*. Cambridge: Polity.

Graber, D. (1996) 'The new media and politics – what does the future hold?', *PS: Political Science & Politics*, 29 (1): 33–6.

Gray, J. (1998) 'Global utopias and clashing civilizations: misunderstanding the present', *International Affairs*, 74 (1): 149–64.

Habermas, J. (1991) *Structural Transformation of the Public Sphere: An Inquiry into a Category of Bourgeois Society*. Cambridge, MA: MIT Press.

Halbwachs, M. (1950) *The Collective Memory*. New York: Harper and Row.

Hall, S. (1998) 'Nowhere man', *Marxism Today*, 20 November: 3–8.

Hannerz, U. (1996) *Transnational Connections*. London: Routledge.

Hay, M. (1999) *The Political Economy of New Labour*. Manchester: Manchester University Press.

Herman, E.S. and McChesney, R.W. (1997) *The Global Media*. London: Cassell.

Herring, S. (1996) 'Gender democracy in computer-mediated communication', in R. Kling (ed.), *Computerization and Controversy: Value Conflicts and Social Choices*, 2nd edn. San Diego: Academic Press.

Howes, D. (ed.) (1996) *Cross-Cultural Consumption: Global Markets – Local Realities*. London: Routledge.

Jamieson, K. Hall (1992) *Dirty Politics: Deception, Distraction and Democracy*. Oxford: Oxford University Press.

Johnson, S. (1997) *Interface Culture: How New Technology Transforms How We Create and Communicate*. New York: HarperCollins.

Keane, J. (1995) 'A reply to Nicholas Garnham', *The Communications Review*, 1 (1): 27–31.

Kellner, D. (1999) *Postmodern Theory – Chapter 1: In Search of the Postmodern*. http://ccwf.utexas.edu/~kellner/pm/ch1.html

Kenis, P. and Schneider, V. (1991) 'Policy networks and policy analysis: scrutinizing a new analytical toolbox', in B. Marin and M. Mayntz (eds), *Policy Networks: Empirical Evidence and Theoretical Considerations*. Frankfurt: Campus Verlag. pp. 25–59.

Krieger, J. (1999) *British Politics in the Global Age: Can Social Democracy Survive?* Cambridge: Polity.

Lekhti, R. (1999) 'The politics of African-America online', unpublished. University of Warwick. pp. 1–25.

Lekhti, R. (2000) 'The politics of African-America online', *Democratization*, 7 (1). Special issue on the Internet, *Democracy and Democratization*, pp. 150–72.

Lipow, A. and Seyd, P. (1995) 'The politics of anti-partyism', *Parliamentary Affairs*, December: 273–84.

Luke, T. (1998) 'From nationality to nodality: how the politics of being digital transforms globalization', paper presented at the annual meeting of the American Political Science Association, San Francisco, 3–6 September.

Martin-Barbero, J. (1993) *Communication, Culture and Hegemony*. London: Sage.

Munson, W. (1993) *All Talk*. Philadelphia: Temple University Press.

Negroponte, N. (1996) *Being Digital*. London: Hodder and Stoughton.

Norris, P. (1996) 'Does television erode social capital?: a reply to Putnam', *PS: Political Science and Politics*, 24 (3): 474–80.

Norris, P., Curtice, J., Sanders, D., Scammell, M. and Semetko, H. (1999) *On Message: Communicating the Campaign*. London: Sage.

O'Shaughnessy, N. (ed.) (2000) *Readings in Political Marketing*. Westport, CT: Praeger.

O'Tuathail, G. (1998) *Re-Thinking Geopolitics*. London: Routledge.

Putnam, R. (1995) 'Bowling alone: America's declining social capital', *Journal of Democracy*, 6 (1): 65–78.

Rex, J. (1998) 'Transnational migrant communities and the modern nation-state', in R. Axtmann (ed.), *Globalization and Europe*. London: Pinter.

Rheingold, H. (1994) *The Virtual Community: Finding Connection in a Computerized World*. London: Verso.

Ritzer, G. (1993) *The McDonaldization of Society*. Newbury Park, CA: Pine Forge Press.

Ritzer, G. and Liska, A. (1997) ' "McDisneyization" and "Post-tourism" ', in C. Rojek and J. Urry (eds), *Touring Cultures: Transformations of Travel and Theory*. London: Routledge.

Robins, K. and Webster, F. (1999) *Times of the Technoculture*. London: Routledge.

Ruggie, J. (1992) 'Territoriality and beyond: problematizing modernity in international relations', *International Organization*, 47 (1): 149–74.

Sassen, S. (1999) 'Digital networks and power', in M. Featherstone and S. Lash (eds), *Spaces of Culture: City–Nation–World*. London: Sage. pp. 49–64.

Scammell, M. (1999) 'Political marketing: lessons for political science', *Political Studies*, 47 (4): 718–40.

Schiller, H. (1976) *Communication and Cultural Domination*. New York: International Arts and Sciences Press.

Schiller, H. (1989) *Culture, Inc.* Oxford: Oxford University Press.

Schiller, H. (1995) 'The global information highway: project for an ungovernable world', in J. Brook and I.A. Boal (eds), *Resisting the Virtual Life*. San Francisco: City Lights. pp. 17–33.

Schudson, M. (1998) 'Democracy and digital media: changing concepts of democracy', presented at the conference on 'Media in Transition', MIT. http://media-transition.mit.edu/conferences/democracy/schudson.html

Shapiro, M. (1995) *Bowling Blind: Post Liberal Civil Society and the Worlds of Neo-Tocquevillian Social Theory*. Baltimore: Johns Hopkins University Press.

Slevin, J. (2000) *The Internet and Society*. Cambridge: Polity.

Snow, D. and Benford, R. (1992) 'Master frames and cycles of protest', in J. Morris and E. Mueller (eds), *Frontiers in Social Movement Theory*. London: Yale University Press. pp. 136–52.

Taguieff, P.A. (1996) 'Political science confronts populism: from a conceptual mirage to a real problem', *Telos*, March: 9–45.

Tarrow, S. (1996) 'Fishnets, Internets and catnets: globalization and transnational collective action', Estudios Working Paper 1996/78, pp. 1–32.

Thompson, J. (1995) *The Media and Modernity*. Cambridge: Polity.

Tomlinson, J. (1999) *Globalization and Culture*. Cambridge: Polity.

Turkle, S. (1996) 'Virtuality and its discontents: searching for community in cyberspace', *American Prospect*, 24: 51–67.

Vattimo, G. (1988) *The End of Modernity*. Cambridge: Polity.

Virilio, P. (1991) *Lost Dimension*. New York: Semiotexte.

Virilio, P. and Lotinger, S. (1997) *Pure War*, trans. Brian O'Keefe. New York: Semiotexte.

Wernick, A. (1991) *Promotional Culture*. London: Sage.

Wolfe, T. (1970) *The Electric Kool-Aid Acid Test*. London: Fontana.

2 The Transformation of Political Communication?

Sandra Moog and Jeffrey Sluyter-Beltrao

Introduction: the question of communicative transformation revisited

From the core countries of the global economy to the emerging democracies of the former 'second' and 'third' worlds, from the top ranks of government and business to the grassroots networks of civil society, political communication is being transformed by global processes of liberalization and deregulation and by the diffusion of new media technologies. Intensifying and unleashing forces of media commercialization and conglomeration, these processes are giving rise to a series of general tendencies at the level of national politics – altering the ways in which social actors and issues are represented in the mass media, the ways in which political actors attempt to communicate with one another as well as with potential supporters, and, as a result, the very forms of those organizations, such as political parties, interest groups and social movements, which have long shaped modern political processes. In country after country, as competing national broadcasters merge information and entertainment formats in pursuit of ever more elusive audience shares, they are increasingly subordinating political coverage to the imperatives of speed and spectacle, heightening the projection of personality and image over issue and idea. In their attempts to adapt to this media climate, individual as well as collective actors are coming to rely on professional image-management techniques and apparatuses, as political negotiation, competition and appeal – even within government, party or movement organizations – become increasingly 'mediatized'.

Critical observers of national politics in regions as diverse as North and South America, Eastern and Western Europe, East Asia and the Middle East have been voicing concerns about these tendencies. Many journalists, politicians and academics worry that the transformation of political communication is bringing about not only a deterioration in the quality of public discourse, but also rising levels of public cynicism and the erosion of civic participation. Of course, alarmist outcry about the transformation of the media and its implications for the quality of public communication is hardly unprecedented. Concerns about the commercialization of the media can be traced at least as far back as the development of the first advertising-supported mass circulation dailies in the early 1800s. And the diffusion of each new media technology has inspired its own generation of social critics, worried about the effects of these new technologies on community, culture and public discourse. Indeed, one might argue that the transformations we are witnessing in this age of new media are themselves nothing new, but simply represent the continuation of commercialization processes and the maturation of political marketing techniques that have been unfolding throughout the last two centuries. Andrew Wernick, for example, argues that the 'promotionalism' so prominent in contemporary political communication, though it has been developing at an accelerated pace in the last few decades, is essentially little more than the natural evolution of competitive processes inherent in mass electoral democracy. After all, Wernick points out, electoral politics is essentially a 'system of competitive exchange', a periodically erected market for votes. Thus, 'the changes of the past thirty years, and the longer arc of change to which they belong,' he claims, 'have themselves only expanded, rationalized, institutionalized and made more fully self-conscious a characteristic of the electoral process which has always been intrinsic to it' (Wernick, 1991: 143).

Nevertheless, as Wernick himself recognizes, the developments in political communication witnessed in the last few decades have been profoundly transformative, constituting a 'qualitative shift' in contemporary political culture (Wernick, 1991: 134). At a very rapid pace, the institutions and norms of discourse characteristic of political 'high modernity' are being transformed, and this transformation seems to be leaving many disenchanted with, if not alienated from, national political processes. In both long-consolidated and newly established democracies around the world, surveys report increasing frustration with politicians, institutions of government and with the mass media as well. Though it may well be that in their capacity as consumers individuals are driving the current trends in political communication, this does not necessarily mean that in their capacity as citizens they will come to accept these new political modalities as legitimate. As Habermas reminds us in *The Structural Transformation of the Public Sphere*, the seminal figures of the liberal democratic tradition, from Rousseau and Burke to Tocqueville and Mill, shared the conviction that the long-term legitimacy and stability of representative government would depend upon the capacity of an active and informed citizenry to sustain open, rational deliberation about crucial issues of their day. These expectations have formed the cornerstone, not only of more theoretical formulations about the legitimacy of representative government, but also of popular ideals about democracy. How citizens and democratic institutions will ultimately adjust to the current transformations in the realm of political communication remains an open and critical question as we begin the new century.

Global restructuring processes and their implications for democratic politics

The recent evolution of political communication should first be understood within the larger context of global economic change. Critical here is the decline of long stable state-centric growth models – of the Keynesian compromise in the first world, state planning in the second and variations of developmentalism in the third. With world-wide economic stagnation in the 1970s contributing to the welfare state's increasingly acute fiscal imbalances over the course of that decade and the next, post-war economic models eventually gave way to a set of reinvented *laissez-faire* commitments, such as trade liberalization, deregulation and the privatization of state-run firms and services. The unprecedented sweep and rigour of free market ideas at an international level quite dramatically restricted the range of viable economic policy options available to national leaders. Political actors in fiscally beleaguered states, some under pressure from the IMF or new multilateral trade agreements such as those of GATT and the EU, increasingly implemented policies in accordance with *laissez-faire* principles. This provided expanding political bases for those leaders and entrepreneurs who insisted upon the necessity of opening up the telecommunications and broadcasting industries to increased privatization and competition, in order to invigorate the cutting-edge information-based enterprises presumed to lie at the heart of the 'post-industrial' economy. With their wealth and international reach growing, new media conglomerates became both more powerful advocates of neo-liberal ideas and less circumspect challengers to the status quo. Meanwhile, defenders of long-standing state prerogatives over the electronic media – which had treated broadcasting as a cultural collective good legitimately supervised and regulated, if not also directly managed, by the people's representatives – were placed on the defensive. By the mid-1980s governments were beginning to fundamentally alter the terrain of national communications policy. Though the rhythm, degree and precise nature of these processes of deregulation and commercialization varied, by the mid-1990s the general trend everywhere involved a recasting of the communications sector ever more as a private market, ever less as a public service domain.

Concurrent with this shift in national and international thinking about the optimal balance between states and markets, the development of new media technologies has also been working to undermine the regulated and controlled broadcasting systems established in many countries during the post-war period. The spread of cable television in the 1980s undermined the legal rationale for much of the post-war regulation of broadcasting – especially that justifying the public service commitments of the American and Western European broadcasting systems. It had been argued that, due to a limited number of available channels, governments had a right to treat the airwaves as a public good, and therefore to hold broadcasters to certain standards regarding the quality and variety of public service and political programming. But the possibility of a multitude of new channels eroded the legal foundations of such regulation. The diffusion of new modes of satellite transmission only compounded the challenge, as even countries whose constitutions and regulatory laws included other justifications for various systems of state control or regulation of broadcasting found it harder and harder to police the borders of their national electronic public spheres.

These two global processes, then – the diffusion of the neo-liberal paradigm and the wave of new media technologies – have precipitated a transformation of national communications systems in nation after nation around the world. Private, commercial television has now appeared in national broadcasting configurations formerly subordinated to strict regulation and managed by the state, by political parties, or by public service organizations. Remaining state or public channels have been increasingly subjected to market pressures, forced to depend more and more on advertising revenues as licensing fees and other state subsidies have dwindled, their programming evaluated increasingly in terms of audience share rather than by traditional measures of quality. In addition, long-standing regulations meant to assure that television would both serve an educational role for citizens and provide a level playing field for political actors have begun to be dismantled in many nations.

This transformation of national broadcasting systems has had profound implications for the form and content of political communication in many countries. As their broadcasting systems approach more fully commercialized configurations – in terms of ownership structure, sources of financing and rules and norms for programming content – this has begun to transform the ways in which political topics are presented to audiences in news and information broadcasts, as well as the ways in which politicians attempt to present themselves to their citizen-audiences. While the increasingly liberalized and intensely competitive global economy places severe limitations on the range of policy options that are open to states, effacing many of the significant differences between the traditional Left and Right in terms of their concrete political offerings, parties have been losing much of the centrality they long enjoyed as organizers of political life. And as parties have weakened in many nations, losing the commitment of their traditional social bases of support, many of whom join the growing ranks of independent, floating voters, politicians have become more and more reliant on the media as a central arena for political communication with the citizenry. At the same time, within the mass media, television has come to play a central role, quickly replacing both radio and the written press as the leading source of entertainment and information for the majority of people in both the most advanced and the emerging nations. Politicians have come to realize that if they want to reach the citizenry, they must do so primarily through television. As Manuel Castells points out, in contemporary democracies, the electronic media have become the 'privileged space of politics' (1997: 311). And within that space, television reigns supreme.

However, as political actors are becoming more and more dependent on television as a means of communication, national broadcasting systems are being transformed by the expansion of commercial television. As a result, political coverage increasingly is coming to be dominated by what we will call 'commercial media logic'. As Altheide and Snow suggest in their 1979 work on television coverage of politics in the USA, television, by its very nature, lends itself to certain forms of presentation over others, imposing on communication its own form of 'media logic'. As a visual medium, it is more effective when words are accompanied and illustrated by pictures. And it is most effective when those pictures are moving ones – when they capture the audience's attention through drama, symbolic effect, or emotional appeal. Thus, the mere fact that television has come to be the central medium for communication in so many polities might be expected to favour a shift to more symbolic and image-oriented politics, towards more sensationalism and towards the personalization of politics in the figures of celebrity leaders. After all, neither parties and other complex government institutions, nor the details of policy initiatives lend themselves easily to vivid visual portrayal. However, while it may be true that there is something about the visual emphasis of television that lends it a particular 'media logic', for decades states and parties used television to great effect, while yielding relatively little to any such inherent logic of the medium. Politicians were able to dominate the airwaves with long broadcasts of 'talking heads', often those of not particularly telegenic leaders, by limiting commercial competition through state monopolies and other forms of regulation. Indeed, it is only in the context of intense competition for audience share by a number of different channels with discretionary freedom over content and format that the inherent logic of the medium can flourish, eventually coming to dominate coverage.

Today, however, in this era of media deregulation and privatization, a common 'commercial media logic' does indeed seem to be flourishing in nations all over the world – a set of general tendencies in terms of political and media actors' modes of communication and interaction is coming to dominate political communication in similar ways in a variety of countries. Discussions of politics in news shows and other political programming are dedicating less and less attention to the unmediated presentation of politicians' speeches and statements. As television journalists concerned with maximizing audience share become more savvy about the use of moving images, dramatizing political coverage in order to maximize the visual and emotional appeal of programming, television coverage comes to present new challenges for public figures attempting to promote their agendas. Political actors, in turn, are learning to tailor their communicative efforts according to the dictates of this new commercial media logic. They are learning to supply the kinds of issues and images that will assure them airtime, and to shrink their statements into smaller, soundbite-ready morsels. In their efforts, they are coming to rely more and more upon the guidance of professional strategists and promoters from the ranks of the advertising and public relations professions.

These dynamics, which are developing in many different national contexts around the world, are serving to transform not only the ways in which political actors communicate with the public, but also the ways in which they compete and negotiate with one another, the kinds of policies they are willing and able to pursue and, as a result, even the forms of organizations which structure the political arena.

In the discussion that follows, we examine this transformation of political communication from a global and comparative perspective. We begin with the American case because the USA, a nation which has in many ways gone the furthest towards completely deregulating national broadcasting, has been at the forefront of innovation in new media technologies and formats and in new modes of political presentation. As a result, the USA has often been taken as an archetype: actors in a number of other countries around the world have responded to political developments in the USA, reacting either positively, by adopting new communication strategies first developed there, or negatively, by attempting to avoid the threats posed by the 'Americanization' of their media and political systems. It is also the case that in multilateral negotiations the USA has been the principal advocate of liberalization and deregulation, especially of the telecommunications and culture industries. However, it is important to avoid a facile understanding of this world-wide transformation of political communication as merely a process of 'Americanization'. The trends we are witnessing in countries all over the globe are not due simply to the diffusion of modes of communication first developed in the USA. Indeed, from an inter-national perspective, what demands theoretical emphasis is that these tendencies are rooted in global economic and technological dynamics.

In fact, as we illustrate in the following section, the transformation of political communication in the USA has been propelled by the same fundamental processes that are affecting other countries around the world. This comparative theoretical orientation is essential, as it allows us to account for the evidence that some of the tendencies associated with commercial media logic appear earlier or more prominently in other latitudes: countries as diverse as Australia, Brazil and Hong Kong are also major exporters of new formats and new techniques of communication and some of these trends may, ultimately, be more fully realized in nations other than the USA.

Thus our intent in the following section is two-fold. Through our examination of developments in the USA, we wish to illustrate in some detail the dynamics which we posit are coming to characterize political communication in democracies throughout the world, by looking at a case in which these tendencies are highly developed and have been carefully researched. At the same time, however, our intent is to illustrate that these dynamics do not simply constitute an essential element of the American broadcasting or political system. We argue instead that the driving forces behind these developments in the USA over the last few decades have been the same processes of liberalization, deregulation and the diffusion of media technologies that are at work in nations around the world.

Centre stage: the transformation of American political communication

The beginning of the age of television dominance in American politics is generally considered to be 1960, the year in which a telegenic John F.

Kennedy wowed the majority of the public in the first nationally televised presidential debate, despite the fact that radio listeners judged Nixon to have bested Kennedy with his arguments. From that moment onward, it was clear that television represented a powerful new medium, whose visual logic would become ever more dominant in the coming years. In fact, over the last four decades, the rise of television has had a profound effect on American politics as communication in the public sphere has become increasingly dominated by commercial media logic. A number of features of the American electoral and broadcasting systems conspired to make the USA an ideal environment for the early development of these dynamics. Most obviously, since the very first days of radio and television, the USA has fostered the establishment of a fairly competitive commercial broadcasting system. Equally important, however, were reforms to the electoral system carried out in the late 1960s and early 1970s; these significantly weakened the political parties as primary channels for communication, leaving the mass media as a central arena for political communication. In this environment, commercial media logic gained an early foothold on the American political scene. As we argue below, these tendencies were initially restrained by a strong public service commitment in American broadcasting, which, by the 1970s, had become consolidated in a variety of journalistic norms and broadcasting regulations. This commitment has been undermined, however, in the more intensely competitive broadcasting environment of the 1980s and 1990s. Public discussion of complex social issues and policy issues has become ever more difficult, as the public sphere becomes increasingly dominated by fast-paced, image-oriented and 'hyper-reflexive' promotional politics.

Over the course of the last four decades, television has become a dominant arena for political communication in the USA. With the population increasingly reliant on television as their primary source of news and information (in 1992, 58 per cent of Americans reported it to be their only source of news), television was bound to gain in importance as an agenda-setter for the mass media in general and as a prime target for politicians attempting to communicate with potential supporters (Ansolabehere *et al.*, 1993). The dominance of the electronic mass media was significantly enhanced, however, by a number of political developments in the late 1960s and early 1970s. The political crises surrounding the USA's role in the Vietnam War, the 1968 Democratic National Convention and the Watergate scandal (all heavily televised events) consolidated public opinion and political will in favour of decreasing the power of the political parties, through reforms of the candidate nomination procedures and of campaign finance laws (Polsby, 1983: 16–39). Undermining the capacity of the parties to maintain discipline and provide financial support for candidates, these reforms served, to a significant extent, to cut politicians loose from the parties, forcing them to make more individualized campaign appeals and to develop their own funding operations. As a result, individual office-seekers came to rely heavily on the media, especially television, in their attempts to win financial support and votes (Moog, 1997).

As American politicians began to orient more of their energy towards television, they adopted new communicative strategies. Since politicians in the USA, unlike those in a number of other political systems, had no direct access to the airwaves, they had to find ways to attract the attention of commercially oriented news broadcasts, dominated by the kind of relatively fast-paced fare which provides a suitable setting for frequent commercial breaks. In their efforts to elicit coverage and to harness the visual and emotional power of the medium, politicians increasingly turned to the services of professional pollsters and public relations consultants to help them simplify their messages and to drama-tize their actions. By the late 1970s and early 1980s, new forms of television- and marketing-driven communication were already becoming well entrenched in the USA: pollsters had become key strategists in electoral campaigns and publicity experts were becoming important advisors to politicians once in office, carefully planning their public appearances to control the 'photo-op' images and 'soundbite' phrases available for broadcast.

Reporters, in turn, began to dedicate ever greater attention to the deconstruction of politicians' marketing ploys. As political coverage increasingly focused on the discussion of politicians' image management and media strategies, however, less airtime was dedicated to extended presentation and discussion of policy issues. A vicious cycle has thereby been set in play: as soundbite lengths shrink, politicians re-double their 'spin control' efforts in order to break into the news and get their messages across, but as politicians dedicate more time and resources to this struggle, the real story about American politics is increasingly the story of these very efforts. As a result of these developments, political communication has become increasingly 'hyper-reflexive': political cov-erage has come to focus more and more exclusively on the publicity game as it is played out within the arena of the media itself, while attention to issues and government processes which transpire primarily outside the purview of the electronic public eye fade from view (Moog, 1997: 48–9). This hyper-reflexivity has not only affected the quality of public discourse. As political actors become more focused on the demands of daily public relations battles, this has begun to affect the ways in which they communicate with one another within the executive, within Congress and within the parties, the speed with which they make decisions about matters of public importance and, to a certain extent, even the kinds of policy options they are able and willing to pursue (see Fallows, 1996: 185; Kurtz, 1998; Lieberman, 1994).

During the 1960s and 1970s, these dynamics were held somewhat in check by the commitment to public service journalism which had been established in US broadcasting during the post-war period. By the middle of the century, American broadcast journalism was generally held accountable to what Baker and Dessart (1998: 134) call a trustee-ship model of public obligation, in which 'the owner, in exchange for the use of the public's airwaves, serves as the guardian of the public's interest'. After 1949, the public service commitment of broadcasters was legally established in an amendment to the Federal Communications Act, known as the Fairness Doctrine, which required that broadcasters (1) develop programming that dealt with controversial matters of public importance, and (2) assure balance of views in their presentation of controversial topics. Perhaps more significantly, however (especially given the lack of real regulatory power on the part of the FCC [Federal Communications Commission]), this public service commitment was incorporated into the professional self-understanding of journalists and media owners. A period of unusual post-war political consensus pro-vided an environment conducive to journalists' and media owners' beliefs in the possibility of an objective expertise above politics, despite their close collaboration with the political establishment (Hallin, 1996: 249–51). This supported the development, throughout the 1960s and 1970s, of news programmes which dedicated tremendous resources to the coverage of national politics, despite the fact that the sponsoring networks thereby incurred millions of dollars in losses.

This public service orientation of American broadcast journalism, however, fell prey to increasingly intense commercial pressures during the course of the 1980s. First, the rise of cable television in the late 1970s and early 1980s began to challenge the networks' dominance, restricting the kinds of resources they could dedicate to less profitable programming (Baker and Dessart, 1998). A second blow was dealt by changes in the regulatory environment promoted as part of the Reagan administration's neo-liberal agenda and backed by a new generation of multi-media conglomerates. The repeal of the anti-trafficking law in 1982, which had required owners to hold a station for at least three years before selling it, and the dismantling a few years later of a number of regulations originally intended to limit concentration of ownership, precipitated a wave of mergers and takeovers in the mid-1980s. Local stations were quickly bought up, often by new owners who had taken on large debts to finance their purchases. Between March 1985 and September 1986 all three major commercial networks changed hands as well.

At both the affiliate and network level, the new owners were often managers of multi-sectoral and multi-media conglomerates, who frequently
had no background in, and little commitment to, the public service tradition in broadcast journalism (Baker and Dessart, 1998: 137–8). Like the
new press owners who, in the 1970s, had transformed the nation's newspapers from locally owned, low-profit ventures into extremely lucrative
enterprises, the new broadcast owners set about finding ways to make
their new acquisitions leaner and more profitable as well.

This trend has only accelerated since the passage of the Telecommunications Act in 1996, which precipitated a second, intensified wave of
buyouts and mergers (Hickey, 1998). In this environment, news operations have become a key target in broadcasters' attempts to improve the
bottom line: budgets, especially at the network level, have been cut; staff
and funds for reporting have been reduced; and many foreign news
bureaux have been closed (Davis and Owen, 1998: 37). Originally
protected from Nielsen ratings pressures, news programmes are increasingly submitted to the same criteria of judgement as entertainment
programming. This means that they have been more forcefully obliged
than ever before to reach out to the large percentage of the audience
with little interest in politics. As CBS Evening News anchor Dan Rather
publicly complained in 1993: 'They've got us putting more and more
fuzz and wuzz on the air, cop-shop program stuff, so as to compete not
with other news programs, but with entertainment programs, including
those posing as news programs, for dead bodies, mayhem and lurid
tales' (Hallin, 1996: 243). Indeed, a study in 1997, looking at news
broadcasts in eight major American cities, showed that the coverage of
blood and mayhem has come to exceed coverage of government, education and race relations by a factor of two to one (Baker and Dessart,
1998: 122–3). Viewers uninterested in hard news are also increasingly
being lured by a new advertiser-friendly category of 'you news' (Tucher,
1997) – focusing on apolitical topics with wide resonance and appeal,
such as health and hygiene. Reflecting these trends, a recent study in
California has shown that in five major market areas less than one third
of one per cent of local TV news programming was dedicated to the
1998 governor's race. Moreover, two thirds of that coverage centred on
insider strategy and political manoeuvring rather than substantive issues
(Purdum, 1999).

The virtual abandonment of public service broadcasting has been
facilitated by the 1987 repeal of the Fairness Doctrine. Today, a whole
new breed of 'infotainment' programming is thriving on America's
airwaves. Tabloid news magazines and TV reality shows represent a new
hybrid format which, while mimicking news formats, offers emotionally
rousing entertainment that is cheap to produce and rates well with

audiences but remains largely devoid of news content. Accompanying these shows, new forms of often vitriolic and superficial TV talk shows have developed as well – shows which, in this post-Fairness age, need raise no concerns on the part of broadcasters about balance or public service content (Davis and Owen, 1998). As local and network news-casts become subject to the same kinds of commercial criteria of success as other entertainment programming, they are coming to resemble these infotainment programmes more and more, and in many areas of the mainstream media, boundaries between editorial and marketing deci-sions, traditionally considered essential to journalistic independence, are beginning to break down (see Hickey, 1998). News stories are increas-ingly selected based on their capacity to attract key audiences for advertisers, and self-censorship oriented to business concerns seems to be on the rise as well.

This new, more commercialized broadcasting environment has intensi-fied the dialectics of commercial media logic, eliciting new forms of adaptation over the last decade and a half. Political actors must now struggle even harder than before to break into the news, as the window for political coverage narrows. From 42 seconds in 1968, the average tele-vision news soundbite had shrunk, by 1992, to less than 10 seconds (Patterson, 1993: 74–5). But the problem is not merely that less time is being dedicated to the coverage of politics, but also that new criteria are being used to define newsworthiness. Much of what traditionally served as the staple of news coverage is no longer considered exciting enough to pass muster in the new environment. In search of alternatives, politicians are reaching out to new venues, such as the TV and radio talk-shows, where they are given more space and control of their self-presentation, but where the discussion is often very superficial and highly personalized. In an appearance on an MTV talk-show during the 1992 campaign, for exam-ple, Bill Clinton spent much of his time answering questions about such vital issues as what kind of underwear he preferred.

It remains to be seen how corrosive the effects of this process may ultimately prove to be. Attempts to compete in this new media environ-ment seem to have led many political actors to opt for a more aggressive, camera-eye-catching style of gesture and discourse, contributing to the increasing frequency of bitter *ad hominem* attacks during key legislative debates. The new dynamics of political distinction may even be pushing us into an era in which, according to Manuel Castells (1997: 337), 'scandal politics is the weapon of choice', as political actors attempt to enhance their own influence by tarnishing the reputations of their competitors. In this political environment, it is not surprising that news coverage is becoming increasingly negative and cynical in its presenta-tion of politics. Nor is it surprising that public alienation from both the political process and the media has reached an historical high point. Since 1966, ratings of confidence in government have fallen drastically: by 1994, confidence in the White House had dropped from 46 per cent to 18 per cent, while confidence in Congress had dropped from 34 per cent to 18 per cent. Confidence in the press has dropped as well, falling, for the press in general, from 30 per cent to 13 per cent, and for television news from 43 per cent to 24 per cent (Harris, 1994). In fact, a 1999 study found that 38 per cent of Americans considered news organizations 'immoral', up from 13 per cent in the mid-1980s. This general public frustration, however, may point to the limits of public acceptance of these new modes of political communication, at least in their more virulent forms. The public reaction to the 1999 impeachment hearings was a fascinating demonstration of citizens' reactions to the new political climate. By the time that the hearings were held, the public's tolerance for the whole phenomenon had already been severely strained. Citizens seemed either indifferent or oblivious to the fact that Clinton did, indeed, perjure himself in front of a grand jury. They were tired of investigations and scandal-mongering as a weapon for political competition, and they blamed the media for fueling the process (Hunt, 1998). Clinton's popularity ratings actually rose throughout the ordeal, and in a Gallup poll conducted at the height of the proceedings, he emerged as the most admired man of 1998 (Saad, 1998). A number of prominent journalists have been speaking out in recent years, warning that current media practices threaten to undermine not only public faith in the political process, but the status of the news media as well (Capella and Jamieson, 1996: 84; Fallows, 1996; Janeway, 1999: 125). It seems as if some editors and producers may finally be paying heed to these warnings. Many local TV news programmes, for example, have recently enjoyed ratings success while maintaining or even renewing their commitments to quality news (Rosentiel, Gottlieb and Brady, 1999). Thus, although it is still too early to tell how far these trends will progress, we may be witnessing the early signs of a partial reversal of some of the tendencies connected to contemporary modes of commercial media logic. In any event, the transformation has already been extensive.

The commercialization of broadcasting: regional variations on a global theme

The USA was of course not alone in its experience of rapid expansion and intensification of deregulation and commercialization of its broadcasting system during the 1980s. Over the course of that decade and into the 1990s countries in regions throughout the world have been under-going similar processes. In Western Europe new technologies began to challenge the state's ability to maintain the kind of closely controlled broadcasting systems that had been established since the introduction of television in the 1950s and 1960s. Developments in satellite trans-mission pushed national broadcasting systems to open up to private competition in a number of ways. In France, the threat of competition from satellite transmission helped accelerate liberalization policies in the mid-1980s (Kuhn, 1995: 166). In Sweden, Denmark and Norway, throughout the decade, commercial satellite broadcasts from London and Luxembourg invaded national airwaves, leading to the establish-ment of hybrid commercial channels (Syvertsen and Skogerbe, 1998). The diffusion of cable television, a widespread phenomenon by the 1980s, also served to undermine state control. Partly this was because cable made possible the retransmission of foreign commercial television. But perhaps more important was that by allowing for the multiplication of channels, it undermined legal justifications for state monopolies. As it became apparent that developments in the communications field were leading toward the technical convergence of broadcasting, telecommuni-cations and computing, and as a growing number of domestic actors came to advocate privatization of these industries with an eye towards assuring national and/or global competitiveness, new laws, and new interpretations of old ones, led to the legalization of commercial terres-trial broadcasting throughout Europe. Sometimes, as in Germany, the new regulatory structures were developed and imposed in an orderly fashion; elsewhere, as in Italy and Greece, the law had to scramble to keep up with developments on the ground, and the state essentially lost control of broadcasting regulation. Eventually, even those European states which had managed to hold out longest against the commercializ-ing pressures of transnational broadcasting saw their national control eroded by a series of EU directives, beginning with the 1984 Green Paper, 'Television without Frontiers,' which limited states' capacities to prevent transnational transmissions, or to regulate their content.

The trends toward deregulation and commercialization of the media that dominated North America and Europe during the 1980s and 1990s were not limited to these regions nor to the wider set of core democratic countries such as Japan, Israel, Australia and New Zealand, which underwent similar processes during this period. Indeed, impacts of equal or greater magnitude have been observed in the emerging electoral democracies of Southern Europe, Latin America, Asia and Eastern Europe. In Southern Europe, where transitions to democracy (in Portu-gal, Greece and Spain) took place in the mid-1970s, before the current era of liberalization, national broadcasting configurations initially recast in accordance with the European tradition of state-regulated public service broadcasting have subsequently undergone processes of commercialization similar to, if not more complete than, those of Northern Europe. In the majority of nations that have formed part of democracy's 'third wave', however, laws and regulations have been established in the context of hegemonic global trends toward liberalization and deregulation of the media. Although they vary significantly in the extent to which they have adopted fully commercialized broadcasting configurations, the overwhelming trend among these emerging democracies has, since the middle of the 1980s, been a commercializing one.

In Latin America, where democratization processes took hold in the 1980s, commercializing trends have been predominant throughout the last two decades. At the beginning of the era of global liberalization, most broadcasting configurations in Latin America were 'mixed' systems: although many of the stations throughout the continent were subject to various forms of state ownership and subordination, most remained commercially funded (Schwoch, 1993). Long influenced by American broadcast models, since the introduction of television in the region most channels have been privately owned and commercially financed (Fox, 1988). State-run channels set up by populist regimes in the 1950s and 1960s, for example, were funded by advertising, and although the authoritarian military regimes that dominated most of Latin America from the mid-1960s to the early 1980s succeeded in politically subordinating expanding national networks, they did not alter broadcasting's essentially commercial nature (Waisbord, 1998: 255). In any event, many of the political barriers to commercialization and competition erected during those years were eroded after 1982 by democratic transition processes which expanded access within broadcasting configurations to a range of previously marginalized actors, and by the debt crisis, which compelled even the region's most interventionist states to liberalize trade and privatize state enterprises. In countries with large domestic markets, such as Brazil and Mexico, where quasi-monopolistic national broadcasting conglomerates had established themselves by the 1980s, democratization processes have promoted shifts toward more independent and competitive commercial configurations (Straubhaar, 1997). And in those Latin American countries that had, by the early 1980s, developed public (as in Chile's university-based stations) or state-run networks (as in Colombia, Peru and Argentina) commercialization has generally advanced markedly in two senses. First of all, many formerly publicly owned stations have been privatized, with the larger of these generally bought up by national or regional media conglomerates (Fox, 1997; Fuenzalida, 1988; McAnany and Wilkinson, 1996; Sinclair, 1996; Waisbord, 1996). Secondly, in those countries in which public or state broadcasters remain, growing numbers of domestic and transnational broadcasters have intensified competitive pressures while expanding the private sector's relative command of broadcasting space, reducing any residual differences in form and content between public and private programming (Buckman, 1997; Lavieri, 1997; Mahan, 1996; Mineo, 1999). These trends toward greater competition were only heightened by the spread of cable and satellite in the 1990s, although the direct impact of these technologies has largely been limited to the region's upper crust (Lawson, 1999; Porto, 1998b).

Broadcasting configurations in democratizing Asian nations such as South Korea, Taiwan, the Philippines, Pakistan and Thailand as well as in long-democratic India have also, since the 1980s, been undergoing sweeping processes of commercialization, but within a regional context quite different from the Latin American one. A combination of historically embedded patterns of direct state control over programming and finances – generally legitimated through NWICO New World Information and Communications Order-filtered national-developmentalist ideology, occasionally also by post-colonial mimicry of the BBC model – together with the relative fiscal strength of Asian states, served to maintain high levels of state control and ownership within Asian broadcasting configurations during the 1980s (Lent, 1998). However, although governments throughout the region maintained high degrees of direct influence over broadcast news, for most Asian nations the decade was characterized by processes of creeping commercialism. Countries such as South Korea, Thailand, Malaysia and Indonesia replaced state monopolies with hybrid systems through the transfer of control of some state stations to 'reliable' private ownership and through the licensing of new private stations (Karthigesu, 1994; Youm, 1998). And even countries, such as India, which resisted privatization, allowed steady rises in advertising revenues to help finance major new state broadcasting initiatives (Thomas, 1998: 203). As the wave of Asian democratization got under way in the latter half of the 1980s, it accompanied and interacted with the spread of new media technologies, playing a direct role in expanding broadcasting competition. State control of broadcasting in Asia, however, generally remained strong until the arrival of new transnational media competitors – cable stations and, above all, new satellite networks such as Star TV – in the early 1990s. With the rapidly growing Asian economies attracting major transnational media investment throughout this period and on into the mid-1990s, it became clear to governments in the region that their failure to invigorate ungainly state-run networks and to encourage private national media expansion would inevitably seal the demise of locally controlled broad-casting in the face of international competition. Asian governments' long and varied participation in broadcasting, combined with their relative economic strength and experience in support of other high-tech sectors, has allowed a number of them to undertake innovative state initiatives which have served to forestall transnational penetration. A few appear to have succeeded in husbanding national or joint regional enterprises capable of holding their own with Western transnational conglomerates. Nevertheless, such efforts have entailed a significant deepening of the commercial nature of the region's national broadcasting configurations and associated media logics (Badarudin, 1998; Berfield, 1996; Chan, 1996; Jussawalla, 1996; McDowell, 1997).

In the former Soviet-socialist countries of Eastern Europe, the trans-formation of authoritarian-statist broadcasting configurations was an extended, if occasionally quite dramatic, process which accompanied both the decay of communist rule in the 1980s and the construction of new economic and political frameworks over the course of the 1990s. Driven primarily by the expanding fiscal and legitimation crises of Soviet bloc states, the roots of this fundamental shift go back at least to the early 1980s, by which time the first trickle of advertising revenue and the expansion of Western programming imports had already taken hold. It was furthered by a media environment made increasingly competitive by governments' limited capacity (and declining will) to block widening flows of cross-border broadcasting, by the rise of an alternative, clandes-tine press (*Samizdat*) and by renewed challenges to blindly partisan journalistic ethics (Sparks, 1998: 56–62). While the fall of Soviet-backed regimes generally meant an end to the communist parties' overbearing ideological and political control of the media, the contours of the new broadcasting configurations emerged only gradually. Though some countries experienced wide-ranging public discussions about the new systems during this period, more mundane political struggles soon came to define local variations within the region's emergent commercial framework. The region-wide economic depression of the early 1990s initially created an inhospitable terrain for commercial broadcasting ventures, particularly when combined with resistance to privatization on the part of the region's post-Soviet leaders who, on the one hand, retained a conception of television as an indispensable 'political tool' and, on the other, were justifiably concerned that an immediate commer-cial opening would only lead to the domination of broadcasting by Western transnational conglomerates (Madden, 1996). By the mid-1990s, however, with signs of economic recovery and the likelihood of EU accession particularly for East Central European countries, even the most reticent of governments proved incapable of controlling broader commercialization processes. The expansion of both terrestrial and transnational private broadcasters during this period intensified competitive pressures, compelling retreating states to withdraw ever more toward the realm of regulation. Meanwhile, increasingly commercialized state broadcasters as well as the new private networks have tended to survive through some combination of two basic strategies: the injection of long-term investment through alliances with foreign capital, or the reinvigoration of submission to political interests. The former strategy has been more prevalent in those countries of East Central Europe perceived to be headed for EU accession and, consequently, to offer more attractive markets to transnational media conglomerates (Sukosd and Cseh, 1998). The poorer, strife-torn domestic markets of South-east Europe in general have offered far fewer enticements to foreign media firms; here, as in the East Central European exception of Slovakia, throughout the mid-1990s blunt partisan struggles over broadcasting continued while joint ventures with foreign capital remained limited (Gross, 1998; Ionescu, 1996; Moore, 1995; Skolkay, 1996). These patterns at times appear also to be small-scale versions of the Russian pattern, where domestic business moguls have built multi-sectoral media empires primarily as instruments in the pursuit of wider political and economic influence, rather than as profit-making media ventures per se (Banerjee, 1997; Nivat, 1998). In any case, despite the more ambiguous shift observed in these latter countries, the general trend throughout Eastern Europe is toward increasingly commercial configurations.

While established core democracies as well as the 'consolidating' democracies of the third wave have been undergoing similar processes of broadcasting commercialization over the last two decades, even those regimes which have managed to maintain authoritarian control in the current era have been faced with some of the same pressures examined above. In the Middle East, for example, the governments of Egypt, Saudi Arabia and Iran have had to accede to the expanding commercialization of their national broadcasting configurations, despite potentially destabilizing implications – above all, the intensification of fundamentalist religious opposition – in order to adapt to changing economic and technological challenges (Amin, 1996; Boyd, 1998; Mohammadi, 1998). Similarly, remaining 'socialist' regimes have also been subjected to immense commercializing pressures: China, for example, began to allow commercial funding of broadcasting in the early 1980s in the wake of liberalizing economic reforms, and even the reinvigoration of political controls in the post-Tiananmen years did not reverse this trend. (Chan, 1996; Hong, 1998; Huang, 1994). For the most part, it is only those countries which have been left out of the current global economic transformation – impoverished or war-torn countries such as those of

Sub-Saharan Africa, which have, in the words of Manuel Castells (1998), become part of a new 'Fourth World', increasingly 'switched off' from global flows of capital and technology – which are not being caught up in these processes of commercialization.

The triumph of commercial media logic?: the transformation of national political communication

As commercializing trends sweep the globe, commercial media logic is presently altering many aspects of political communication in nation after nation as well. Due to space limitations we cannot fully explore in this chapter the many nuances that mark the development of these processes, though it is quite clear that they are unfolding in unique ways and at very different tempos in various national contexts. Important sources of variation include divergent institutional features of particular countries' electoral and broadcasting systems, differences in national political culture and journalistic norms and the variant positions that different countries inhabit in the global economy. Thus, for example, presidential, two-party systems seem to be far more susceptible to some of these dynamics than multi-party parliamentary systems characterized by closed list proportional representation. A number of North-west European countries, with relatively rich and strong states, have been fairly successful at finding ways to maintain much of their public service programming and, thus, more classic modes of televised political coverage. A few countries with strong cultural and institutional traditions of rational-critical political discourse have managed to erect a variety of legal bulwarks against the 'Americanization' of electoral campaigns (on France, see Maarek, 1997: 357). And in some nations where commercial television is not profitable due to small linguistic markets and/or weak economies, television stations have been bought up by wealthy political or commercial interests who are willing to incur financial losses due to the influence they can thereby garner; here, obviously, a quite different kind of promotional logic dominates programming (see Nivat, 1998 on Russia; Papathanassopoulos, 1997 on Greece; McEnteer, 1996 on the Philippines). In any case, despite the existence of distinct developmental paths, the general tendency in democracies world-wide is, indeed, the progression of commercial media logic and associated forms of promotional, mediatized political communication. Our intention in this section is to illustrate these general trends, indicating their scope through a scattering of citations from political observers from a number of world regions.

An unsurprising but nevertheless fundamentally important point of departure is that, in most advanced and emerging democracies, citizens have become increasingly dependent on television for their news and information about the world around them. In Spain, for example, the audience for television, in early 1992, was about 90 per cent of the population, whereas only 36 per cent of the population read the daily written press (Vilches, 1996: 178, 186). During the same year in Greece, 69 per cent of the population reported that it got its daily news from TV, whereas only 17 per cent reported newspapers to be their primary source (Papathanassopoulos, 1997: 359). Though assessments vary, some 50–75 per cent of Mexicans indicate that television is their principal source of news, compared to 10–15 per cent for newspapers (Hallin, forthcoming/b); in Brazil those figures for television rise to almost 90 per cent (Porto, 1998b: 3). Again, mirroring trends in the USA, in many countries around the world people report that they trust television more than newspapers. In Israel, for example, 55 per cent reported confidence in television, whereas only 9 per cent reported that they trusted the written press (Liebes and Peri, 1998: 29). With so much of the citizenry depending on television for their political news, the transformation of television coverage should have important implications for the nature of political communication world-wide.

Television programming is, in fact, changing significantly in this new era of widespread commercialization. Private commercial stations as well as public service stations are adopting new formats of news presentation, developing a more fast-paced, aestheticized style. Not only are they spicing up their broadcasts with new logos, graphics and music, but they are cultivating anchor-celebrities who appeal to the public by presenting increasingly mediated news coverage: verbatim reports of parliamentary speeches and politicians' statements are on the decline while soundbite length is shrinking, giving way to the increasing pre-dominance of journalistic interpretation within news coverage (see, for example, Papathanassopoulos, 1998: 8–11 on Greece; Sherman, 1995 on Japan; Blumler et al., 1996: 59 on Britain; Atkinson, 1994 on New Zealand; Chopra, 1998 on India). On commercial and public stations alike, political news is being presented in more dramatized and often sensationalized formats (see, for example, Pfetch, 1996: 439 on Germany; Dader, 1998: 8 on Spain; Porto, 1998a on Brazil). Throughout the world, observers also report that the discussion of politics is tending to become more personalized, not only emphasizing political leaders at the expense of collective actors and political processes, but also focusing on leaders' personal characteristics at the expense of their roles as political actors (see, for example, Rospir, 1996: 163 on Spain; Cavarozzi

and Landi, 1992: 220–5 on Argentina; Mayobre, 1996: 242 on Venezuela; Lent, 1998: 160 on South Korea, India and the Philippines;
Mickiewicz, 1997: 150–2 on Russia). And while news programmes are
being transformed throughout the world, new formats for television
coverage of politics and public affairs are proliferating as well. Tabloid-
style TV newsmagazines and infotainment-oriented TV talk shows, for
example, are thriving (see Dahlgren, 1995: 65 on Sweden; Rondelli,
1998 on Brazil; Hallin, forthcoming/a on Mexico; Madden, 1996 on the
Czech Republic; Hoon, 1997 on South Korea; Badarudin, 1997 on
Malaysia).

Political actors are responding to this new climate for political coverage in similar ways. Throughout the world, politicians and leaders of
organizations in civil society are focusing more of their attention on
attempts to foster positive images in the media, and to tailor their
messages to the new media environment. They are learning to speak in
soundbites, incorporating targeted catchphrases into their public statements. In Brazil, media experts have provided training to militant labour
union leaders aimed at cleansing their public discourse of self-defeating
leftist predilections towards jargon and complexification (Sluyter-
Beltrao, forthcoming). In Spain, politicians will actually break off in
mid-sentence when they see camera links light up at political rallies, in
order to deliver specially prepared soundbites aimed at optimizing their
minute of televised coverage (Dader, 1998: 17). These carefully packaged messages are often little more than oversimplified slogans, such as
Chirac's careful delimitation of his discourse in the 1996 French election
to abstract propositions about overcoming 'la fracture sociale' (Maarek,
1997: 364), or the case of the 1998 Brazilian elections, in which both
Lula and Cardoso, the leading presidential candidates on the Left and
the Right, respectively, incorporated Clinton's slogan 'putting people
first' into their campaign jingles (Campos, 1998: 40).

As politicians focus more of their energies on their media images, they
are coming to rely increasingly on public relations and polling experts to
help them assess public receptivity, to create TV-friendly media events
and to coin catchy slogans that will capture the public imagination (see,
for example, Franklin, 1994, and Scammel, 1995 on Britain; Bernardes
and Netto, 1998 on Brazil; Waisbord, 1996 on Argentina; and Mickiewicz, 1997 on Russia). A whole new market for international consultants has arisen over the last ten years. While American experts have
been hired in campaigns throughout the world, such expertise is hardly
an exclusively American export: French strategist Jacques Séguéla has
worked on campaigns in Eastern Europe since 1990, and was one of the
first international consultants to advise a Swedish campaign in 1991
(Asp and Esaiasson, 1996: 79; Nivat, 1998: 32). British strategists have

been employed in Russia and South Africa during elections in 1993 and 1994 (Blumler *et al.*, 1996: 57). And Latin America has developed its own corps of international campaign consultants (Harwood, 1999). These consultants are helping parties and candidates to moderate their images as they battle for the centre and for the expanding pool of uncommitted voters in this new era of contracting political options. As Sergio Bendixen, Peruvian-born advisor to American and Latin American campaigns observes: 'politics is being restricted to a very narrow lane . . . we are the experts at making campaigns out of narrow points' (Harwood, 1999).

As a result of these changes, negative dialectics similar to those witnessed in the American case are developing in countries around the world. As the airtime dedicated to policy platforms and political statements shrinks, political actors are attempting to dominate the political agenda by offering images and phrases that will command attention in the new media environment. But such manoeuvring, especially when aided by the professional tactics of pollsters and marketing experts, becomes news itself, as journalists' attempts to deconstruct the public relations strategies of politicians become a central staple of news coverage. Consequently, news coverage is coming to frame political struggle more and more in terms of horserace and public relations wars: stories centre on the issue of whose popularity is rising and falling and speculations about the role various public relations efforts might be playing in such developments (see Liebes and Peri, 1998: 29–31 on Israel; Blumler and Gurevitch, 1998: 5 on Britain; Maarek, 1997: 366 on France; Smith, 1999 on Mexico). This kind of coverage, however, is often very cynical and negative in tone, and political observers around the world report increasing negativity in the coverage of national politics (see Asp and Esaiasson, 1996: 83 on Sweden; Papathanassopoulos, 1998: 20 on Greece; Rawnsley, 1997 on Taiwan). In part, this is because leaks to the press and scandal-mongering have indeed become potent political weapons in the current media climate. But the constant attention to horserace and public relations wars inherent in commercial media logic tends to lend to politics, even in calmer times, a somewhat disreputable cast.

With the aim of maximizing media access and circumventing journalistic mediation, political actors in various countries are reaching out to new infotainment formats as well. At times, these trends seem to be following US developments popularized by international media coverage – in some instances, very closely indeed: in 1994 in The Netherlands, echoing Clinton's 1992 saxophone rendition of 'Heartbreak Hotel' on the Arsenio Hall Show, parliamentary candidate Hans Dijkstal, future

Minister of the Interior, took up his own sax to play the blues on a Dutch talk-show (Brants, 1998: 315). However, in many countries, politicians' participation in these shows exceeds the kinds of limited forays into alternative television formats made by American politicians to date. In some Latin American countries, participation in TV talk-shows and infotainment-style programmes predates that in the USA. Carlos Menem, for example, took great advantage of these formats on his path to the Argentine presidency (Cavarozzi and Landi, 1992), four years before the first American presidential candidates ventured into such waters in 1992. In places like Brazil, appearances on these shows are already a regular staple of politicians' communication strategies. And in some countries, the forms such participation is taking are outpacing anything that has been seen in American politics. In Sweden, the Foreign Minister exchanged clothes with an androgenous rock star on a TV talk-show, to illustrate that 'the clothes make the man' (Dahlgren, 1995: 56). On Brazil's *Roda Viva*, politicians are seated upon swivel chairs in a sort of pit, with a circle of journalists perched above, casting provocative questions down upon them, while on *Programa Livre*, candidates risk exposure to the often compromising impertinence of a teenage audience. These may be more pleasant scenarios, however, than those now faced by political leaders in India and South Korea. Indian politicians' nervous faces often gleam with sweat on *Aap Ke Adalat*, which offers them nationwide media projection in exchange for the opportunity to defend themselves against contrived accusations of corruption and other high crimes leveled by a wisecracking prosecutor (Pendakur and Kapur, 1997: 201–2); in South Korea the four leading presidential candidates in 1997 not only had to make the rounds of cooking and singing shows, but also to deal with a late-night talk-show host who asked them with which actress they would most like to perform a love scene (Hoon, 1997: 16). Despite the risks and challenges posed by these infotainment formats, politicians see them as opportunities for more extensive exposure than the shortened soundbites on TV news allow.

As we have seen in the case of the USA, the new communication environment is affecting far more than simply the conduct of national electoral campaigns. It is also transforming the organization and orientation of parties, the conduct of parliamentary politics and the construction and strategies of actors in civil society. The marketing advice of pollsters and other consultants is helping bring parties of the Left and the Right closer to the centre in their iconography as well as their platforms. Brazil's left-wing contender, the PT, for example, in pursuit of swing voters repelled by the party's militant image, substituted white party flags and backdrop for the usual red ones in its 1998 campaign spots – provoking widespread indignation among party members – upon the recommendation of consultants (Campos, 1998: 40). In Spain, the conservative Prime Minister Jose Maria Aznar and his People's Party image makers, at the 1999 party congress, pushed through a shift of message away from traditional right-wing planks towards a new centrism modelled on British Prime Minister Tony Blair's 'Third Way'. The new environment is also changing the power dynamics and modes of negotiation and bargaining within parties. As Panebianco (1988: 266) has argued, the transformation of political communication has 'caused an earthquake' within parties, as media coverage empowers the parties' elected representatives (along with an entourage of media and other professional experts) while undercutting former bases of power enjoyed by members and party bureaucrats. The rise of leader 'celebrities' has been accompanied by the declining role and importance of party activist networks – even in parties with strong participatory-democratic roots (see Frankland, 1995 on the German Greens). And as party bureaucrats lose power to media-savvy representatives, parties risk losing coherence and discipline. Social movement organizations, to the degree they gain prominence and media coverage, tend to evolve along similar lines, marked by patterns of leader 'celebrity', by exacerbated internal conflict, by shifts toward strategic and ideological moderation over 'radical' alternatives and by a tendency of media-oriented leaderships to be cut off from grassroots activists and members (see Gitlin, 1980 on US student movement; Groth, 1996 on Japanese civic movements; Sluyter-Beltrao, (forthcoming) on the Brazilian labour movement). Indeed, because social movements are constructed around collective identities that fundamentally challenge the status quo, integration into the arena of media politics may be expected to contort such movements to a far greater degree than mainstream political organizations.

While observers in the USA have displayed a widely shared concern that the new modalities of political communication are contributing to the decay of democracy – undermining the quality of public discourse, citizens' trust in their governments and leaders' capacity to govern – assessments of these trends in other parts of the world have been more mixed. On the negative side, and particularly in the longer standing, post-industrial democracies of the West, many observers report tendencies toward cynicism and frustration on the part of citizens in new, commercially mediatized communication environments. In Britain, Blumler *et al.*, write of a political climate characterized by 'widespread public mistrust' (1996: 66). National polls in the early 1990s showed high disapproval ratings for political leaders in Canada, Japan, Italy and

France as well (see Castells, 1997: 344). Of course, it is difficult to conclude that rising cynicism is caused primarily by the tenor of political communication. Indeed in the context of the globalization of national economies, government institutions are weaker, with little capacity to offer real economic alternatives, and political parties are hard pressed to present genuine alternatives. Nevertheless, the deterioration of political debate in the mass media adds to public frustration and alienation.

On the positive side, however, political observers report a number of potentially beneficial effects of the new communication regime. One aspect of the transformation of political communication which is being welcomed is the rise of politically independent television journalism, a relatively new phenomenon in a number of countries. Traditionally, television journalists, not only in authoritarian regimes, but on public service news programmes in many democracies as well, have been staid conveyors of official pronouncements and positions. In their news presentations, they followed the political agenda set by political leaders, reading official announcements and covering official events as they were provided by political elites. The new media environment, however, is helping to establish new forms of broadcast journalism in a number of countries. Like Spain's new commercial Antena3, these stations are more likely to conceive of themselves as public 'watchdogs', to provide news analysis and interpretation, and to put together issue packages covering topics that they consider to be politically important (on Spain, see Semetko and Canel, 1997; on Greece, see Papathanassopoulos, 1998: 10). This is a trend which has affected not only new commercial stations, but public channels as well (see, for example, Stratham, 1996: 519 on Italy's RAI; Blumler and Gurevitch, 1998 on Britain's BBC).

Perhaps equally important, in attempting to reduce their prolonged reliance on mainstream politicians and boost identification with a mass audience, many news programmes are reaching out to alternative sources, from average citizens to civic movement activists and opinion leaders previously marginalized from the elite spheres of mediated political commentary. This tendency to include more voices from civil society is what Blumler and Gurevitch (reporting on trends in recent coverage at the BBC) have referred to as a 'populist undercurrent', which might offer some sort of remedy to the hyper-reflexive battles that draw journalists and politicians into the dialectics of commercial media logic (1998: 1). In this regard, it is the role of the mass media in the recent democratic transitions in non-core countries that has received the greatest accolades. In Mexico and Brazil, in South Korea, Thailand, Taiwan and Indonesia, in Poland, Rumania and Russia observers have identified positive contributions to democratization processes by the new media venues which have frequently served as sites for the expanded public expression of opposition to authoritarian regimes (Chen, 1998; Cohen, 1998; Lawson, 1999; Lee, 1996; Mollison, 1998). Numerous studies have shown not only how growing domestic access to international news coverage via cable, satellite, fax machines and the Internet has bolstered regime opponents, but how private stations, as well as increasingly commercial public ones, in countries such as Brazil (Straubhaar, 1997: 227), Yugoslavia (Condit, 1994), Indonesia (Cohen, 1998) and Thailand (Eng, 1997) have become key points of political access and empowerment. However, while broadcast media have often played a role in the transition phase, the ensuing phase of democratic consolidation has generally been marked by quite precipitous declines into familiar patterns of access for political elites and of marginalization for actors from civil society. Thus, the new broadcast media do not assure the maintenance – much less the promotion – of the kind of vibrant, democratic public sphere which many had anticipated (Gross, 1998; Jakubowicz, 1995). They do, however, offer more plural representation than had their predecessors.

Another potentially positive effect which many observers of the recent transformations have noted is the fact that the new, more entertaining, modalities of communication are cultivating political interest among segments of the population which had previously shown little interest in political issues (see Donsbach, 1997: 150 on Germany; Stratham, 1996: 519 on Italy). These developments, however, are hardly unmitigated blessings for contemporary political systems, despite their potential to draw wider segments of the population to news programming. For one thing, rising interest on the part of the least engaged is often accompanied by the disaffection of those who had traditionally followed politics closely and who presumably bear higher expectations for political discourse. Papathanassopoulos (1998: 29), using Eurobarometer data, illustrates this tendency quite succinctly for the case of Greece: from 1980 to 1994, while the percentage of the population reporting that they were 'not at all' interested in politics decreased from 30 per cent to 21 per cent, the percentage reporting 'a great deal' of interest declined as well, from 18 per cent to 11 per cent. Habermas would hardly be cheered by the prospect of an increasing number of citizens making voting decisions based in good part on criteria such as how politicians handle themselves when faced with embarrassing personal queries on TV talk shows. The important question is, of course, what kind of interest these new forms of communication are piquing and whether the new modes of 'participation' are ultimately conducive to democratic vitality.

Gearing up for the next wave of new media technologies: conglomeration and audience segmentation, continuing challenges to civic communication

Ultimately, the kinds of pressures brought to bear on classical modes of political discourse in different countries will depend to a great extent on the particular forms that commercializing trends take there. Currently, we find ourselves in an era in which global conglomerates are rapidly gearing up for the development and provision of a wave of new media technologies. As digital television and new broadband Internet connections bring the convergence of broadcasting, telecommunications and computing into view, multi-media and telecommunications conglomerates are scurrying to position themselves in what promises to be a whole new communications landscape (Duncan, 1998; Yang *et al.*, 1998). This will probably only intensify current trends toward increasing commercial pressures within the media of the most advanced countries of the world. The high stakes and uncertainty involved in the rapid transformation of media technologies and the industries which provide them have already fostered an environment in which national (and supranational) regulatory bodies are wary of limiting powerful processes of horizontal and vertical integration in the communications industry, for fear that they might cripple their own capacity to cultivate globally competitive technologies and companies (see Hickey, 1998 on the FCC in the USA; Kaitazi-Whitlock, 1996 on the EU). As processes of relatively unregulated conglomeration sweep more and more media outlets into subordination to intense bottom line pressures, current trends toward the intensified domination of commercial media logic should be expected to continue apace.

On the other hand, new communications technologies offer new opportunities for political communication as well. As Internet access spreads wider across the globe, and deeper into national societies, it brings new opportunities for direct access to politically relevant information, for unmediated communication between political organizations and potential members, and for interactive discourse among citizens themselves (Moog, 2000). Nevertheless, for the majority of the population, television, in whatever new forms it may take, will probably remain the most important source of political information. As channels of distribution multiply, continued segmentation of television audiences can be expected. While market segmentation may mean that some providers will tailor new products for the more politically interested segments of national audiences, which, along the lines of C-Span or The

History Channel, offer viewers rich new sources of political information, the vast majority of national audiences will likely find themselves surfing the waves of programming options characterized by ever-increasing levels of commercial media logic. How far audience segmentation proceeds may well depend on the relative size and wealth of national audiences and therefore of national advertising budgets. Thus, smaller countries (with limited linguistic markets) and poorer countries (which cannot support as many providers through advertising) may be less subject to the kind of stratification of political audiences that we will probably see in the USA in the coming decades. But in countries at the core of the world economy, we can expect to witness the increasing ghettoization of informed debate and classical modes of journalism. Such trends hardly bode well, of course, for the future of rational critical discourse in the public sphere.

References

Altheide, David L. and Snow, Robert P. (1979) *Media Logic*. Beverly Hills, CA: Sage.

Amin, Hussein (1996) 'Egypt and the Arab world in the satellite age', in J. Sinclair, E. Jacka and S. Cunningham (eds), *Peripheral Visions: New Patterns in Global Television*. Oxford: Oxford University Press. pp. 101–25.

Ansolabehere, Stephen, Behr, Roy and Shanto Iyengar (1993) *The Media Game: American Politics in the Television Age*. New York: MacMillan.

Asp, Kent and Esaiasson, Peter (1996) 'The modernization of Swedish campaigns: individualization, professionalization, and medialization', in D. Swanson and P. Mancini (eds), *Politics, Media and Modern Democracy*. Westport, CT: Praeger. pp. 73–90.

Atkinson, Joe (1994) 'The state, the media and thin democracy', in Andrew Sharp (ed.), *Leap Into the Dark: The Changing Role of the State in New Zealand since 1984*. Auckland: Auckland University Press. pp. 146–77.

Badarudin, Noor Bathi (1997) 'Programming content in Malaysian television', *Media Asia*, 24 (3): 131–48.

Badarudin, Noor Bathi (1998) 'The changing Malaysian TVscape: road to regionalisation and globalisation', *Media Asia*, 25 (1): 131–48.

Baker, William F. and Dessart, George (1998) *Down the Tube: An Inside Account of the Failure of American Television*. New York: Basic Books.

Banerjee, Neela (1997) 'Russia: big business takes over', *Columbia Journalism Review*, Nov./Dec.: 27–39.

Berfield, Susan (1996) 'Asia's no pushover: in the fight for the region's television audiences, the satellite giants are meeting tough resistance', *Asiaweek*, 8 Nov.: 38–46.

Bernardes, Ernesto and Vladimir Netto (1998) 'Os Bruxos das Eleicoes: Os homens que criam as imagens dos candidatos e mudam o rumo dos votos', *Veja*, 16 September: 41–7.

Blumler, Jay G. and Gurevitch, Michael (1998) 'Change in the air, campaign journalism at the BBC, 1997', in I. Crewe, J. Bartle and B. Gosschalk (eds), *Political Communications: Why Labour Won the General Election of 1997.* London: Frank Cass. pp. 176–94.

Blumler, Jay G., Kavanagh, Dennis and Nossiter, T.J. (1996) 'Modern communications versus traditional politics in Britain: unstable marriage of convenience', in D. Swanson and P. Mancini (eds), *Politics, Media and Modern Democracy.* Westport, CT: Praeger. pp. 49–72.

Boyd, Douglas (1998) 'The Arab world', in A. Smith with R. Paterson (eds), *Television: An International History.* Oxford: Oxford University Press. pp. 182–7.

Brants, Kees (1998) 'Who's afraid of infotainment?', *European Journal of Communication,* 13 (3): 315–36.

Buckman, Robert T. (1997) 'Birth, death, and resurrection of press freedom in Chile', in R. Cole (ed.), *Communication in Latin America: Journalism, Mass Media and Society.* Wilmington, DE: Scholarly Resources. pp. 155–81.

Campos, Cintia (1998) 'A hora do espetaculo', *Veja,* 26 Aug.: 40–3.

Capella, Joseph N. and Hall Jamieson, Kathleen (1996) 'News frames, political cynicism and media cynicism', *Annals of the American Academy of Political and Social Sciences,* 546: 71–83.

Castells, Manuel (1997) *The Power of Identity.* Oxford: Blackwell.

Castells, Manuel (1998) *The End of Millennium.* Oxford: Blackwell.

Cavarozzi, Marcelo and Landi, Oscar (1992) 'Political parties under Alfonsin and Menem: the effects of state shrinking and the devaluation of democratic politics', in E. Epstein (ed.), *The New Argentine Democracy.* New York: Praeger. pp. 203–27.

Chan, Joseph Man (1996) 'Television in Greater China: structure, exports and market formation', in J. Sinclair, E. Jacka and S. Cunningham (eds), *Peripheral Vision: New Patterns in Global Television.* New York: Oxford University Press. pp. 126–61.

Chen, Sheue Yen (1998) 'State, media and democracy in Taiwan', *Media Culture and Society,* 20: 11–29.

Chopra, Mannika (1998) 'TV wins the elections: this year's all-out coverage redefined Indian journalism', *Columbia Journalism Review,* May/June: 1–4.

Cohen, Margot (1998) 'Acid test: the media corrode Suharto's legitimacy', *Far Eastern Economic Review,* May (28): 18–20.

Condit, E. (1994) 'Food for thought: how an independent television station survives in Belgrade', *Columbia Journalism Review,* Nov./Dec.: 14–31.

Curran, James (1996) 'Mass media and democracy revisited', in J. Curran and M. Gurevitch (eds), *Mass Media and Society,* 2nd edn. London: Arnold. pp. 81–119.

Dader, Jose Luis (1998) 'European communication in comparison: some perspectives on Spain', paper presented at the Workshop on Media and Politics in Europe, Center for German and European Studies, University of California at Berkeley, 17 and 18 April.

Dahlgren, Peter (1995) *Television and the Public Sphere: Citizenship, Democracy and the Media.* London: Sage.

Davis, Richard and Owen, Diana (1998) *New Media and American Politics.* New York: Oxford University Press.

Donsbach, Wolfgang (1997) 'Media thrust in the German Bundestag election,

1994: news values and professional norms in political communication', *Political Communication*, 14 (3): 149–70.

Duncan, Emma (1998) 'Wheel of fortune: a survey of technology and entertainment', *The Economist*, 21 Nov.: 1–18.

Eng, Peter (1997) 'Thailand: media rising – how the press is bolstering democracy', *Columbia Journalism Review*, May/June: 5–7.

Fallows, James (1996) *Breaking the News: How the Media Undermine American Democracy*. New York: Pantheon.

Fox, Elizabeth (1997) 'Media Politics in Latin America: an overview', in E. Fox (ed.), *Media and Politics in Latin America: The Struggle for Democracy*. London: Sage. pp. 6–35.

Fox, Elizabeth (1988) 'Media politics in Latin America: an overview', in E. Fox (ed.), *Media and Politics in Latin America: The Struggle for Democracy*. London: Sage. pp. 6–35.

Frankland, E. Gene (1995) 'Germany: the rise, fall and recovery of Die Gruenen', in D. Richardson and C. Rootes (eds), *The Green Challenge: The Development of Green parties in Europe*. New York: Routledge. pp. 23–44.

Franklin, Bob (1994) *Packaging Politics: Political Communications in Britain's Media Democracy*. London: Edward Arnold.

Fuenzalida, Valerio (1988) 'Television in Chile: a history of experiment and reform', *Journal of Communication*, 38 (2): 49–58.

Gitlin, Todd (1980) *The Whole World is Watching: Mass Media in the Making and Unmaking of the New Left*. Berkeley, CA: University of California Press.

Gross, Peter (1998) 'Inching toward integrity: after helping spark a revolution, Romania's media struggle in the aftermath', *Transitions*, 5 (3): 82–5.

Groth, David Earl (1996) 'Media and political protest: the bullet train movements', in S. Pharr and E. Krauss (eds), *Media and Politics in Japan*. Honolulu: University of Hawaii Press. pp. 213–35.

Habermas, Jurgen (1989) *The Structural Transformation of the Public Sphere: An Inquiry into a Category of Bourgeois Society*. Trans. T. Burger, with F. Lawrence. Cambridge, MA: MIT Press.

Hallin, Daniel C. (1996) 'Commercialism and professionalism in the American news media', in J. Curran and M. Gurevitch (eds), *Mass Media and Society*, 2nd edn. London: Arnold. pp. 243–61.

Hallin, Daniel C. (2000a) '*La Nota Roja*: popular journalism and the transition to democracy in Mexico', in C. Sparks and J. Tulloch (eds), *Tabloid Tales*.

Hallin, Daniel C. (2000b) 'Media, political power and democratization in Mexico', in J. Curran and M. Park (eds), *De-Westernizing Media Studies*.

Harris, Louis (1994) 'Changing trends in American politics: what in the world is going on in this nation?', *Vital Speeches*, 60 (21): 663–7.

Harwood, John (1999) 'A lot like home: campaign strategists give foreign elections that American cachet', *Wall Street Journal*, 24 March: A1, A18.

Herman, Edward S. and McChesney, Robert W. (1998) *The Global Media: The New Missionaries of Corporate Capitalism*. Washington: Cassell.

Hickey, Neil (1998) 'Money lust: how pressure for profit is perverting journalism', *Columbia Journalism Review*, July/Aug.: 7–11.

Hong, I. (1998) *The Internationalization of Television in China: the Evolution of Ideology, Society and Media since the Reform*. Westport, CT: Praeger.

Hoon, Shim Jae (1997) 'Candid(ate) camera: TV brings political change – but is it for the better?', *Far Eastern Economic Review*, 23 Oct.: 16–17.

Huang, Yu (1994) 'Peaceful evolution: the case of television reform in post-Mao China', *Media, Culture and Society*, 16 (2): 217–41.

Hunt, Albert R. (1998) 'Washington events fuel disdain for media, politics: in scandal, no one escapes blame, especially the media', *Wall Street Journal*, 17 Sept.: A12.

Ionescu, Dan (1996) 'Tele-revolution to tele-evolution in Romania', *Transitions*, 2 (8): 42–4.

Jakubowicz, Karol (1995) 'Media as agents of change', in D. Paletz, K. Jakubo-wicz and P. Novosel (eds), *Glasnost and After: Media and Change in Central and Eastern Europe*. Cresskill, NJ: Hampton Press. pp. 19–47.

Janeway, M. (1999) *Republic of Denial*. New Haven: Yale University Press.

Jussawalla, M. (1996) *Telecomms: a Bridge to the Twenty-first Century*. The Hague: North Holland.

Kaitazi-Whitlock, Sophia (1996) 'Pluralism and media concentration in Europe: media policy as industrial policy', *European Journal of Communication*, 11 (4): 453–83.

Karthigesu, R. (1994) 'Broadcasting deregulation in developing Asian nations: an examination of nascent tendencies using Malaysia as a case study', *Media, Culture and Society*, 16 (1): 73–90.

Kuhn, Raymond (1995) *The Media in France*. London: Routledge.

Kurtz, Howard (1998) *Spin Cycle: Inside the Clinton Propaganda Machine*. New York: The Free Press.

Lavieri, Omar (1997) 'The media in Argentina: struggling with the absence of a democratic tradition', in R. Cole (ed.), *Communication in Latin America: Journalism, Mass Media and Society*. Wilmington, DE: Scholarly Resources. pp. 183–98.

Lawson, Chappell (1999) *Building the Fourth Estate: Media Opening and Democratization in Mexico*, unpublished PhD dissertation, Stanford University.

Le Duc, Don R. (1987) *Beyond Broadcasting: Patterns in Policy and Law*. New York: Longman.

Lee, Jae-Kyoung (1996) 'A crisis of the South Korean media: the rise of civil society and democratic transition', *Media Asia*, 23 (2): 86–8, 94–5.

Lent, John A. (1998) 'The mass media in Asia', in Patrick H. O'Neil (ed.), *Communicating Democracy: The Media and Political Transitions*. Boulder, CO: Lynne Rienner. pp. 147–70.

Lieberman, Trudy (1994) 'The Selling of Clinton Lite', in the *Columbia Journalism Review*, March/April: 12–14

Liebes, Tamar and Peri, Yoram (1998) 'Electronic broadcasting in segmented societies: lessons from the 1996 Israeli elections', *Political Communication*, 15 (1): 27–43.

Maarek, Philippe J. (1997) 'New trends in French political communications: the 1995 presidential elections', *Media, Culture and Society*, 19 (3): 357–68.

Madden, Normandy (1996) 'The business of broadcasting', *Transition*, 2 (8): 6–17, 64.

Mahan, Elizabeth (1996) 'Media, politics and society in Latin America', *Latin American Research Review*, 31 (2): 138–62.

Mayobre, Jose Antonio (1996) 'Politics, media, and modern democracy: the case of Venezuela', in D. Swanson and P. Mancini (eds), *Politics, Media and Modern Democracy*. Westport, CT: Praeger. pp. 227–45.

McAnany, Emile G. and Wilkinson, Kenton T. (1996) 'Introduction', in E. McAnany and K. Wilkinson (eds), *Mass Media and Free Trade: NAFTA and the Cultural Industries*. Austin, TX: University of Texas Press. pp. 3–29.

McDowell, Stephen D. (1997) 'Globalization and policy choice: television and audiovisual services policies in India', *Media, Culture and Society*, 19: 151–72.

McEnteer, James (1996) 'Guns, goons, gold, and glitz: Philippine press coverage of the 1995 national elections', *Press/Politics*, 1 (1): 113–20.

Mickiewicz, Ellen (1997) *Changing Channels: Television and the Struggle for Power in Russia*. New York: Oxford University Press.

Mineo Tudela, Liz (1999) Personal communication with authors, Lima, Peru, 10 April.

Mohammadi, Ali (1998) 'Electronic empires: an Islamic perspective', in D.K. Thussu (ed.), *Electronic Empires: Global Media and Local Resistance*. London: Arnold. pp. 257–72.

Mollison, Thomas A. (1998) 'Television broadcasting leads Romania's march toward an open, democratic society', *Journal of Broadcasting and Electronic Media*, 42 (1): 128–41.

Moog, Sandra (2000) 'The transformation of American political communication in the information age', in *Vox Populi – Vox Dei?* Slavko Splichal (ed.), Hampton Press.

Moog, Sandra (1997) 'Television, mass polling and the mass media: the impact of media technologies on American politics, 1960–1996', *Javnost: The Public*, 4 (2): 39–55.

Moore, Patrick (1995) 'War as the centerpiece in Bosnia and Croatia', *Transition*, 1 (18): 30–3.

Nivat, Anne (1998) 'His master's voice: Russian journalists feel the grip of the media moguls', *Transitions*, 5 (6): 42–7.

Panebianco, Angelo (1988) *Political Parties: Organization and Power*, trans. Marc Silver. New York: Cambridge University Press.

Papathanassopoulos, Stylianos (1997) 'The politics and the effects of the deregulation of Greek television', *European Journal of Communication*, 12 (3): 351–68.

Papathanassopoulos, Stylianos (1998) 'Media journalism and politics in Greece', paper presented at the Workshop on Media and Politics in Europe, at the Center for German and European Studies, University of California at Berkeley, 17 and 18 April.

Patterson, Thomas (1993) *Out of Order*. New York: Knopf.

Pendakur, Manjunath and Kapur, Jyotsna (1997) 'Think globally, program locally: privatization of Indian national television', in M. Baille and D. Winseck (eds), *Democratizing Communication?* Cresskill, NJ: Hampton Press. pp. 195–217.

Pfetch, Barbara (1996) 'Convergence through privatization? Changing media environments and televised politics in Germany', *European Journal of Communication*, 11 (4): 427–51.

Polsby (1983) *The Consequences of Party Reform*. Berkeley, CA: Institute of Governmental Studies Press.

Porto, Mauro (1998a) 'Globo's evening news and the representation of politics in Brazil (1995–1996)', paper presented at the 48th Annual Conference of the International Communication Association, Jerusalem, July.

Porto, Mauro (1998b) 'Novas tecnologias e politica no Brasil: a globalizacao em uma sociedade periferica e desigual', paper presented at XXI Congress of the Latin American Studies Association, Chicago, Sept.

Purdum, Todd S. (1999) 'TV political news in California is shrinking, study confirms', *The New York Times*, 13 Jan.: A11.

Rawnsley, Gary D. (1997) 'The 1996 presidential campaign in Taiwan: packaging politics in a democratizing state', *Press/Politics*, 2 (2): 47–61.

Rondelli, Elizabeth (1998) 'Televisao aberta e por assinatura: consumo cultural e politica de programacao', *Lugar Comun*, May–Dec.: 33–58.

Rosentiel, T., Gottlieb, C. and Brady, L. (1999) 'Local TV: what works, what flops, and why', *Columbia Journalism Review*, Jan./Feb.: 17–23.

Rospir, Juan I. (1996) 'Political communication and electoral campaigns in the young Spanish democracy', in T. Weymoth and B. Lamizet (eds), *Markets and Myths: Forces for Change in European Media*. Harlow, Essex: Addison Wesley Longman Limited. pp. 155–69.

Saad, Lydia (1998) ' "Most admired" poll finds Americans lack major heroes', *Gallup Poll Monthly*, 388: 2–3.

Scammel, Margaret (1995) *Designer Politics: How Elections are Won*. New York: St. Martin's Press.

Scammel, Margaret (1998) 'The wisdom of the war room: U.S. campaigning and Americanization', *Media, Culture and Society*, 20 (2): 251–75.

Schudson, Michael (1978) *Discovering the News: A Social History of American Newspapers*. New York: Basic Books.

Schwoch, James (1993) 'Broadcast media and Latin American politics: the historical context', in T. Skidmore (ed.), *Television, Politics and the Transition to Democracy in Latin America*. Baltimore, MD: Johns Hopkins University Press. pp. 38–54.

Semetko, Holli A. and Canel, Maria Jose (1997) 'Agenda-senders versus agenda-setters: television in Spain's 1996 election campaign', *Political Communication*, 14 (3): 459–79.

Sherman, Spencer A. (1995) 'Hiroshi who?', *Columbia Journalism Review*, July/Aug.: 8–9.

Sinclair, John (1996) 'Mexico, Brazil, and the Latin World', in J. Sinclair, E. Jacka and S. Cunningham (eds), *Peripheral Vision: New Patterns in Global Television*. New York: Oxford University Press. pp. 33–66.

Skolkay, A. (1996) 'An analysis of media legislation: the case of Slovakia', *International Journal of Communications Law and Policy*, 6 (2): 1–13.

Sluyter-Beltrao, Jeffrey (forthcoming) 'Old Vinegar, New Bottles: Factional Competition and Democratic Thinning in Brazil's New Unionism, 1978–1995', unpublished PhD dissertation, University of California at Berkeley.

Smith, Geri (1999) 'Mexico's next election could be a real horse race', *Business Week*, 15 March.

Sparks, Colin with Anna Reading (1998) *Communism, Capitalism and the Mass Media*. London: Sage.

Stratham, Paul (1996) 'Television news and the public sphere in Italy: conflicts at the media/politics interface', *European Journal of Political Communication*, 11 (4): 511–56.

Straubhaar, Joseph D. (1997) 'The electronic media in Brazil', in R. Cole (ed.), *Communication in Latin America: Journalism, Mass Media and Society*. Wilmington, DE: Scholarly Resources. pp. 217–43.

Swanson, David and Mancini, Paolo (eds) (1996) *Politics, Media and Modern Democracy*. Westport, CT: Praeger.

Sukosd, Miklos and Cseh, Gabriella (1998) 'Hollywood's Hungarian Offensive', *Transitions*, 5 (4): 42–7.

Syvertsen, Trine and Eli Skogerbe (1998) 'Scandinavia, Netherlands, and Belgium', in A. Smith with D. Paterson (eds), *Television: An International History*, 2nd edn. Oxford: Oxford University Press. pp. 223–33.

Thomas, Pradip N. (1998) 'South Asia', in A. Smith with D. Paterson (eds), *Television: An International History*, 2nd edn. Oxford: Oxford University Press. pp. 201–7.

Tucher, Andie (1997) ' "You news": it's not your father's newscast anymore', *Columbia Journalism Review*, May/June: 7.

Vilches, Lorenzo (1996) 'The media in Spain', in T. Weymoth and B. Lamizet (eds), *Markets and Myths: Forces for Change in European Media*. Harlow, Essex: Addison Wesley Longman Limited. pp. 173–201.

Waisbord, Silvio R. (1996) 'Secular politics: the modernization of Argentine electioneering', in D. Swanson and P. Mancini (eds), *Politics, Media and Modern Democracy*. Westport, CT: Praeger. pp. 207–25.

Waisbord, Silvio R. (1998) 'Latin America', in A. Smith with D. Paterson (eds), *Television: An International History*. 2nd edn. Oxford: Oxford University Press. pp. 254–63.

Wernick, Andrew (1991) *Promotional Culture: Advertising, Ideology and Symbolic Expression*. London: Sage.

Yang, Catherine, Gross, Neil, Siklos, Richard and Brull, Steven (1998) 'Digital D-Day', *Business Week*, 28 Nov.: 144–58.

Youm, Kyu Ho (1998) 'Democratization and the press: the case of South Korea', in P. O'Neil (ed.), *Communicating Democracy*. Boulder, CO: Lynne Rienner. pp. 171–90.

3 The Transformation of Democracy?

Peter Dahlgren

Observers note the paradox that in the world today innumerable people who have not attained democracy are willing to risk their lives to achieve it, while so many in the West who have it seemingly switch off when the topic is brought up. In many corners of late modern society a profound debate is under way on the current state of democracy and the potential for renewal. Scholars, journalists, politicians and citizens are asking themselves if and how the democratic character of societies can be maintained and enhanced. The current moment attests that we are rather far from the original ideals of liberal democracy and are experiencing what many term a democratic deficit.

Trying to evaluate the contemporary status of democracy and comprehend the forces that shape it is no easy task. Democracy is complex and multidimensional, both as a concept and as a phenomenon. While elections are a vital feature of all functioning democracies, there is a civic and political life beyond elections that must also measure up to our democratic ideals, not least the character of public discursive communication between citizens (cf. Benhabib, 1996). Democracy requires a public culture, anchored in some minimum of shared values and manifested in everyday practices, where people can experience themselves as members and potential participants of a democratic society.

We find varying – and often competing – diagnoses about the present situation (Beck, 1998; Dahl, 1998; Hirst, 1997; Resnick, 1997). Virtually everybody will agree on the importance of the media of communication in shaping the democratic character of society, but fewer, unfortunately, emphasize the importance of democratizing the media (Bailie and Winseck, 1997, offer some exceptions). In the modern era, their role in making politics (and society) visible, in providing information, analysis, forums for debate, a shared civic culture – in short, a public sphere – is beyond dispute. They appear ubiquitous and continue to expand. Certainly the media have been instrumental in globalizing the normative vision of democracy. In Western democracies they have been both praised and vehemently criticized, but however we judge them, the media are an integral part of our contemporary reality, a major historical force. At the macro, societal and micro level of everyday life, the modern world – and democracy in particular – would be totally unrecognizable without the media of communication (Thompson, 1995).

There are many factors shaping late modern democracy, and we would be foolish to lapse into media-centrism and reduce all these dynamics simply to the workings of the media: their impact is effected through their interplay with other forces. How we think about public issues, for example, is not simply a mirror of media output, but the result of an array of variables, as media research has argued from the beginning. Moreover, the media do not function as a unified societal force, but as a complex set of institutions. They are shaped by internal organizational features as well as by external societal conditions. Consequently, there is nothing inherently deterministic about the way the media function, nor about their impact on democracy and on the way that we think about the world and about ourselves.

That said, I still want to underscore the media's key position in the transformation of democracy. I would also support the counter-argument, that the media help maintain continuity for democracy, providing stability via their established ways of covering politics, the collective frames of reference they foster and the rather ritualistic elements that characterize their modes of representation. The two positions are obviously not mutually exclusive: democracy and society manifest both stability and change in varying ways. In part it is a question of time frame: from day to day we tend to recognize the recurring features of democracy and society generally. As we increase the temporal span of our perspective, the changes come more clearly into view. Here I will be emphasizing the alterations in democracy over the recent decades. And if democracy has been evolving, the media too can be said to be undergoing dramatic transformation.

In what follows, I will set the stage by sketching a few dominant trends in both the theory and practice of contemporary democracy. Thereafter I take up a number of themes concerning the media's role and how this relates to democracy. First, I highlight a few key trends that are dramatically altering the traditional media – the press, radio and television – at a structural level. I then turn my attention to the Internet, which has engendered nothing less than a media revolution during the 1990s. From there I go on to explore how such changes in media structures are impacting on the nature of journalism, changing its logic. Then I will offer some reflections on how the polity, being media audiences, is also in transition. Finally, from the standpoint of democracy as a whole, I discuss how the media have come to constitute the dominant sites for political life and what the implications of this might be.

Late modern democracy

If the functioning of democratic systems in Western democracies varies between countries, some general trends over the past few decades can nonetheless be specified. Many of these trends can fuel pessimism, but we should remind ourselves that trends are not necessarily identical with the overall reality. There are still many democratic forces and resources operating in society, but we would be misguided to ignore contemporary developments, since they do call into question some of our basic assumptions about democracy.

We can note, first, at an overarching level, the altered contract between capital, labour and the state. Capitalism has been a precondition for liberal democracy and yet remains chronically problematic for it, in that it generates social power that lies beyond democratic control. The post-war welfare state structures and the Keynesian policies associated with them were a successful strategy in their time for dealing with such tensions; the various shades of social democratic measures served to extend democracy and citizenship. By the 1970s this model was encountering serious difficulties. Since then, particularly during the 1980s, we have witnessed in Western democracies a political turn where market forces and private enterprise have been given much greater rein to define the social landscape, with a concomitant decline in democratic accountability. This has in turn shifted the ideological climate to emphasize the congruence between democracy and capitalism while downplaying the dilemmas.

Secondly, we can observe that the formal political system of most Western nations appears stagnant, reactive rather than proactive, eclipsed by developments in the realms of large-scale capitalism and technological innovations and outpaced by socio-cultural developments. The margins of governmental manoeuvrability are narrowing. Institutions central to democratic life, in particular political parties, have become unresponsive in the face of the major changes of late modernity. The sovereignty of the nation-state itself is being downsized in the face of global circumstances, in particular the role of transnational corporations, as well as – in the European context – the EU. In the case of the latter this opens up the challenge of developing democracy at the regional level.

Thirdly, among citizens, the arena of official politics does not command the degree of support and participation it has in the past. Voter turnouts are decreasing, even in countries such as Sweden, which has had considerable stability in its electoral patterns over the earlier post-war decades. Party loyalty is in decline, especially among the young (Huggins, Chapter 6 in this volume). One also sees signs of a growing contempt for the political class. A corrosive climate of cynicism is emerging in some places. The extensive disenchantment with formal politics is a theme addressed by many today (Norris, 1999; Putnam, 1993; Sandel, 1996). In the West we have a crisis of civic culture and citizenship (Blumler and Gurevitch, 1995), that can be linked to a more pervasive cultural malaise (Bellah *et al.*, 1985). Many people in Western societies seem to have at best very rudimentary identities as citizens, as members and potential participants of political society. This atmosphere of 'anti-politics' must be understood as the consequence of the inability of the political system to meet social expectations and an absence of an alternative and compelling political vision. Economic insecurity, unemployment, low wages, declining social services, growing class cleavages, ecological dilemmas and a sense of powerlessness among many citizens are all part of the picture.

Fourthly, the polity itself is becoming more heterogeneous and, seen sociologically, is fragmenting. In the 'great retreat' (Boggs, 1997) from the arena of common concerns and politics, we see a concurrent withdrawal into 'enclave consciousness', away from larger collective identities and community sensibilities. These enclaves may or may not have a political focus. This fragmentation has several origins, but for our purposes here, two are most significant. The first has to do with the pluralization of lifestyles in late modernity. Generally, advanced consumer culture fosters increasing 'nichification', or even 'neo-tribalism', as some observers put it, as the multiplicity of tastes, interests and social orientations accelerate (Axford, Chapter 1 in this volume). The second has to do with multiculturalism, as the ethnic and religious pluralism of many Western countries increases. These centrifugal forces problematize a democracy predicated on a nation-state characterized by homogeneity, sharing a unified public culture. Both of these tendencies also serve to promote frames of reference and engagement beyond the borders of the nation-state (e.g. global youth culture, transnational social movements, diasporic communities).

Lastly, there is counter-evidence that evokes a different, more optimistic train of thought, at least in regard to citizen engagement. It is in a sense the flip side of the previous point, and can be said to represent a form of 'new politics' (Giddens, 1991, speaks of 'life politics'). The ostensible political apathy and disaffiliation from the established political system may not necessarily signal a disinterest in politics per se. That is, if we look beyond formal electoral politics, we can see various signs that suggest that many people have not abandoned engagement with the political, but have rather refocused their political attention outside the parliamentary system. Or they are in the process of redefining just what constitutes the political (Mulgan, 1994), often within the context of social movements. The boundaries between politics, cultural values, identity processes and local self-reliance measures become fluid (Beck, 1998); civil and political society become less differentiated from each other. Politics becomes not only an instrumental activity for achieving concrete goals, but also an expressive and performative activity (Street, Chapter 10 in this volume).

This new politics is characterized by personalized rather than collective engagement and a stronger emphasis on single issues than on overarching platforms or ideologies (Bennett, 1998). Some claim that part of this development can be understood as a move away from politics based on production to one focused on consumption; political attention is geared more towards the needs of clients, customers and consumers than in the past (Gibbens and Reimer, 1999). Further, political activity within the new politics is more ad hoc, less dependent on traditional organizations and on elites mobilizing their standing cadres of supporters. It is more typified by decentralized networking. Along with social movements, particularly in the areas of ecology, feminism, peace and social self-help, we find a large number of non-governmental organizations (NGOs) that also can mobilize and absorb citizens' engagement, even across national borders. Whether or not these developments are genuinely fruitful for the enhancement of democracy is of course under debate, but they do open the door for new ways to think about the contemporary political landscape.

Restructuring the traditional media

Most fundamentally the media are social institutions, largely organized commercially for profit. As institutions, what they do is to provide the dominant symbolic environment of society, with patterns of communication criss-crossing the social terrain in complex fashion. Their activities are enabled and constrained by their political economy, as well as by the social and cultural environments in which they operate (such as the behaviour and views of their audiences). Also, their organizational structures and routines, and the occupational horizons and ambitions of the people who work within them are important elements. For example, the professional ideals of journalists at times come into conflict with those who make financial decisions. The legal parameters for their operations derive from regulatory policies, itself a key political terrain. Not least are the technical developments that impact on how media institutions operate and develop (e.g. television can do different things from the press; both are being modified by digitalization).

Some of what is presented in the media derives from the media's own initiatives and professional mores (e.g. investigative journalism). Much arises from the symbiotic relationship the media have with external actors, notably the mutual dependence of journalists and political elites. Some of the media's output is a direct result of external initiatives (a politician calling a press conference, for example). Popular discourses tend to mythologize journalists as heroes (and sometimes villains). The answers to the classic questions of *why* the media's output looks the way it does generally, or why they covered a particular event in a given way, however, are to be found in a complex interplay of institutional circumstances. (See Schudson, 1996 for a classic overview of sociological perspectives on news production.)

A key to understanding the media's role in the transformation of democracy is to grasp how the structural conditions of the media are changing and what this means for the way they operate. Socio-cultural changes among audiences are having an impact, as I will discuss below. More immediate are five mutually reinforcing trends that are dramatically changing the media landscape: commercialization, concentration, globalization, deregulation and proliferation. Digitalization is of course also a profoundly important trend, but for the sake of exposition, I take up digitalization in the following section.

Commercialization

All media have to arrange for their financing, and with the exception of public service broadcasting, which has been strong in the Western European context and comparatively weak in the USA, the media have been organized as commercial ventures from the start. They are institutions in the business of making money for their stockholders. In regard to the press, the profit incentive has traditionally been balanced – with varying degrees of success – by a sense of public purpose and responsibility. For private radio and television, there had been a similar sense of social responsibility, though backed up by regulatory frameworks that, among other things, demanded a minimum of news and current affairs output.

For a variety of reasons commercial imperatives have hardened over the past few decades, and the balance between public responsibility and private profit has been steadily tipping in favour of the latter. Normative goals are increasingly giving way to economic calculation (McManus, 1994; Underwood, 1995. For a concise statement on the political economic perspective of the media, see Golding and Murdock, 1996; for a more extensive presentation see Mosco, 1996.) In the current commercial climate, many daily newspapers are having a hard time attracting readers, especially younger ones, as other media successfully compete for their attention. The elite press in most countries is in decline, and popular forms of journalism are on the increase.

Concentration

For the press and for private broadcasting, commercialization is inseparable from the concentration of ownership and the media's expanding character as big business; the media are following general patterns found in the economy. Massive media empires have emerged on a global scale, concentrating ownership in the hands of a decreasing number of corporations. Such giants as Time Warner and AOL, Disney, Rupert Murdoch's News Corporation and Bertelsmann are among the dozen or so leading global media corporations, followed by another three or four dozen somewhat smaller corporate actors. Together they dominate the media landscape of the modern world. The holdings of these corporations encompass all phases of media activity, from production to distribution, hardware and software, across virtually all media forms and technologies.

Significantly, via mergers and co-operative ventures, the media industries are integrating with telecommunications (e.g. AT&T with DirecTV) and the computer industry (e.g. Microsoft and NBC; Time Warner with AOL). These trends and their implications for democracy are analysed in a growing literature (Alleyne, 1997; Herman and McChesney, 1997; Lacroix and Tremblay, 1997; McChesney, 1999; Schiller, 1999; Sussman, 1997). In the words of Baldwin *et al.*, journalism and the functions of information distribution 'will come into the hands of businesspeople and managers who have only a layperson's exposure to the traditions and ethics of journalism' (1996: 397). The culture of journalism, with its critical watchdog functions and its protection of freedom of expression, is not the culture of these institutions. The forces of concentration are even felt on the local level: in the USA, most areas now have only one newspaper and most of these are owned by non-local corporations whose journalistic commitments are minimal.

Globalization

Michael Tracey (1998: 46) observes that among the top 500 corporations in the USA, half proclaim that they belong to no single nation.
Within the communication field we see also an increasingly global
character of media ownership and activities. The major media corporations are global actors, operating transnationally. In regard to media,
globalization can mean transnational ownership, which can raise problems about responsiveness and accountability. However, globalization
also can mean transnational media activities (Barker, 1997, for the case
of television). For example, European countries had to relinquish claims
to national sovereignty of their airwaves with the advent of satellite
television, and the Internet certainly is indifferent to national boundaries. The implications of such developments are complex, yet we should
not ignore the potential positive contribution of such developments for
enhancing citizens' frames of reference and social engagement (Coleman,
Chapter 5 in this volume). For example, public engagement with many
international events – political repression, environmental disasters, famine, and so on – has been made possible by globalized media coverage,
especially on television. This remains true even while much criticism is
justifiably aimed at the nature of the coverage (e.g. the Gulf War) and
the vast black holes of non-coverage of much of the world.

Deregulation

If economic developments have given birth to intensified commercialism,
concentration and globalization, deregulation has been the midwife.
Deregulation is the policy process whereby the various laws, rules and
codes that governments use to shape media ownership, financing and
ongoing activities are withdrawn or weakened, a process which at
bottom is a political one, reflecting the power and interests of various
actors. Regulation and deregulation of the media are of course an area
of intense concern in a period of profound restructuring of the media
landscape (McQuail and Siune, 1998).

Deregulation has been most strongly manifested in the area of broadcasting, with the transition in most Western European countries in
recent decades from public service monopolies to mixed systems. Public
service broadcasting itself was in need of institutional renewal. Virtually
all such broadcasting organizations were facing financial difficulties by
the 1980s, and charges of paternalism and stagnation, as well as in some
countries a too close relationship with the state, were not without
validity. However, as many have argued (cf. Tracey, 1998) the question is
whether or not the politics of deregulation have contributed to the

erosion of the public service mission, which mission included enhancing democracy (Graham and Davies, 1997).

Public service broadcasting is predicated on the ideal of universalism – it is intended as a right for all citizens, and strives to serve society in its entirety via the diversity of its programming. Its premise is to address audiences as publics, not markets. Clearly its degree of success in achieving these aspirations varied, but there remained, significantly, a normative consensus regarding its mission and mechanisms of social accountability. The alterations in broadcasting's circumstances have significantly weakened this consensus and any possibility of account-ability. While public service in most countries has restructured and streamlined itself, today it comprises a declining proportion of the overall broadcasting output, and its *raison d'être* is less self-evident. The new commercial broadcasters, for their part, had fewer restrictions placed on them in regard to programming, and enforcing the regulations that remained at times proved difficult.

Proliferation

An important upshot of these developments is that we have many more channels of communication today than we had twenty years ago. Cable and satellite television offers packages with dozens of channels; in some cities the number available is nearing 100. If the number of daily newspapers is contracting somewhat, the growth in magazines has been explosive over the past two decades. And the Internet (see below) offers not only a seemingly endless supply of information on its own, but is also increasingly relaying the output of traditional media. The mediati-zation of society and culture is proceeding at a rapid pace, as the density of our symbolic environments and the accessibility of information mushrooms. While much of the media environment is geared to enter-tainment, leisure and consumption, it would be unfair to say that news and current affairs have been left in the dust; they too are proliferating, primarily on the Net and on television. Are these trends good for democracy? Herman and McChesney (1997: 1) describe the overall situation succinctly:

> Since the early 1980's there has been a dramatic restructuring of national media industries, along with the emergence of a genuinely global commer-cial media market. The newly developing global media system is dominated by three or four dozen large transnational corporations (TNC's), with fewer than ten mostly US-based media conglomerates towering over the global market. In addition to the concentration of media power, the major feature of the global media order is its thoroughgoing commercialism, and

an associated marked decline in the relative importance of public broad-casting and the applicability of public service standards. Such a concentration of media power in organizations dependent on advertising support and responsible primarily to shareholders is a clear and present danger to citizens' participation in public affairs, understanding of public issues, and thus to the effective working of democracy.

I would reiterate that we are talking about trends: these developments do not mean that the mediated public sphere in Western democracies is beyond all hope, but the direction of the developments is significant. Thus, while journalism is proliferating, it is increasingly losing its privileged status as an institution whose purpose is to serve – and help define – the common good. In the context of commercial logic it is becoming a media commodity among others. These structural changes in the media have arisen reciprocally with other societal trends, including the crisis of the welfare state, the dilemmas of the national project in a globalizing world and the enhanced power of market forces. Together these challenge us to rethink the definitions and possibilities for democracy in the future. But to better understand the present, let us now look at the Internet, in which not inconsiderable democratic hope has been invested.

Net promises and uses

Digitalization is unquestionably the major technological trend in the media today. This means that a common electronic language, based on the 'bits' of the computer, is emerging for all mediated communication. Thus, text, sound and voice, as well as still and moving images, are increasingly being translated into a common digital form (Fidler, 1997). The traditional media are all using digital technologies in various phases of their activities. A major threshold that has been anticipated in recent years is the transition from analogue to digital television transmission, currently a commercially uncertain development that is now just starting to take off (Steemers, 1998). We see digitalization firmly entrenched in other media, for example in the CD-ROM formats of games and educational materials, the newly launched DVD technology (digital versatile disk) and of course on the Internet.

The Internet has emerged during the 1990s as a major media revolution (see Kitchin, 1998, for a useful overview). While its spread globally is very skewed (the developing nations have only a few per cent of the world's computers) and its spread in the industrialized West is still

skewed by socio-economic factors, its growth has exceeded most prog-
noses. Ascertaining the extent of Net access and use is tricky and some
claims should be met with scepticism, but it is clear that its spread has
been nothing short of phenomenal. In Sweden it was recently announced
that half the population has access to the Net. Even if figures vary
among countries, the Net has unquestionably become a major medium
in all industrialized societies. While there is a strong bias towards
affluent males with a high degree of cultural capital among Net users,
this group is far from alone in cyberspace. If the economics and cultural
competencies required to become an on-line citizen will prevent the Net
from becoming genuinely universal for the foreseeable future, its present
reach is still of much relevance for democracy.

From the beginning there were many who hoped that the Internet
would somehow manifest an alternative to the kinds of tendencies I have
sketched in regard to the traditional media. But a lot of Net history has
transpired in a short time. Today, not only is the commercialization of
the Net a fact, but the Net itself has become a central tool and arena for
the global marketplace (Schiller, 1999). The Net is increasingly being
used for economic transactions, and the majority of new Web sites these
days are commercial. If the initial 'cyber-euphoria' has by now faded,
there are still key features of the Internet that are of direct relevance for
democracy. In particular the notions of community and public sphere in
cyberspace are now getting a more nuanced treatment in the literature
(Holmes, 1997; Jones, 1998; Smith and Kollock, 1999; Sassi and
Coleman, Chapters 4 and 5 in this volume). But the basic point to be
made about the Internet in regard to democracy is that its consequences
today appear quite mixed (see, for example, the special issue of *Constellations*, 1997) – this holds true even for the results of explicit
experiments in Net use in urban settings (Tsagarousianou *et al.*, 1998).
Ambivalence will no doubt remain even as the Net continues to expand
in its reach and develop in its technical possibilities. We cannot reduce
the complexity of the Net and its impact to a singular, unequivocally
positive or negative evaluation.

The several kinds of communication possibilities that the Net today
offers underscore this complexity. First of all, though not part of its
original profile, the Net in its current phase can be seen as an extension
of the mass media. On-line versions of television, radio stations, news
services and daily newspapers constitute a considerable degree of Net
activity, with many major mass media now having an on-line presence.
Secondly, the Internet also offers one-to-many communication via the
Web sites that in principle (though not in practice) anybody can set up,
including governments, businesses, financial actors, interest groups,

political and civic activists, hobbyists and fan clubs. Similarly, individuals can search the countless data banks available. These banks constitute an enormous domain within cyberspace, even if many of them charge fees for access.

Thirdly, we have the interactivity typified by Usenet news groups and chat rooms. Globally, there are tens of thousands of such discussion groups, with many fading out and new ones taking off all the time. Also, all the various forms of networking, enacted by an endless variety of institutions and collectivities, are an important aspect of this many-to-many communication. People link up not just to talk, but also to get things done, including achieving political goals. Finally, with e-mail, we have basically one-to-one communication for which the post office is the paradigmatic model. As with the post office, mass mailings are often done via e-mail, but the core of this part of the Internet remains dyadic in its communicative form.

How is the Net used? There are many answers to this question, but for our purposes we should note that the use of the Internet for serious information searches or for political engagement appears to be a minor sideline. This becomes apparent when compared to the massive flows of commerce, trivia, entertainment, chatting, role playing and other games, and, not least, of pornography. The percentage of Web sites and news groups oriented towards politics is a small minority (Hill and Hughes, 1998). Thus, we are talking about a limited and rather elite segment of the population in Western societies whose use patterns of the Internet as a political arena and information source are very much of a minority. The small numbers, however, are to a degree offset by the sociological profile of the group: affluence and high education are important variables in the shaping of opinion and political climates. Along with the many discussion groups in the civic and political domain, we have thousands of NGOs, organized social movements, lobby groups and political activists who make use of the Net. Cyberspace is thus becoming a vital link and meeting ground for a civically engaged and politically mobilized stratum of the polity. In this regard, it fosters the emergence of multiple mini-public spheres.

At the same time, we must be alert to qualities of the Net that can actually hinder citizen engagement. Democracy requires not just a formal system, but also certain cultural prerequisites in everyday life. Forms of interaction between citizens (which is the discursive core of any 'public'), minimal shared feelings of belonging to a democratic community, minimal identity as a citizen (Clarke, 1996) – as a member and potential participant of a larger entity – are necessary for a democratic civic culture (Dahlgren, 1995, 1997). Without such a healthy civic culture, democracy as a system has no future. If we look at the Net's possible contribution to generating publics, we must take into account these cultural dimensions. What contributions and limits to civic culture arise from the disembodied character of cyber communication? What are the implications of the absence of physicality in social contact and in regard to geographic position? How does this impinge on people's sense of shared purpose and collective self-understanding? What place can we find for commitment within the playful environment of the Net, when we can so easily switch off if we feel bored? These are not facile rhetorical questions, but rather central themes for the future of democracy that we must grapple with, conceptually, empirically and normatively, as more and more communication takes place within cyberspace.

Virtual reality raises many issues about communicative ethics, about discourse strategies. We are by now quite used to the notion of 'virtual', but we need to remind ourselves that it points to a difference, a distinction, while at the same time minimizing the importance of that distinction. Alternatively, it might be said to emphasize the difference, heralding it as something new (and possibly better). My point here is precisely the issue of the distance from – or the approximation of – 'real life' within virtual reality: the status or quality of its representations, modes of interaction and social bonds. They *are* different, yet tantalizingly similar. The implications of this tension continue to engage current analyses of cyberspace (Fornäs, 1998; Jordan, 1999; Robins and Webster, 1999).

In an early study of Net use among politically engaged citizens, Fisher *et al.* (1996) were able to distinguish several ideal types of civic interaction on the Net. These include what they call the communitarian, which emphasizes the ideal of participatory democracy and mutuality, democratic mobilization, in which cyberspace is used by activist interest groups to organize themselves, and like-minded exchange, where discussion reinforces the values and perceptions of groups and discourages contact with those who think differently. Like-minded exchange can give rise to decidedly uncivil interaction ('flaming'), as insiders strive to mark boundaries against outsiders who do not share their fundamental assumptions. More significantly, the drive toward like-mindedness ties in with the pattern of ever-increasing small and isolated mini public spheres that do not necessarily link up with larger forums of discussions. In other words, the public sphere on the Net risks generating a very fragmented public sphere that consists of increasingly private discussions.

However, Hill and Hughes (1998), in the largest study thus far on the political uses of Internet, note that the Net does add something significant for those who use it. Of the sites which had to do with politics, they find that about 20 per cent fell outside the political mainstream reflected by the traditional media. In other words, for its users, the Net can expand the political margins of the public sphere. In the USA, Hill and Hughes note the paradox that most Internet users lean towards the liberal end of the political spectrum; conservatives are minority in terms of numbers. However, in looking at the political activity among Usenet groups and other manifestations of political engagement on the Internet, there is a clear conservative dominance. The conclusion they draw is that thus far the right-wing has been more ambitious, organized and well-financed, and taken more initiatives in terms of using the Net.

In the use of the Net as extensions of the older media, Hill and Hughes observe that people favour a few specialized news providers, much as they do with the mass media. Also, they are often probing deeper into something that they have seen in the traditional mass media; they are getting more, but largely not very different information. In contrast to some postmodern theorizing, this suggests that the Internet does not change people so much, it tends rather to allow them to do what they usually do, but do it better. We should add, however, that this might change with increasing experience of the Net and its capacity for interactivity. It seems that few people become political information junkies via the Net; rather, if they are, they in all likelihood already were before they became Net users.

The picture that comes into focus counsels sobriety in regard to easy optimism or pessimism. A massive sea change in political life is not yet apparent. Politics as we know it is still recognizable in cyberspace (Barnett, 1997). As indicated, access to the Net is far from universal, and only a small portion of those who use the Net do so in ways which seemingly pertain to the public sphere. However, looking to the decades ahead, the 'cyberspace divide', based as it ultimately is on material conditions (Loader, 1998), may well prove to be a key issue regarding the social grounds of citizenship. The growing gap between information haves and have-nots in the digital age threatens to become a serious destabilizing factor for democratic life.

The evolving contours of journalism

Journalism is in many ways emblematic of the modern era. Yet many of the historical, taken-for-granted premises of modernity itself have come into question – for example, the links between political, economic and/or technological progress on the one hand, and human freedom, happiness and general well-being on the other. At the start of a new millennium, the future looms more uncertainly than of yore. The optimism for a democratic society once reflected in the role and capacity of modern journalism has become more ambivalent. This ambivalence does not decrease as journalism moves into cyberspace.

As an institutionalized set of practices located within the media, journalism of course does not remain unaffected by the transformations of society, culture and the media themselves. The 'high modernist' or 'classical' paradigm of journalism, a product of specific historical circumstances, is waning, as a number of authors have argued (cf. Altheide and Snow, 1991). This historical mode took shape early in the last century and based itself on traditional liberal ideals of democracy and citizenship. In this framework, journalism in the mass media is seen as providing reports and analyses of real events and processes, and contributing to defining the public agenda (Dearing and Rogers, 1996).

Through its narratives, classical journalism lays claim to accurate and impartial renderings of a reality that exists independently of its telling, and which is external to the institutions of journalism. It is aimed at a heterogeneous citizenry that basically still shares the same public culture, and where citizens use journalism as a resource for participation in the politics and culture of society. Journalism in this mode serves as an integrative force and as a common forum for debate. Even if journalism in the real world has never operated quite like this (see Bennett, 1996, for an analytic overview of journalism's contradictions), it is this paradigmatic model of how it should be that has guided our understanding of it and our expectations of it. This model has also been fundamental for journalism's daily practices, guiding the news values that lay behind the two kinds of questions that journalism must continuously answer. These are: *what* to present about the world and *how* it is to be represented, i.e. what modes of representation and what 'angle' to take.

To say that this mode of journalism is waning is not to suggest it has vanished, or that it will. Rather, it is to call attention to the fact that the ensemble of historical factors on which it has been predicated are changing, as we move from high modernity to late modernity. We can already see the signs of new developments, but they are by no means clear, and we cannot say with any certitude how they will evolve. What we have at present are the contours of an as yet incomplete and even at times contradictory portrait of classical journalism in transition. I would underscore in particular the following mutually reinforcing trends as indicative of the present trajectories within the broad field of journalism.

Overabundance

The sheer amount of information available to citizens is increasing obviously enough, but so is its density. Information within the media environment is so ubiquitous, so crowded, that the competition for attention is becoming an ever-important feature of public culture. At the same time, the vast majority of media output is not journalistic in nature, and the competition for attention to the media must also be understood as one between journalism and non-journalism. Among the oceans of information flowing through the traditional media and the Net, only a small portion can be deemed journalism, and the attention it gets may be even disproportionately smaller.

Popularization

The media are increasingly blurring the distinctions between journalism and non-journalism; generic hybridization through 'infotainment' (e.g. talk shows and docu-dramas) is by now an established concept within the mass media, and we see an increasing trend toward the populariza- tion of journalism. The shift away from print (e.g. decline in 'elite' press) to audio-visual formats in much public culture, at least within the media aiming at large-scale audiences, can also be understood as an expression of popularization. Popularization can be and often is a positive develop- ment when it makes the public sphere available to larger numbers of people, via more accessible formats and styles of presentation, as exemplified in the better versions of some newer TV news formats. Alternatively it takes up topics and experiences from the realm of private experience and introduces them as important and contestable topics within the public sphere.

All too often, however, popularization reflects commodification, and in practice means sensationalism, scandal, personification and excessive dramatization. Such trends are at the heart of much of the controversy within journalism today, and they have evoked vehement critique from journalists committed to journalistic ideals (Fallows, 1997), not least because these trends promote a climate of cynicism towards politics and toward the media. Reactions have also included calls for – and the practice of – civic, or public, journalism, in an effort to set journalism back on a suitable course (Black, 1997; Merrit, 1998). Unfortunately these are the exceptions. More common is, for example, the growing avoidance of placing cerebral demands on audiences, resulting in a kind of 'newzak' (Franklin, 1997).

Shifting representation

Within the traditional media, an increasingly self-referential symbolic world is emerging, which is to various degrees removed from the actual experiential world of most people. Such a position can be and has been subject to facile overstatement (Baudrillard, 1983), but there is no necessary denial of an extra-media reality in noting that collective memory, for example, is increasingly a memory of shared media experiences. Of course, in cyberspace, we have forms of virtual reality which provide fuel for various theories of the postmodern. For example, problematic issues of documentary representation have been with us for some years as a result of digital photography.

Professional pluralization

In the mass media, the self-understanding of journalism as a professional culture and the professional identity of journalists are becoming increasingly protean, as the boundaries of the profession become permeable to related media occupations such as public relations, advertising, editing and lay-out, and information brokerage. Given the commercialization of the media, the professional identity of journalists often becomes sundered, between loyalty to journalistic ideals and loyalty to the economic advancement of the media organization for which they work. In cyberspace, the definition of 'journalist' may soon be merging with a number of other possible information-handling functions.

In fact, the information sharing going on in cyberspace increasingly tends to bypass the classical role of journalism. The hierarchical, top-down mass communication model of journalism is being challenged in this new media environment. These citizens are more and more circumventing the packaging of journalism as stories and retrieve – and produce – information for themselves, thus 'eliminating the middleman'. The traditional storytelling of journalism is being complemented by large flows of socially relevant, non-journalistic electronic information between people and organizations outside journalism. Who is and who is not a journalist in this context may not always be so clear in the years ahead, as a variety of information functions arise to sort, sift and funnel data electronically. The boundaries between journalism and non-journalism in cyberspace may become even more problematic than it has become in the mass media.

Spin and targeting

In a related vein, 'spin doctors' are altering the way journalism gets done and the way political communication takes place. An expanding occupational group of professional communicators, media advisors and political consultants using the techniques of advertising, market research, public relations and opinion analysis help economic and political elites shape media messages to their advantage. (It is claimed that in the USA the number of public relations workers now outnumbers the working journalists.) Elite groups, often in competition amongst themselves, have long been able to influence the output of the media in subtle and sometimes not so subtle ways, though in liberal democracies direct intervention in media output is the exception. 'Spin', or public relations, has a long history (Ewen, 1996), but in recent years its entwining with political communication and journalism has intensified (Stauber and Rampton, 1995). Increasingly, politicians, political parties, corporations and other large organizations, including unions, are making use of the media to further their own particular interests. Thus, while the media serve as resources for a majority of the population in their roles as audiences, they have increasingly become a resource, or more aptly, a tool, for powerful social actors.

One of the consequences of this development is that while the media have amplified visibility in modern society, their own transparency is now diminishing. These strategically formulated and carefully placed communications are seldom identified as such, reducing the open, dialogic character of the media. The boundaries between journalism, public relations, advertising and political commentary become more porous. Another consequence is that political communication is increasingly being geared to smaller and smaller specific target groups, defined according to particular variables (Gandy, 2000). This is altering the nature of the public sphere, further fostering its fragmentation (Mayhew, 1997).

Life-worlds and niches

People use the media and vice versa; the media are resources for their audiences, while audiences are in part constructed by the media (Ettma and Whitney, 1994). People make use of the media in various ways. In the history of media research, early studies tended to emphasize questions about media effects, that is what the media do to people, how they shape our attitudes, opinions and behaviour. This perspective was gradually modified by an emphasis on what people do with the media, the uses and gratifications they derive – such as information seeking and relaxation. More recently, beginning in the early 1980s, research informed by qualitative methodologies, cultural studies and also newer trends in cognitive psychology have underscored active sense-making processes; how people make meaning from their media encounters. All three perspectives still have validity, as well as limitations. The concept of the 'audience' has been evolving along with the media and with researcher's shifting theoretical and empirical orientations (Abercrombie and Longhurst, 1998; McQuail, 1997; and see Huggins, Chapter 6 in this volume). Today, there is a good deal of discussion about the concept and status of audiences, as the mediazation of society takes on all the more complex forms. Also, the relationship that people have with the media – both the traditional mass media and the newer digital media – is becoming more multidimensional, as media encounters become contextualized in new ways within people's life-worlds (Dickinson *et al.*, 1998; Hay *et al.*, 1996).

Audiences today reflect the major tendencies in train within the socio-cultural sphere of society at large. The structural changes in the traditional media and the rise of the Internet are in turn inseparable from important developments in society at large. I will not attempt an extensive analysis of late modern society here, but only mention a few interrelated themes that are important backdrops for understanding trends in media audiences. The first has to do with cultural differentiation. This has in part to do with the large immigrant populations in many Western European countries that have contributed to giving these societies a more pluralistic composition. Many countries, in short, have become multiethnic. Some, such as The Netherlands, have had long experiences of immigration as part of their colonial legacy, while others, such as Sweden, have experienced relatively recent immigration via the labour market and refugee measures.

Yet cultural differentiation has emerged on other fronts, and the domain of consumption and leisure constitutes an even greater momentum towards differentiation. (There is a very large and recent literature, reflecting many orientations, on consumption and the consumer society. See, for example, Corrigan, 1997; Miles, 1998; Slater, 1997.) Individualization of lifestyles has moved more and more to the centre stage of people's life plans. With the general growth in affluence of the populations of Western society (despite the economic difficulties) more people are in a position to engage in consumer-based leisure. As markets expand, more people feel that they have a greater range of choices they can make in this regard. Travel and tourism are also domains that have increasingly helped promote new ways of seeing the world and oneself. The popular magazine market can serve as a mirror for this development. If one walks into a well-stocked newsagent today one is struck by the vast array of categories among the magazines: computing, gardening, skate-boarding, music, musical instruments, tattoos, cigar-smoking, fishing, antiques, skiing, UFOs, boating, romance fiction, science fiction, popular psychology, celebrities, and so on. And within each category there are often many sub-categories, further defining and specifying interests.

In short, the popular cultural landscape has become more differentiated, our social worlds that bit more pluralistic and our identities – our sense of who we are and what we want – somewhat more heterogeneous. The cultural commonality of national populations – as manifested in everyday leisure activities and lifestyle identities – has declined, but by no means vanished. If we situate these developments in relation to audiences, it suggests that, increasingly, audiences are expecting more choices in media consumption. It also means that media audiences are becoming more fragmented. Indeed, the notion of a national audience is fading rapidly, as audiences split into smaller groups. This undercuts the notion of a shared public culture and common knowledge. Clearly there are exceptions and variations here, not least in regard to specific media, with terrestrial national television channels still representing the best approximation of national audiences.

Among media audiences we can note a general decline in 'reading publics' in most Western countries, as television becomes the dominant medium of news and current affairs, and also the medium more people tend to trust the most. Also, while citizens are becoming increasingly socially fragmented amongst themselves (i.e. seen horizontally) as specific market niches emerge from continuing sociological segmentation, a hierarchical (i.e. vertical) differentiation is also becoming more pronounced. The distinction between 'informed elites' and 'entertained majorities' is on the increase in many countries, supported not least by media economics, as access to deeper information and knowledge beyond the popular media becomes more of a significant economic factor (Golding and Murdock, 1996). Overall, the strong concept of 'the public' as the voice of the inclusive citizenry moves more toward a weak version of media spectatorship, complemented by a plethora of smaller, more exclusive 'interpretative communities'. The citizen becomes marginalized by the consumer.

The space of politics

In terms of the state of democracy, where have we arrived after this rather brisk tour of many aspects of the modern and postmodern media? It should be clear that democracy in late modern society is at a turning point, and even if we cannot predict exactly which directions it will take in the new century, there is legitimate cause for concern. Moreover, the transformations we see in how democracy functions stand in complex relation to the dramatic changes in the structures of the media. Changes are apparent in both the traditional media and the Internet, in the conditions and practices of journalism and in the social trends of cultural differentiation, individualization and consumption. Major social trends, in turn, connect with the increasing fragmentation and stratification of media audiences and the polity in general. The stagnation of formal political systems, the emerging climate of 'anti-politics', the retreat to enclave consciousness, but also the growth of extra-parliamentary 'new politics', are not simply caused by the media, but do articulate in myriad ways, with media developments.

Against this background, I would suggest that an important theme that can help us to better grasp present and future developments is that, fundamentally, the media have become the major sites, the privileged space of politics in late modern society. Here we have the key to understanding the media's role in reshaping democracy. As Castells (1997) and others forcefully argue, the media are transforming democracy because political life itself today has become so extensively situated within the domain of the media. This view does not mean that politics does not exist outside the media, or that politics has been reduced to a mere media spectacle. It does, however, posit that political actors who want to accomplish things requiring public visibility will always turn to the media. Political and economic elites make use of the media for the daily routines of governing, for opinion- and image-management, as well as for major initiatives or troubleshooting in times of crises. Moreover, it suggests that the structures, organization and strategies of politics are increasingly adapting themselves to the media. This shift is manifested in everything from the strategic targeting of messages for specific audience niches to the rhetoric of press conferences and to the conscious adaptation of public discourse to soundbites of suitable length and visuals with dramatic impact. Established elites as well as alternative or oppositional groups trying to shape public opinion (Greenpeace is a paradigmatic example) must all follow the same path. 'If it wasn't in the media, it didn't happen', as they say.

Further, this view emphasizes the emergence of an increasingly coherent media logic (Altheide and Snow, 1991) that sets the conditions for participating in the media. These conditions comprise such features as timing and scheduling, forms of expression, tempo, informational density and modes of address. Factors like these have important consequences for how politics is organized and expressed. It is important to bear in mind that we are talking about the media as sites in the plural. While we can point to a rather coherent media logic, there are important distinctions to be made. Firstly, the various branches of the mass media – press, radio and television – have somewhat differing logics. Television as a medium, for instance, is visual and exists in time; the press is a textual medium that takes up space (though the processes of digital-ization are pushing all media toward a technical convergence). The communicative logic and the processes of production are significantly different, and hence political actors using these media will have to use different approaches. Moreover, within any given medium there are important genre differences: a local radio talk-show is not the same as a national news broadcast, a popular television magazine operates differ-ently from a highbrow debate programme.

The concept of media logic contains an element of modest post-modern reasoning. It suggests that the traditional way of understanding the media's relationship to politics is being called into question; namely that the media simply represent, with varying degrees of accuracy, politics and, more generally, the real world 'out there'. What is asserted here is that politics no longer exists as a reality taking place outside the media, to be 'covered' by journalists. Rather, politics is increasingly organized as a media phenomenon, planned and executed for and with the co-operation of the media. Note that I called this a 'modest' form of postmodern reasoning. It does challenge the traditional notion of media practices aiming to represent an external reality, but it does not claim that there is no real world outside the media, or that everything we see in the media is merely a form of simulation. The argument instead can be understood sociologically: in the modern world, many institutions, including religion and sports, but especially politics, have adapted their activities to the logic of the media, and in the process transformed themselves.

Finally, in regard to the media becoming the prime site of politics, this view does not deny that politics takes place in other settings as well. It does, however, underscore the increasing marginality of other forums. This is in keeping with what was said above about the general political disengagement we are witnessing. In everyday life, in civil society, people are of course still discussing public affairs – and this is of great importance for the democratic development of opinion – but these contexts tend normally to have relatively less bearing on politics when compared to the massive presence of the media. I would underscore that this is not a question of the extent to which people accept or reject the views they encounter in the media, but rather where we find the centre of gravity for politics in late modern society. Clearly this development is not unproblematic, nor does it proceed uncontested; the emergence of 'new politics', that I noted earlier, can be seen in part as a challenge to this trend, an effort to return the political to the domain of people's experiences and practices. From a Habermasian perspective (Habermas, 1989), we could say that the media are increasingly becoming the dominant institutions of the public sphere and increasingly integrated into the logic of the system, at the same time as they then colonize the realm of the political within the domain of the life-world.

We will have to continue to grapple with democracy, both conceptually and in our concrete life circumstances. Any and all such activity must have the media clearly in focus; indeed, we would do well to consider the media themselves as key focal points for struggles to enhance democracy. If the media have become the privileged sites of politics, then they must also become central objects of democratic engagement.

References

Abercrombie, Nicholas and Longhurst, Brian (1998) *Audiences*. London: Sage.

Alleyne, Mark D. (1997) *News Revolution: Political and Economic Decisions about Global Information*. London: Macmillan.

Altheide, David and Snow, Robert (1991) *Media Worlds in the Post-Journalism Era*. New York: Aldine de Gruyter.

Bailie, Mashoed and Winseck, Dwayne (eds) (1997) *Democratizing Communication?* Cresskill, NJ: Hampton Press.

Baldwin, Thomas, McVoy, David and Steinfield, Charles (1996) *Convergence: Integrating Media, Information and Communication*. London: Sage.

Barker, Chris (1997) *Global Television*. London: Blackwell.

Barnett, Steven (1997) 'New media, old problems: new technology and the political process', *European Journal of Communication*, 12 (2): 193–218.

Baudrillard, Jean (1983) *Simulations*. New York: Semiotext(e).

Beck, Ulrich (1998) *Democracy Without Enemies*. Cambridge: Polity.

Bellah, Robert, Madson, Robert, Swidler, Alan and Tipton, Samuel (1985) *Habits of the Heart*. New York: Perennial Library.

Benhabib, Seyla (ed.) (1996) *Democracy and Difference: Contesting the Boundaries of the Political*. Princeton, NJ: Princeton University Press.

Bennett, Lance (1996) *News: The Politics of Illusion*, 3rd edn. New York: Longman.

Bennett, Lance (1998) 'The uncivic culture: communication, identity, and the rise of lifestyle politics', Ithiel de Sola Pool Lecture, annual meeting of the American Political Science Association, Boston.

Black, Jay (ed.) (1997) *Mixed News: The Public/Civic/Communirtarian Journalism Debate*. Mahwah, NJ: Lawrence Erlbaum Associates.

Blumler, Jay and Gurevitch, Michael (1995) *The Crisis of Public Communication*. London: Routledge.

Boggs, Carl (1997) 'The great retreat: decline of the public sphere in late twentieth-century America', *Theory and Society*, 26 (2): 141–80.

Castells, Manuel (1996) *The Rise of the Network Society*. Oxford: Basil Blackwell.

Castells, Manuel (1997) *The Power of Identity*. Oxford: Basil Blackwell.

Clarke, Paul Barry (1996) *Deep Citizenship*. London: Pluto Press.

Constellations (1997) 4 (2), with special section 'Democratizing technology/ technologizing democracy'.

Corrigan, Peter (1997) *The Sociology of Consumption*. London: Sage.

Dahl, Robert (1998) *On Democracy*. New Haven and London: Yale University Press.

Dahlgren, Peter (1995) *Television and the Public Sphere*. London: Sage.

Dahlgren, Peter (1997) 'Enhancing the civic ideal in TV journalism', in K. Brants, J. Hermes and L. van Zoonen (eds), *The Media in Question*. London: Sage.

Dearing, James W. and Rogers, Everett (1996) *Agenda-Setting*. London: Sage.

Dickinson, Roger, Harindranath, Ramaswami and Linnné, Olga (eds) (1998) *Approaches to Audiences*. London: Edward Arnold.

Eliasoph, Nina (1997) ' "Close to home": the work of avoiding politics', *Theory and Society*, 26 (5): 605–47.

Ettma, James S. and Whitney, D. Charles (eds) (1994) *Audiencemaking: How the Media Create the Audience*. London: Sage.

Ewen, Stuart (1996) *PR! A Social History of Spin*. New York: Basic Books.

Fallows, James (1997) *Breaking the News*. New York: Vintage Books.

Fidler, Roger (1997) *Mediamorphosis: Understanding New Media*. Thousand Oaks, CA: Pine Forge Press.

Fisher, Bonnie, Margolis, Michael and Resnick, David (1996) 'Breaking ground on the virtual frontier: surveying civic life on the Internet', *American Sociologist*, 27 (1): 11–25.

Fornäs, Johan (1998) 'Digital borderlands. Identity and interactivity in culture, media and communication', *The Nordicom Review*, 19 (1): 19–35.

Franklin, Bob (1997) *Newzak and News Media*. London: Edward Arnold.

Gandy, Oscar (2000) 'Dividing practices: segmentation and targeting in the emerging public sphere', in L. Bennett and R. Entman (eds) *Mediated Politics: Communication and the Future of Democracy*. Cambridge: Cambridge University Press.

Gibbens, John R. and Reimer, Bo (1999) *The Politics of Postmodernity*. London: Sage.

Giddens, Anthony (1991) *Modernity and Self-Identity*. Cambridge: Polity Press.

Golding, Peter and Murdock, Graham (1996) 'Culture, communications, and political economy', in J. Curran and M. Gurevitch (eds), *Mass Media and Society*. London: Edward Arnold.

Graham, Andrew and Davies, Gavyn (1997) *Broadcasting, Society and Policy in the Multimedia Age*. Luton: John Libby.

Habermas, J. (1989) *The Structural Transformation of the Public Sphere*. Trans. T. Burger. Cambridge: Polity.

Hay, James, Grossberg, Lawrence and Wartella Ellen (eds) (1996) *The Audience and its Landscapes*. Boulder, CO: Westview Press.

Herman, Edward and McChesney, Robert (1997) *The Global Media*. London: Cassell.

Hill, Kevin A. and Hughes, John E. (1998) *Cyberpolitics: Citizen Activism in the Age of the Internet*. Lanham, MD: Rowman & Littlefield.

Hirst, Paul (1997) *From Statism to Pluralism*. London: UCL Press.

Holmes, David (ed.) (1997) *Virtual Politics: Identity and Community in Cyberspace*. London: Sage.

Jones, Steven G. (ed.) (1998) *Cybersociety 2.0*. London: Sage.

Jordan, Tim (1999) *Cyberpower: The Culture and Politics of Cyberspace and the Internet*. London: Routledge.

Kitchin, Rob (1998) *Cyberspace: The World in the Wires*. New York: John Wiley and Sons.

Lacroix, Jean-Guy and Tremblay, Gaëtan (1997) 'The "information society" and cultural industries theory', special issue of *Current Sociology*, 45 (4).

Loader, Brian D. (ed.) (1998) *Cyberspace Divide*. London: Routledge.

Mayhew, Leon H. (1997) *The New Public*. Cambridge: Cambridge University Press.

McChesney, Robert (1999) *Rich Media, Poor Democracy: Communication Politics in Dubious Times*. Champaign, IL: University of Illinois Press.

McManus, John H. (1994) *Market-Driven Journalism*. London: Sage.

McQuail, Denis (1997) *Audience Analysis*. London: Sage.

McQuail, Denis and Siune, Karen (eds) (1998) *Media Policy: Convergence, Concentration and Commerce*. London: Sage.

Merritt, Davis 'Buzz' (1998) *Public Journalism and Public Life*. Mahwah, NJ: Lawrence Earlbaum and Associates.

Miles, Steven (1998) *Consumerism as a Way of Life*. London: Sage.

Mosco, Vincent (1996) *The Political Economy of Communication*. London: Sage.

Mulgan, Geoff (1994) *Politics in an Antipolitical Age*. Cambridge: Polity.

Putnam, Robert (1993) *Making Democracy Work*. Princeton, NJ: Princeton University Press.

Norris, P. (ed.) (1999) *Critical Citizens: Global Support for Democratic Governance*. Oxford: Oxford University Press.

Resnick, Philip (1997) *Twenty-first Century Democracy*. Montreal and Kingston: McGill-Queens University Press.

Robins, Kevin and Webster, Frank (1999) *Times of the Technoculture*. London: Routledge.

Sandel, Michael (1996) *Democracy's Discontent*. Cambridge, MA: The Belknap Press of Harvard University Press.

Schiller, Dan (1999) *Digital Capitalism*. Cambridge, MA: MIT Press.

Schudson, Michael (1996) 'The sociology of news production, revisited', in J. Curran and P. Gurevitch (eds), *Mass Media and Society*. London: Edward Arnold.

Slater, Don (1997) *Consumer Culture and Modernity*. Cambridge: Polity.

Smith, Marc A. and Kollock, Peter (eds) (1999) *Communities in Cyberspace*. London: Routledge.

Sparks, Colin (1998) *Communism, Capitalism and the Mass Media*. London: Sage.

Stauber, John and Rampton, Sheldon (1995) *Toxic Sludge is Good For You: Lies, Damn Lies and the Public Relations Industry*. Monroe, Maine: Common Courage Press.

Steemers, Jeanette (ed.) (1998) *Changing Channels: The Prospects for Television in a Digital World*. Luton: University of Luton Press.

Sussman, Gerald (1997) *Communication, Technology and Politics in the Information Age*. London: Sage.

Thompson, John B. (1995) *The Media and Modernity*. Cambridge: Polity.

Tracey, Michael (1988) *The Decline and Fall of Public Service Broadcasting*. Oxford: Oxford University Press.

Tsagarousianou, Roza, Tambini, Damian and Bryan, Cathy (eds) (1998) *Cyberdemocracy: Technologies, Cities and Civic Networks*. London: Routledge.

Underwood, Doug (1995) *When MBAs Rule the Newsroom*. New York: Columbia University Press.

4 The Transformation of the Public Sphere?

Sinikka Sassi

The Internet as a new medium of civic engagement

When I began to study the Internet in the middle of the 1990s my main interest was in emerging forms of grassroots politics and the way social bonds were created on and through the Internet. I wanted to know how the Net affects non-institutionalized politics. Does it give more room and prominence to new initiatives and new forms of politics, or does the significance of new kinds of political activism get lost in the whimsy of virtuality? As a theoretical framework the concepts of civil society and public sphere served as an appropriate starting-point for my investigation because they define the realm wherein political initiatives from below can grow. At that point I also turned to the Habermasian system model to make sense of the whole network structure. In Habermas's terms the Net is a special kind of medium, differing from earlier modalities in the range of its applications and impact. For example, as well as being a realm of social integration, it has important steering functions in both material production and administrative practices which should not be neglected in examining its role as a medium. Indeed, if the Net passes for an arena of citizen activity, it must still be seen in a much larger context comprising all other networks including both corporate and military ones. The whole is sometimes called the 'Matrix' (Gibson, 1984), that is, the network of all the networks.

To broaden the interpretative framework, I also applied the discourse of the 'cultural turn', now much in vogue, which implies a radical shift in modern society and culture. The Net seems to fit very neatly into this scheme since it is a powerful driving-force behind the changes taking place in both the political and cultural terrains. At this point a tension between different theoretical approaches emerged. New media, new forms of politics and the trend to culturalization are expressions of and intrinsic to the same profile of epochal change. But how can a framework of civil society derived from Enlightenment traditions be applied in quite other conditions, and in a study having the Net as its primary focus? In other words, how can a modern tradition be applied to late modern circumstances?

The tension between different theoretical approaches was accompanied by another dilemma. In seeking for an empirical case study I decided to use my own experiences of using the Net for political purposes instead of studying the activities of others. So I was obliged to look at the world simultaneously through two particular lenses: as a researcher eager to make sense of the Net, and as a citizen devoted to having an impact on local city planning. This tension between the roles of observer and actor obliged me to alternate consciously between them in order to get the critical distance needed for reflection. In the end, the present story emerges much as a debate between two academic discourses, the macrosociological tradition of civil society and the cultural approach with its postmodern overtones, with each having a great deal of appeal. In what follows, the 'researcher' has the leading part but, bearing in mind the practical implications of Net technology for creating new discursive spaces, the 'actor' will not be neglected. While the researcher is concerned about academic discourses, the actor's stance is more pragmatic, seeking new prospects of empowerment. Raymond Williams once pointed out that the 'long revolution' is the process by which people take the circumstances of their lives into their own hands (see Hall, 1984), and his sentiment comes very close to this actor's concerns.

In principle, the Net permits a new arena of grassroots politics, but the question is whether it really works as such in practice. With some justification it can be understood as a vast public sphere or, more accurately, as a plethora of public spheres. Possessing an open and public nature is its most promising quality for any theory of democratic renewal since, at the very least, it has the potential to replicate the old ideal of a debating public. However, any sustained reflection upon civil society must lead to a comprehensive critique of the concept and of the entire tradition. And because the concepts of civil society and public sphere are closely related – the former being the organizational basis for the latter – when one is the subject of critique, the other will be challenged too. Keeping this articulation in mind, two themes will be discussed here, using the Net as the focus of discussion: the assumption of essential changes in the character and forms of politics, and the shifts in discourse and in theorizing necessary to comprehend these changes.

The discourse of civil society

As I have noted, in the first instance the need to understand the basic characteristics of the meta-network pushed me towards Habermas's system model (1987: 320). Habermas's distinction between the *system*, consisting of the economic realm and administration, and the *life-world*, consisting of the private sphere and public sphere, proved helpful in teasing out the elements and organizational principles of the Net as a social system. Whereas the political system is driven by administrative power and rules and the economic system is guided by money and exchange, the life-world and its self-organized public spheres are based on communication. The concepts of life-world and civil society are related but not fully overlapping, since the former also includes the private sphere of mutual (intersubjective) understanding. Habermas's distinction identifies civil society as the realm of societal organization and shared political efforts. Use of his schema allows the complex and contradictory functions and qualities of various networks to be described.

The concepts of public sphere, civil society and citizenship all belong to a tradition of democratic theory dating back to the eighteenth century. Although together they form a relatively coherent discourse, the tradition combines elements of two schools of thought: the liberal Anglo-American strain and the German Hegelian. These intellectual accounts share many basic tenets, but in existing political cultures their features are variably mixed (Sassi, 2000b). Civil society itself is an historical construct and the child of that long and complex series of transformations called modernity. At the heart of the process is the distinction between state and civil society that became established in the early nineteenth century.

Today, civil society, as summarized by Keane (1998: 5–6), is seen mostly as the dynamic, sometimes unruly and conflict-ridden social realm of private institutions, organizations, associations and individuals linked to, but separate from, the state and the market economy. For Habermas (1996: 366), the institutional core of civil society comprises those non-govermental and non-economic connections and voluntary associations that anchor the communication structures of the public sphere in the social component of the life-world. Although Keane and Habermas differ with respect to economics, which Habermas leaves outside the realm of civil society, they both point to a particular kind of modern, non-violent political order in which political authorities are accountable to the sovereign people and their mission is to service the needs of society. All hitherto existing and present-day civil societies contain specific characteristics that ensure that the exact demeanour of civil society is very context dependent. But everywhere civil society is the sphere of actors who legally and voluntarily engage in civic activities, which means that they are able to reproduce, and also to reinterpret and to transform, the social and political structures within which they interact.

But the received concept of civil society has little resonance with the everyday lives of individuals and has come under criticism for this reason. Part of the critique arises from the tendency to conceptualize it as a homogeneous entity, which tendency has the effect of concealing the fact that our social world consists of conflicting opinions and contradictory interests – in other words, it is irredeemably pluralist. The same shortcoming applies to the concept of the public sphere which in reality never was singular and homogenous, but consisted of a variety of public spheres and publics which were sometimes in direct opposition to each other. Paradoxically, the continued attraction of the holistic ideal stems from the fact that it was only ever a simulacrum of real life. In short, it has been widely accepted as a convenient means of highlighting shortcomings in current social and political life, and in the quality of democracy in those parts of the world undergoing rapid change. In Europe, for example, new interest in civil society began to arise during the 1970s in the Central-Eastern half of the continent. The aim of the Polish workers' movement was to develop a plurality of self-governing civil associations capable of pressuring the state from without and enabling various groups to attend peacefully to civic activities. Keane (1998: 12–20) calls this the second phase of the renaissance of the idea of civil society, while the first was a short-lived period in Japan during the late 1960s. In Central-Eastern Europe, public criticisms of despotic state power developed and a healthy civil society was bruited as the crucial element of a new democratic political and social order. In Western Europe the concept was reintroduced in everyday language and in initiatives such as 'Citizens' Europe' during the 1990s.

During the past decade the language of civil society has spread to an unprecedented variety of geographic contexts beyond the boundaries of Europe. Although it is used sometimes just as a rhetorical device, it has nevertheless re-emerged as a key item on the democratic agenda. Keane (1998: 24) addresses current developments in South Africa, where talk of a renewal in civil society has attracted attention across society. Apartheid itself gave rise to networks of power-sensitive citizen groups that initially functioned as 'dual power' organizations, designed to disrupt the dominant ideology. In the post-apartheid regime, these organizations, now deemed legitimate expressions of pluralism, still try to play the role of watchdogs on the ANC-led government. So, to sum up, civil society could be broadly defined as the self-reflexive, self-organizing, non-governmental activities of citizens. Between the core terms of the discourse another distinction can also be made, that if citizen associations and social movements form the organizational basis of civil society, then the public sphere accounts for its forms of communication, and politics for its content.

Old paradigm—new paradigm

Along with its revival as a feature of an ideal of democratic society, a scholarly debate between the macrosociological tradition and cultural theorizations of civil society has taken place. Some contributions have provided an overview (see e.g. Friese and Wagner, 1999; Stevenson, 1999) highlighting the difference between structural and cultural, and sociological and semiotic studies. Others, more germane to this chapter, have focused more precisely on the perspective of the public sphere and the role of the media in it (e.g. Alexander and Jacobs, 1998). The dominant paradigm consisted of those theories which focus primarily on the formal political arrangements and legal procedures, that is, the institutional structures of civil society. Civil society was narrowly conceived as those institutional structures necessary for appropriating power from the state and toward the civil sphere of voluntary action. However, the new approach to civil society emphasizes the dimensions of culture and media as these are experienced in everyday life, a viewpoint neglected in many of the earlier discussions. Although it was commonly agreed that freedom of communication is impossible without networks of non-state communications media, the growing significance of the media and media texts in people's lives remained largely a non-issue. While the precise meaning of civil society is far from settled, it is now generally agreed that the mass media have an extraordinary impact on its forms and functions.

Although many earlier democratic thinkers, such as Dewey (1927) or Tönnies (1922), have recognized the importance of the cultural sphere, today it has acquired more autonomy than before and established itself as a separate arena of social experience (Featherstone, 1995: 15–33) as well as a category of analysis. If culture is understood as being concerned with the dialogic production of meaning through a variety of practices, then media and communication, being essentially about language and the process of signification, themselves belong to the field of culture. So the 'cultural turn' in academic discourse means that there is a quest for a theory of civil society more sensitive to various forms of communication and to multiple publics and multiple sites of reception. Rather than limiting the concept to the scope of actor autonomy from the state, civil society is also made up of those social and cultural relations that constitute the basis of belonging and the sense of sharing. A common cultural code and common narrative structure would thus allow for intersubjectivity and cross-communication between different publics. Alexander and Jacobs (1998) define civil society in this sense as a communicative space working for the imaginative construction and reconstruction of collective identities and solidarities. Consequently, it should no longer be conceived solely as a world of voluntary associations, elections, or even legal rights, but also, and most significant of all, as a realm of symbolic communication.

How do we explain the shift to a more culturally informed discourse on civil society? Friese and Wagner (1999) suggest two possible reasons for the shift occurring, the first being what they call intellectual progress. Scholars in the social sciences are now more sensitive to the cultural and motivational dynamics of communities and other collectivities. The other reason they suggest is that major social change has occurred. Until recently our societies were structurally ordered and tied together by formal roles and interests, but now they manifest a predominance of cultural relations and the more fragmented grouping of individuals according to identity. All of this is central to the much debated transformation of modern society into a new phase that has been variously labelled the 'communication society', 'media society' or 'cultural society' (e.g. Lash, 1994; Schwengel, 1991). But has there been a real change in the character of modernity or just a less portentous shift in the academic discourse?

Stuart Hall may provide an answer to the question of intellectual progress. For Hall (1996), the metaphor of language constitutes *the* theoretical revolution of our time, in the sense of reorganizing the theoretical universe. It is not only the discovery of the discursive that is important, but the metaphorically generated capacity to reconceptualize other kinds of practice as operating like a language in a number of important ways. The discursive perspective has also generated a very important insight; namely, the whole area of subjectivity, particularly in the ideological domain. It has required us to think about reintroducing the subjective dimension in a non-holistic, non-unitary way. This change has resulted in the deconstruction of the received wisdom that political subjectivities do flow from the integrated ego, which is also the integrated speaker. Hall finds the discursive metaphor extraordinarily rich analytically and having massive political consequences.

Ulrich Beck (1999) would no doubt endorse the idea of massive social change. Beck defines the contemporary age as the second modernity, and conceives of it as radically different from first modernity. In his view, we face a structural and epochal break, a paradigmatic change, which has little to do with gradual increases in knowledge and reflection. Flows of cultural commodities, numbers of telecommunication transactions and permanence of migration are among the empirical indicators of a cosmopolitan process which, in another guise, appear as aspects of an ecological crisis. The term 'cosmopolitan' focuses attention on the ways people's cultural, political and biographical self-assertions can change when they no longer locate themselves within the confines of the nation-state and the identities tied to it, but globally. The second modernity not only transforms the relations between nation states, but challenges the received concepts of politics and society alike. The main question is how we can imagine, define and analyse post-national and transnational political communities. What categories and theories of politics, of state and democracy are relevant – if any? Who are the agents and what are the political institutions? The cosmopolitan process has advanced both on the micro-level – in life-worlds and ways of living and as a growing awareness of multiculturalism – and on the macro-level as interdependence created by the world market and international and transnational networks which supersede the political power of nation-states. Beck proposes that in these conditions the relations between the state, corporations and civil society should be redefined. If we do not think of civil society as confined within the nation-state, we can perhaps better discover its capabilities for reviving politics and democracy. Such considerations underscore the practical and theoretical importance of the cultural turn in the experience of and in the analysis of civil society.

Culturalizing the discourse

Just how has the culturally informed perspective affected the study of civil society? There are two ways of answering the question. The first is to reject the civil society discourse altogether, while the other, more germane to this chapter, is to revise it in terms of the predominance of the media and the sphere of culture. I will explore two versions of the cultural option. One of the new versions available is Appadurai's notion of 'scapes' (1990). He studies the complexity of the current global economy through five dimensions of cultural flow, termed: (1) 'ethnoscapes', the movement of peoples evident within diasporas, tourism and migrations; (2) 'technoscapes', the uneven distribution of global technology; (3) 'finanscapes', the operation of global commodity speculation;

(4) 'mediascapes', the transportation of semiotic cultures; and (5) 'ideo-scapes', which means the transnational mobilization of hegemonic and counter-hegemonic ideologies which are then recombined in a variety of contexts to produce different effects. Appadurai describes these scapes as disjunctive, as they have no necessary relation to each other. Of these terms, 'mediascapes' and 'ideoscapes' are the most interesting for this chapter and also the most closely related. Mediascapes tend to be image-centred, narrative-based accounts of strips of reality, offering those who experience and enact them a set of resources from which the scripts of imagined lives can be formed. Ideoscapes are also chains of images, but they are often directly political and frequently express the ideologies of states and the counter-ideologies of movements explicitly oriented to capturing state power or a piece of it. These ideoscapes are composed of elements of the Enlightenment world-view, which encompasses a set of key ideas, terms and images, including 'freedom', 'welfare', 'rights', 'sovereignty' and 'representation', as well as the master-term 'democracy'. In the master-narrative of the Enlightenment, the basic terms were intimately related to each other and presupposed a relationship between reading, representation and the public sphere.

The use of the suffix '-scape' suggests that these are not objectively given relations but rather deeply perspectival constructs, greatly influenced by the historical, linguistic and political situatedness of various actors. Among the actors are nation states, multinationals, diasporic communities, as well as sub-national groupings and movements and even intimate face-to-face groups. Finally there is the individual actor, since these landscapes are also navigated by agents who both experience and constitute larger formations. Appadurai's construct looks productive for the examination of the current cosmopolitan and increasingly contingent environment of the individual, since we are deeply embedded in the changing flows of images and ideologies. The upshot is that the terms 'mediascape' and 'ideoscape' in particular have become popular in academic discourse and are, on occasion, used instead of, or alongside, the concepts of civil society and the public sphere. The appeal of these concepts may be due in part to their relative openness and flexibility. For example, a study of citizen experiences of, and reactions to, the process of membership of the EU was inspired by Appadurai's concepts (Kivikuru, 1995, 1996). By examining both mediascapes and ideoscapes, feelings of frustration were revealed along with a divergence between the views of citizens and elites. From the perspective of democracy, the appeal of the Enlightenment world-view and the diffusion of its tenets across the world are also explainable in Appadurai's terms.

The narrative construction of civil society

Another kind of cultural approach is Alexander and Jacobs's semiotic study of civil society (1998). They find the narrative elaboration of events and crises crucial for providing an understanding of the historical and moral construction of civil society. They see the mass media as providing the cultural environment from which common identities and solidarities can be constructed. This shared cultural environment – the discourse of civil society – consists of two structural levels. In terms of 'deep structure', there is a common semiotic system through which public actors speak and through which public readers interpret what is being communicated. Alongside this deep semiotic structure there is a 'temporal structure', a set of common narrative frameworks through which public actors chart the movement of themselves and others in real historical time. These two cultural environments simultaneously con-strain and enable public actions in civil society.

The deep semiotic structure supplies the structured categories of *pure* and *impure* into which every member, or potential member, is made to fit. Just as there is no developed religion that does not divide the world into the saved and the damned, so there is no civil discourse that does not conceptualize the world into those who deserve inclusion and those who do not. For this reason, they say, the discourse of civil society constitutes a language system that can be understood semiotically, that is, as sets of homologies and antipathies which create likenesses and differences between various terms of social description and prescription. This semiotic structure develops not so much through the agency of individual speech, but rather through the historical and cultural process of semiosis. Thus civil society becomes organized around a bifurcating discourse of citizen and enemy, defining the characteristics of both worthy, democratic citizens and of unworthy, counter-democratic enemies. Alexander and Jacobs apply the semiotic tools to an analysis of big media events such as the Watergate crisis and the Rodney King affair in order to understand the cultural dynamics of civil society. An approach like this, that looks for the shared semiotic codes through which an event is filtered and interpreted, seems to be very useful for understanding media events that develop into social drama.

Both these approaches are discursive in the sense that they identify and interpret discourses or segments of discourses. They both present individual actors as being immersed in their mental landscapes, that is, as being part of the same unified world. This holistic quality is important since in more systemic approaches the individual and various societal entities are conceived as being distanced from each other. What these cultural approaches do not reveal directly is the intentional political action and active civil resistance that are key elements in the politics of, for example, environmental protection. The semiotic perspective helps us to find the narrations of civil society and to position the citizen in them, but when the story does not proceed to a media event and then to a social drama such binary oppositions are not apparent. In non-dramatic or more routine situations, the positions of actors often remain as complex and shifting constellations of relations, and their narrative elaboration as neatly juxtaposed pairs may not contribute much to the analysis. Similarly, the seeming advantage of Appadurai's conceptualiza-tion, that is, the holistic view of the actor and his/her world, becomes an obstacle if the subject stays enmeshed in the flows of communication instead of reacting to them via practical effort. While the metaphor of flow may describe the current global transfers of ideas, technologies and human beings at an aggregate level, it cannot assist much in revealing how active subjects plan and accomplish their goals.

Searching for mediation

So, it seems rather obvious that the sociological and cultural approaches explore the world differently and do not address the same questions. Therefore, in order to locate the sphere of politics and social change, the actor in local politics may have to turn back to the more sociologically inclined tradition of civil society. This remains useful, especially in spotlighting the area of self-organization of social life, where the polit-ical dimension and citizen identity with its attached rights and duties are essential. Here the questions of agency, power, resistance and intention-ality arise as something other than discursive formations, finding expres-sion through institutional practices and conflict. At the same time they still have to be understood as linguistically produced and mediated. Consequently, while the old tradition is valuable on its own merits, it should not be left unvarnished. Stuart Hall's notion of the linguistic turn also deserves due attention, but not simply as a nod in the direction of culture.

Here a double twist emerges: we need the cultural approach to deconstruct both the universalist assumptions and the critical-rational actor model inherent in the old paradigm, and to articulate a more pluralistic civil society with more emotion-bound deep cultural struc-tures. At the same time we should also retain something of the old paradigm, since denying the value of critical debate would be absurd. One possibility of renewing the tradition of civil society may be to focus on the concept of citizenship and to examine the rights and duties it involves, and, in addition to the reflections offered here, Stephen Coleman's chapter in this book traverses some of the same ground. The concept of cultural citizenship (Stevenson, 1999) can provide us with a potential linkage between the two traditions. Citizenship has long been defined in political terms as a matter of membership, rights and obligations. However, there are more informal considerations about membership of a community, about who will be included and who excluded, and these considerations are part of the routines of all political cultures.

In institutional terms the terrain of citizenship is usually marked out by abstract legal definitions as to who is to be a member of a political community. For Alexander and Jacobs (1998), membership is defined in terms of certain 'timeless' qualities of personal motivation, social relationship and group organization. In the present communication or media society a new aspect of citizenship – identity – becomes important. Cultural citizenship is basically about mechanisms of exclusion and inclusion based on cultural distinctions and shared meanings. Stevenson (1999: 61) finds that cultural citizenship is realized to the extent that a society makes semiotic cultures available. These are necessary in order to make social life meaningful, to enable criticism of practices of domination and to allow for the recognition of difference under conditions of tolerance and mutual respect. Exclusions from cultural citizenship can appear as attempts to erect rigid boundaries between insiders and outsiders, and as a tendency to subject the distribution, circulation and exchange of symbolic forms to practices that reinforce relations of dominance.

The combination of social, political and cultural aspects of citizenship becomes especially relevant in considering individual experiences. The sense of dignity in being an accepted member of a community is fully realized only when a person is tied to a network of social interaction, has political rights and duties towards the community and can fulfil them, and has the knowledge that his/her particular cultural characteristics are approved. It goes almost without saying that in certain circumstances these conditions are not met. In order to suggest how the prevailing conditions should be changed we need the information that cultural studies can offer about the subtle mechanisms of exclusion employed both by the members of a community and in administrative practices alike.

The changing public sphere

In the present communication or media society, the nature of the public sphere is a matter of growing concern to students of democracy. To lessen the ambiguity inherent in the concept, a few distinctions should be made. As mentioned earlier, if civil society in the main equates to the diversity of grassroots organizations and forms of societal self-organization, then it must also equate to the communication dimension of these organizations and practices. Thus the concepts of civil society and public sphere are inherently interconnected, the former standing for structures and the latter for shared meanings emerging through these structures. The second distinction concerns the difference between the public sphere and the mass media, where the concepts are overlapping but not identical. In common-sense understanding, the mass media as the prevailing form of circulating texts, ideas and images would obviously stand for actual publicness. From the civil society perspective, the public sphere comprises the mass media but it is larger than that, taking in the realm of alternative and specialized media and a plurality of civic conversations. Today a paradox emerges: while it seems as though the civic public sphere has become fragmented, and even insignificant in its original political sense, contemporary civil society seems to consist more and more of diverse public spheres than of free associations and other citizen organizations. This situation, one that is troubling to many commentators on democracy, reflects the fact that current social and organizational ties seem to be weak in their form and stability, whereas the sphere of mediated communication, especially through the Net, appears to be widening and strengthening. At the same time, the political public sphere, as Habermas calls it, seems to have lost its significance at the expense of the more cultural one.

In his most recent writing on the public sphere, Habermas (1996: 374) has sought to define its dynamic and spatially complex nature. He differentiates it into levels according to the density of communication, organizational complexity, and range – from the episodic publics found in taverns, coffee houses or on the streets; through the occasional or 'arranged' publics of particular functions and events; up to the abstract public sphere of isolated readers, listeners and viewers scattered across large geographical areas and brought together only through the mass media. Both civil society and the public sphere appear today as more plural by nature than before, revealing a more agonistic realm consisting of extremes in movements and groups hostile towards each other. These contradictions emphasize the continuing need for 'zones' or 'spaces' for the non-violent and communicative settlement of disputes. Yet for a variety of reasons, the public sphere reveals a strong tendency towards fragmentation (Sassi, 2000a) or, worse, towards mutually exclusive forms of segregation.

Diasporic communities, such as Somali refugees, represent a development in the construction of an ethnoscape and illustrate the tendency to fragmentation. Roughly ten years ago a few thousand Somalis arrived in Finland, a culturally homogeneous country on the rim of the northern hemisphere. Because of the continuing warfare in Somalia, they had not been left with much choice but to try to settle down in a strange and culturally distant environment. Quite recently, some members of the community have discovered the Net and started to exploit it to maintain family contacts and to discuss politics and the future of the Somali nation. When a husband lives in Finland, his wife in the UK, some relatives in Australia and still others in Canada, regular contacts are of vital importance. Through the Net they can keep their social ties alive while also attending to a larger imagined community of Somali people. These contacts help them to reproduce their identities and strengthen the sense of membership. On the other hand, there are very few contacts between them and other cultural groups whether native or not, and this appears to be a modal phenomenon where such groups are concerned. The prevalent global ideal of multiculturalism, however, is not based on segregation and separation, but on the assumption of interaction relations between groups. Thus, from a policy perspective, an urgent question is whether such dialogue and reciprocal relations can be created and sustained through the Net.

Ideally the aim would be to create a common sense of belonging to a larger community of different cultural groups, but without suppressing cultural diversity. Theoretically this suggests a fragile and chronic balancing act between universalistic conceptions and particular ways of life. The task is not made easier in circumstances where individualization and differentiation have reached a very high level in most Western societies, and on some accounts are exacerbated by the spread of information technologies. A community movement serves as a further example of the difficulties involved. Some years ago a parents' association was initiated in Finland due to perceived difficulties with some youth whose behaviour was considered anti-social and undesirable by both families and schools. With a mother at its head, a group of parents launched a co-operative network whose aim was to help solve disputes between adults and teenagers and to agree on shared rules of behaviour. It turned out that parents succeeded in dealing with their teenagers much more easily once they could appeal to the rules and the authority of the association. However, it soon became apparent that these groups still developed in a markedly different direction: some revived traditional codes of behaviour and expected the young to accede to these entirely, whereas some acted in an extremely liberal way, for example negotiating with 12-year-olds on the proper amount of beer at their school disco. As a response to the trend to differentiation, the organizers published a founding document with excerpts from civil law and aimed at providing a joint basis of action. This example illustrates the tensions between the opposing trends of universalism and particularism. It also shows that universalistic principles are not bound to result in cultural homogeneity, since the groups involved still developed specific features and independent practices even after approving the general rules.

In media cultures in the media age, the primary task of the public sphere is to identify problems of common concern and provide room for their expression. This requires a functional connection between the public sphere and democratic procedures, in which the former detects and highlights matters of public interest that should then be fed into the procedures and deliberations of representative institutions and the state. Not only are the structures of representative democracy vital but – because of the dissolution of the union between state and individual and between societal guidance and individual choice – more dispersed forms of democracy and more intensive participation in the social life of a locality are needed. Habermas (1996: 371) sees this process as linking the increasing individualism evident in ethical decisions with a moral discourse at community level. An informed public culture and a strong civil society should be built upon the complex interaction between a number of different public realms and arenas. Today public spheres are mediated by modes of communication which seem to make face-to-face interaction obsolete and which are characterized instead by small, diverse and dispersed networks employing digital means of production and distribution. These mediated forms are not necessarily inferior to face-to-face interaction but radically different and they are still fairly poorly understood. In fact, the idea of the Net as a political public sphere is hardly considered by the greater public and, as the medium is subject to increased commercialization and attempts at regulation by private and public bureaucracies, the prospects may be remote for some time to come.

What is new about politics and the public sphere

Although the conception of a major cultural change is still much contested, suggestions have been made about the need to rethink what constitutes the sphere of the political and the forms of politics (Beck, 1997; Melucci, 1996). Both Beck and Melucci focus on political activities originating from below and urge us to subject them to more study. In Melucci's view, new social movements are more media-like in the sense that they do not directly strive for changes in the political field. Instead they seek to question the modes of representation, along with the linguistic and cultural codes used to define a matter as political. In this context, the Net appears to be strongly symptomatic of the transformation of politics since it is essentially about communication and the process of signification.

An interesting, if somewhat exotic, example of potential new forms of politics is the so-called 'Future State of Balkania'. The idea for its foundation emerged from a meeting of cultural practitioners in Budapest in spring 1999, when a working group discussed the establishment of an alternative to the fractured and hostile patchwork of countries and nations of the Balkan region (Broeckmann, 1999). Discussing possible scenarios which might follow the war in Kosovo, the group founded the Future State of Balkania, also called the Cultural State of Balkania, to be established on the Net (see www.kiasma.fi/temp). This state has no territory, but is a state of mind, rooted in people's ideas and ideals for the future. This parallel and virtual reality, although deriving its rationale from the history and problems of the Balkans, will investigate what will be needed to form a synthesis of conflicting views and colliding identities. The general aim is to formulate strategies that will help to create a Europe which is less divided, less egotistical, less closed to the rest of the world.

The tone of the Balkania project is utopian and, of course, it is only a virtual reality, but does this mean that it can have no practical consequences? The symbolism of the enterprise is powerful, even if the goal of unity which lies behind it is fanciful at present. The creation of flags, slogans and other virtual cultural signs of unity is a way of addressing the question while avoiding the more sensitive political implications. For all that, the project is certainly political, but it strives to approach the idea through less controversial means. It is also a long-term attempt to imagine a new sort of Europe, emphasizing the principles of similarity and equality rather than difference and plurality as the ethical basis of people's coexistence. At the same time, it reveals the tension between universalism and particularism that is prevalent in actual societal development. In the virtual public space the task is to create frames of reference through which people's personal security will be wrested free from the imagining of an ethnically pure nation, an historically legitimate territory and a culturally and linguistically homogeneous neighbourhood (Broeckmann, 1999). As such, the project highlights the issue of cultural citizenship, since not only are political rights important in this simulation, but the symbolic and material cultures necessary for the full membership of a community also become central to the endeavour. In former Yugoslavia, the reconstruction of the broken social ties may also be more easily initiated in the cultural sphere.

A rough distinction between the former socialist countries and Western Europe can be made too in their application of the Net to political purposes. In Western Europe the Net is largely used as a medium for election and single-issue campaigns, whereas in the former socialist countries it is used in the main as a means of organizing people and creating social movements (Garcia and Lovink, 1999). Following the collapse of the socialist system, there is a crucial need to rebuild citizen associations in Eastern Europe. While broad-based social movements questioning the way of life in consumer societies have always been highly visible in Western Europe, nowadays a plethora of single issue campaigns have grown without much of a link to broader emancipatory movements. Among present Net-activist groups it is hoped that a campaign could gain enough electronic visibility to appeal to a greater public and thus turn into a broader movement. Net campaigns are often criticized for being merely talk and creating empty signs instead of promoting real action and this is a substantial criticism. However, the mediated nature of the whole society is also accountable for the development. The need for mediation obviously springs from the societal complexity produced by the process of modernization, a processs that invites technological forms of assistance. The media, the Net included, is primarily focused on symbols and meanings, using its discursive power for questioning established conventions. In addition, many struggles have moved off the streets and factories into the space of representation, changing socially bound action into mediated ones. However, in the media age it is of little value to make strict divisions between the real and the symbolic because it is doubtful whether any meaningful new politics can emerge outside the media realm. Instead it would be sensible to ask in what conditions a virtual campaign can achieve political influence and under what circumstances an effective movement can be created on and through the Net.

The soil of politics

The Balkania project shows what is meant by the intermingling of the political and aesthetic aspects in new forms of politics. On the Net, artistic experiments become crucial since they can test the extremes and the potentialities of the technology. In the social sphere the importance of the Net revolves around its capacity to function as a common ground for creating and maintaining social ties. Frequently, in the history of communication technology it has turned out that people use new media creatively, adapting them to the perfectly ordinary purposes of keeping in touch with each other, of building sociality. The needs of sociality should not be overlooked since they are the soil in which political activities can thrive. The Argentine mailing list (Boczkowski, 1999) is a good example of the sociality characteristic of the Net. The list was founded in 1989 by a small group of people, and has evolved over the years into a larger community. By 1995 the majority of the members were Argentine nationals living abroad and interacting mostly in Spanish. It was divided into six sublists, which were Sport, Literary Corner, Musical, Charter, News and Cafe. The last one was a tribute to the Argentine social practice of going to a cafe and informally talking about any kind of issue – a less mannered form of cafe society. Eventually a CD-ROM was put together to 'immortalizing' this important moment in the evolution of the network. It was called Morel's Cafe, after Adolfo Bioy Casare's novel, *The Invention of Morel*. One aspect of the novel central to the endeavour, and to the very essence of national virtual communities, was the dialectic between memory, materiality and immortality.

Discussions on the CD-ROM frequently turned toward experiences and memories of various cafes and cafe culture. The joint evocation of actual places and symbols was accompanied by sharing stories about childhood, dreams and migration. Thus talking about the CD-ROM became a vehicle for perpetuating a sense of nationhood. As one member wrote: 'A couple of months ago I was in Argentina and felt more than ever a kind of exile syndrome in which one looks for spaces, people and a country that aren't there. It's painful and bewildering. That's why it seems to me that the cafe is also this, a place . . . where one finds oneself.' Through the processes of collective recall, members strengthened their identities and their sense of belonging to a nation. Boczkowski sees Morel's Cafe as expressing the idea of the cafe as a social institution, reaffirming the subjective presence of the Argentine nation among its afficionados. For him, Morel's Cafe represents an 'infinite babel', composed of furniture and other objects, social roles and stereotypes, magazines and newspapers, foods and beverages, posters and paintings, bathroom graffiti and conversation topics drawn from myriad real and imaginary cafes, with the whole attached to meaningful moments in the lives of participants through virtual exchanges.

What has Morel's Cafe to do with politics? Directly not much, but indirectly a great deal, because it shows us sociality in action, which is the soil of politics. While it has now become almost routine to speak of the uncertainty and contingency of life and society, it should be as important to study the formation of social ties under these conditions. Although many of the social bonds built upon the Net remain fluid, narrowly confined and ever-changing, it can still assist in creating collectivities. And yet it is now commonly accepted that to be stable and effective, virtual communities also need face-to-face encounters. From the perspective of a locality, the formation of social ties is even more crucial since, to establish a political community, some kind of social coherence has to be presupposed. Thus, when seeking the still embryonic forms of the new politics we should first turn our attention to the kinds of social bonds necessary for their emergence. Conversation and remembered conversation seem to be crucial in this respect and are characteristic of the sociality of neighbourhood associations on the Net as well. In an age of more intensive globalization and greater mobility, people today seem to be more attached to place. It may be possible to employ the Net to build their local roots and create their shared histories and to equip them as competent sojourners in a variety of imagined worlds.

Why is politics important?

One of the most conspicuous characteristics of our time is the expansion of the media realm, resulting in the corresponding enlargement of the public sphere. In addition it seems as though the media are contributing to further fragmentation rather than unification of society, and that the emergent public sphere(s) has not produced an equivalent growth in political activism. However, behind the political public sphere there is a broader publicness, the literary public sphere in Habermas's terms (1996: 365), which is growing in scope. Problems first experienced in the life-world can find their expression in artistic and literary forms, that is, in the broader public sphere. The literary and political public sphere are intertwined, the former articulating values and disclosing the world, the latter focusing on shared activities. Here we see again the interaction between politics, sociality and culture, emerging in relations of mutual dependency. If the public sphere is about achieving understanding and resolution in everyday matters, the social and cultural spheres provide the essential basis for such engagements.

Civil society is the sphere where common concerns can be identified and made political. Today, many scholars and activists see a strong civil society as a crucial component of an inclusive and democratic society. Although ambiguous and full of contradictions, it seems a relevant and, for some, the only counter-force against globalized economies and the remoteness of decision-making. Under certain circumstances, civil society could express itself as a form of communicative power and be able to exert influence upon, for example, the policy of a multinational corporation or the administrative practices of a municipality. As a public sphere, the Net gives us incredible potential to express our views and debate common matters, while it also shifts politics towards more discursive and linguistic forms. It is obvious that for future democratic development, linkages between Net discussions and formal political procedures should be established and new democratic forms created that can address the complex transformations of late modern society.

But why is it so important to seek new arenas and emerging forms of politics? Why is it vital, after all, to delineate the functions and expressions of civil society and make them visible? One answer has to do with the Net itself. While the political potential of the Net, as well as its importance as the soil of social interaction are recognized, it is also crucial to understand that the same technology operates as a ubiquitous and yet imminent mechanism of surveillance and control. Network technology, contributing essentially to new divisions of wealth and its accumulation into fewer hands, thereby invites pervasive forms of surveillance and violations of our rights to privacy. Here we address the major social change and paradox of our time: the need to equip ourselves with the skills to work the Net and to use that knowledge to enhance the promise it reveals and protect against the threats it creates.

References

Alexander, J. and Jacobs, R. (1998) 'Mass communication, ritual and civil society', in T. Liebes and J. Curran (eds), *Media, Ritual and Identity*. London: Routledge. pp. 23–41.

Appadurai, A. (1990) 'Disjuncture and difference in the global cultural economy', in M. Featherstone (ed.), *Global Culture: Nationalism, Globalisation and Modernity*. London: Sage.

Beck, U. (1997) *The Reinvention of Politics. Rethinking Modernity in the Global Social Order*. Cambridge: Polity Press.

Beck, U. (1999) 'Kosmopoliittinen perspektiivi – toisen modernin sosiologiasta', *Tiede & Edistys*, 3 (2): 177–99.

Boczkowski, P. (1999) 'Mutual shaping of users and technologies in a national virtual community', *Journal of Communication*, 49 (2): 86–108.

Broeckmann, A. (1999) *Changing Faces, or Proto-Balkanian Dis-Identifications. Reference text for the Temp Media Lab*. Helsinki. http://www.kiasma.fi/temp

Dahl, G. (1999) 'The anti-reflexivist revolution: on the affirmation of the New Right', in M. Featherstone and S. Lash (eds), *Spaces of Culture. City, Nation, World*. London: Sage.

Dewey, J. (1927/1994) *The Public and Its Problems*. Athens: Swallow Press.

Featherstone, M. (1995) *Undoing Culture. Globalization, Postmodernism and Identity*. London: Sage.

Friese, H. and Wagner, P. (1999) 'Not all that is solid melts into air: modernity and contingency', in M. Featherstone and S. Lash (eds), *Spaces of Culture. City, Nation, World*. London: Sage.

Garcia, D. and Lovink, G. (1999) 'The DEF of tactical media', in *Next 5 Minutes 3 Workbook*, Tactical Media Event, 12–14 March, Amsterdam.

Gibson, W. (1984) *Neuromancer*. London: Grafton Books.

Goff, P. (ed.) (1999) *The Kosovo News and Propaganda War*. Vienna. Geneva: The International Press Institute.

Habermas, J. (1987) *The Theory of Communicative Action. Volume 2. Lifeworld and System: A Critique of Functionalist Reason*, trans. Thomas McCarthy, first published 1981. Cambridge: Polity Press.

Habermas, J. (1996) *Between Facts and Norms; Contributions to a Discourse Theory of Law and Democracy*, trans. W. Rehg. Cambridge: Polity Press.

Hall, S. (1984) 'The Culture Gap', *Marxism Today*, January: 18–23.

Hall, S. (1996) 'On postmodernism and articulation: an interview with Stuart Hall', in D. Morley and K.-H. Chen (eds), *Stuart Hall. Critical Dialogues in Cultural Studies*. London: Routledge. pp. 131–50.

Keane, J. (1998) *Civil Society: Old Images, New Visions*. Palo Alto, CA: Stanford University Press.

Kivikuru, U. (1995) 'From public opinion to popular sphere? Theme interviews tell a different story of Finnish EU opinion', paper presented at the IAMCR Conference, Portoroz, Slovenia.

Kivikuru, U. (ed.) (1996) *Kansa Euromyllyssä. People in the Euromill*. Helsinki: Yliopistopaino.

Lash, S. (1994) 'Reflexivity and its doubles: structure, aesthetics, community', in U. Beck, A. Giddens and S. Lash (1994) *Reflexive Modernization*. Cambridge: Polity Press. pp. 110–73.

Melucci, A. (1996) *Challenging Codes. Collective Action in the Information Age*. Cambridge: Cambridge University Press.

Sassi, S. (2000a) 'The controversies of the Internet and the revitalization of local political life', in K. Hacker and J. van Dijk (eds), *Digital Democracy*. London: Sage.

Sassi, S. (2000b) 'Public opinion as local opinion', in S. Splichal (ed.), *Public Opinion and Democracy: Vox Populi – Vox Dei?* Cresskill, NJ: Hampton Press.

Schwengel, H. (1991) 'British enterprise culture and German kulturgesellschaft', in R. Keat and N. Abercrombie (eds), *Enterprise Culture*. London: Routledge. pp. 136–50.

Stevenson, N. (1999) *The Transformation of the Media. Globalisation, Morality and Ethics*. London: Longman.

Tönnies, F. (1922) *Kritik der Öffentlichen Meinung*. Berlin: Verlag von Julius Springer.

The Transformation of
   Citizenship?

Stephen Coleman

The idea of citizenship

It is all rather new and strange for the British to be considering
themselves as citizens. Historically, the British were subjects and that
status needed little elaboration. But what does it mean to become a
citizen? The current New Labour Secretary of State for Education has
resolved that school pupils should be educated for citizenship and
schools instructed to teach democracy. But how do you teach people to
become democratic citizens? Do you teach them to obey bad laws or to
break them? Are good citizens deferential or challenging? When is
teaching citizenship about politics and when is it about morality? None
of these questions will be answered directly here, although many others
have given much thought to them. In this chapter I shall look at the
convergence of two seismic changes germane to the subject matter of this
book: the birth of an agenda for citizenship and the emergence of new
media of communication which present scope for change in the traditional relationship between citizens and power-wielding elites.

Citizenship was largely conspicuous by its absence as a characteristic
of most of the twentieth century's grand social experiments. The Left,
particularly those who worshipped the Leninist 'god that failed', sought
to free the people's state from meaningful accountability to the citizenry,
and in turn sneered at citizens' rights as if these were contemptible tricks
of *bourgeois* rhetoric. The Right endeavoured to strip people of all but
their atomized status as ever-consuming members of the species, *homo
economicus*. The culmination of this debilitating ideology was the
glorification in the 1980s of all that could be private and purchasable,
matched by derision of civic solidarity and, ultimately, a pathological
denial that society existed. As these delusions imploded, the envelopment of all life – cultural, economic, political – by unstoppable globalization has resulted in mass dislocations of civic identities, giving rise to
a new tribal pursuit of roots. Nationalist longings, ostensibly benign
though often malignant, rhetorically liberationist as well as brutally

divisive and racist, have all been manifested by those who felt displaced from inclusive citizenship and who are trying to discover an illusory sense of community. There is nothing more likely to stimulate a desire to be a citizen of somewhere than to be denied the chance to be a citizen of anywhere – or being forced to be a citizen of a place where one feels like an alien. So, citizenship has attracted those who have perceived them-selves as outsiders in some way (such as immigrants from the poorest lands driven to richer pastures by the search for homes and jobs) and others who feel themselves sucked into discomforting new relationships signifying only geopolitical place (Eurosceptics who fear the loss of ancient national sovereignties to the EU; Canadians faced with NAFTA and CNN; Quebecois discontented by Anglophone dominance; blacks in countries where white skins are the required collateral for stable citizenship).

In the closing decades of the twentieth century Britain began to embrace a new lexicon of citizenship. In 1990 the then Speaker of the House of Commons established a Commission on Citizenship. There followed the creation of the Citizenship Foundation and the Institute for Citizenship Studies. The Conservative ex-Deputy Prime Minister, Doug-las Hurd, promoted the ideal of 'the active citizen' who would join Neighbourhood Watch and use confidential hotlines on which dole cheats could be named. Politically this drive was accelerated by the creation of over forty Citizen's Charters: a series of government-endorsed guarantees of the quasi-rights of the consumer against the inefficiencies of bureaucracies and the labyrinthine procedures of service providers. Rights of citizenship came to be equated with a consumerist ethos that 'the customer is never wrong'. Those who could not afford to be customers or entered into relationships with authorities operating beyond the market (notably, the coercive aspects of the state) found little solace in this consumerist enfranchisement. Meanwhile, New Labour embraced no less zealously a commitment to stakeholding citizenship: a New Citizenship, offering rights that were largely cost-free to the Treasury, with responsibilities too often cast in terms of moral incanta-tion and not always matched by policies that would empower the deprived or excluded. Nonetheless, the more we are told that we are all citizens now, the more the elusive goal of engaged citizenship attracts those inured to political disenchantment. Despite its undoubtedly amor-phous nature, at least two cheers for citizenship were heard in most quarters.

Enthusiasm for the values of citizenship is in part a reaction to the experience of their palpable absence. Hyperbole and even hysteria aside, there prevails a real sense of chronic social decomposition, manifesting itself in ways that commentators have come to recite in a nightmarish litany. This litany includes the drugs culture; gratuitous violence against the harmless, the defenceless and the environments in which people do their best to make a life; hooliganism which has often transformed the communal loyalties of sport into tribal petty-terrorism; the lager-loutishness of tourists for whom travel narrows the mind, just as economic opportunity extends their intimidating reach. It extends to the fraudulence and callousness now endemic within the core capitalist activity of making money; the utter disdain for political discourse (the Independent Television Commission (ITC) reported that in the 1997 general election 4 out of 10 people switched channels or switched off their TVs rather than watch any political coverage); the banality, brutality and sourness of much that passes for entertainment; and finally – overwhelmingly – symbolic of civic breakdown, the appalling aware-ness of assaults of various forms against children.

Out of a fear of the unfolding consequences of such routine incivility, movements to encourage citizenship have gained life and momentum. But citizenship is not something that can just be switched on. If one defines the concept in accordance with the best-known books, the Speaker's Commission and the excellent Crick Report on *Education for Citizenship and the Teaching of Democracy in Schools* (1998), citizen-ship concerns a relationship between members of the public, in political, economic and civic terms, with the communities in which they live and the states within which their democratic lives are played out.

Mass communication and citizenship

To be an active citizen is to be a communicative agent. The socially estranged citizen is a contradiction in terms, for citizenship derives its significance from communicative acts between individuals and their civic, political, economic and moral environments. There can be no community without communication. This is why tribal communities affirmed their identities through public displays of ritual that served to communicate a common language of history and belonging. Central to the initiation rites of the Elena of Papua New Guinea (Knauft, 1999) and the Australian Aborigines (Morphy, 1992) was a belief in the unfolding nature of cultural identity via visual art and orality.

Writing of the origins of national-civic consciousness, Benedict Ander-son points to the seminal importance of the fifteenth century's new technology: 'mechanically-reproduced print-languages' (1983: 47). We need not agree entirely with Anderson's thesis that 'the convergence of capitalism and print technology . . . created the possibility of a new form of imagined community, which in its basic morphology set the stage for the modern nation' (49) to recognize the huge impact of print culture in framing a secular European conception of citizenship. From vernacular languages, Bibles and dictionaries to the dissemination of national accounts of history, the lexicon of modern citizenship, as well as modernist historical consciousness, relied upon the printed word as a communicator of social identity.

The emergence of the mass-produced newspaper accelerated this process of shared civic identity. The newspaper is a daily updated history textbook. Through an unfolding account of 'our' country, state or city, revealed via the implicit or explicit bias of a shared ideology, the press provides a point of connection between atomized readers and the community of which they want to feel part. As an individual one sits at one's window cursing the incompetence of the town council; as a consumer of news one learns of an impending election and feels momentarily empowered by the chance to become an active citizen. As well as civic nourishment, newspapers are often accused of providing their readers with misinformation, distraction and irrelevance. The community imagined for us by journalists is sometimes far from the one we experience (see Peter Dahlgren's Chapter 3 in this book). Civic relationships may come to be impoverished, enervated and poisoned by mistrust in response to the journalistic depiction of the civic network as a precarious web of selfishness and intrigue. Paradoxically, the mass media can both bring together and tear asunder social threads.

In the nineteenth century a press battle ensued for the soul of citizenship. The well-resourced, commercial newspapers adhered to the constitutional claim that sovereignty resided in the state and that the public were subjects of its unelected, crowned head. The radical press addressed itself subversively to a sovereign citizenry and pursued a news agenda based upon popular-democratic interests. The state retaliated, first by licensing newspapers and then by taxing them, as a means of constraining their readership and resources.

The birth of radio, and later television, as channels for the organization of national communication highlighted this tension between the media as forces of civic connection and disconnection. The BBC, as the national broadcaster, representing a national voice and national interest, had a unique civic responsibility placed upon it. More than any newspaper could ever do, it presented itself as a publicly accountable civic space. But this accountability has always been flawed and partial. Politically, the BBC's dependence upon the state, in the form of the government that licensed it, was stronger than its need to belong to the public. So, at the point of its crucial political test of impartiality in the General Strike of 1926, when it could have opted for authentic balance between the strikers and the government, the BBC's Director-General, John Reith, adopted the view that 'since the BBC was a national institution, and since the Government in this crisis were acting for the people . . . the BBC was for the Government in this crisis too' (Scannell and Cardiff, 1991: 33). This undisguised toadyism enabled the British Broadcasting Company to be licensed as a Corporation in 1927, and to enjoy the subsequent trust of government.

The technology of broadcasting provides for monological channels of communication. The public is spoken to as an audience. Neither radio nor television are well suited to two-way communication. Culturally, the production of radio and television has come to be associated with a process of mass consumption which does not sit easily with the require-ments of active citizenship. The couch potato is rarely an engaged citizen. Since the inception of broadcasting, however, a stream of social commentators have pointed to its potential role in educating the public for democratic citizenship. John Scupham, the BBC's first Controller of Educational Broadcasting, regarded 'the field of politics' as being where 'radio and television are making by far their most significant educative contributions', adding, with sanguine innocence, that 'Radio and tele-vision have shifted the emphasis of political controversy in the demo-cratic countries from abuse to argument' (1967: 132–6). This was not an isolated perception. McCallum and Readman, in their study of coverage of the 1945 general election, concluded that 'radio campaigning has revolutionized the nature of British elections' because 'The exposition of policy which is offered . . . tends to be more lucid and intellectually able than that delivered from the local platform' (1945: 173). TV coverage of elections was also seen as providing 'a new quality', according to Treneman and McQuail in their study of the 'first TV election' of 1959: 'The party manifestos, which had once been shouted from public platforms by speakers well used to coping with hecklers, must now be directed to the family by the fireside' (1961: 15).

Such optimism about the impact of television upon civic life did not prevail. In the 1960s McLuhan (1964) and others expounded a critique of the mass media which emphasized the spectacular, voyeuristic, alien-ating, atomizing and distracting nature of broadcast culture. McLuhan, and later Poster, located the root of the malady in the technology of the televised image, whereas Raymond Williams (1974) placed critical emphasis upon the collusion of media producers with elitist political structures and ideologies. Groombridge (1972), writing in the Williams tradition, argued for a new 'mission for television' to become a stimulus to participatory democracy. In the spirit of the Skeffington Report (1968), which argued for more inclusive public involvement in planning and policy-making, Groombridge called for television 'to be considered as candidate for a major part in the civilizing of our arid communal existence and in the improvement and enlivenment of our democracy, such that more people have the opportunity, the aptitude, the incentive and the desire to play an active personal part in what is with unconscious irony called "public life" ' (1972: 25). In the radical manifesto for participatory broadcasting, which formed the concluding third of his magisterial study, Groombridge argued that 'viewers should have greater access to the medium, so that it is much less a one-way medium through which a select band of communicators may address everyone else, and much more a medium through which the heterogeneous sections of a society . . . may effectively communicate with each other' (1972: 163).

A number of experiments in more participatory media formats were tried in the last quarter of the twentieth century. These included local radio, established with a brief to 'combine popular programming with fostering greater public awareness of local affairs and involvement in the community'; cable television, which inspired early hopes of realizing the communal and interactive potential of media technology; phone-ins, or talk-programmes, which promised to turn the microphones over to the voice of the public; and various versions of audience participation discussions and deliberative polls, intended to show how informed and vocal citizens could use television as a forum for deliberative reflection. We shall briefly examine each of these developments.

Local radio stations existed in North America, Australasia and parts of Europe before the 1960s, but only came to the UK, on an experimental basis, in 1969. They were established with an explicit civic brief and were regarded by many as providing platforms for wider local debate and experimentation in coverage of 'council debates . . . or the meetings of tenants' associations, civic societies or neighbourhood councils'. In reality, not much of this happened. As Tony Wright observed in his 1979–80 report on *Local Radio and Local Democracy*: 'the amount of public affairs broadcasting on local radio was found to be disappointingly (and surprisingly) meagre . . . Comments from local broadcasters reflected a widespread antipathy on their part to political broadcasting, while local politicians, public officials and community groups testified to the small impact of local radio on civic affairs . . . A listener survey confirmed . . . this by revealing that local radio had contributed little to the promotion of local political awareness' (1980: 172). With the emergence of commercial local radio in the 1970s and the growth of fierce competition for audiences in the following two decades, scope for a civic role for local media has declined to the point of being almost forgotten.

Cable TV in the USA gave rise to much enthusiasm from some democratic and media theorists. Much of this anticipated similar hopes associated with the new media; indeed, some contemporary optimists are still using examples from cable TV as their examples of how the new media will reshape civic life (Barber, 1998). Arterton (1987) studied 13 'teledemocracy' projects which sought to utilize new media technologies, including cable TV, to facilitate public involvement in decision-making. He concluded that such initiatives could 'improve the quantity and quality of citizen participation in politics', could 'mitigate the inequalities now found in the rates of participation of different social groups', but could not lead to a transition towards direct democracy, as desired by many of those promoting and supporting them (184).

Phone-ins are the closest formats within traditional broadcast media to the interactivity which is characteristic of the new media. To some media theorists who have despaired at the civic impoverishment of most political broadcasting, phone-ins offer a refreshing opportunity to bring the people into the political equation. For Blumler and Gurevitch (1995), who outline eight clear benefits of the phone-in format, it has the joint advantages of restoring 'the ordinary citizen as a significant point of reference for political communicators and as a properly active participant in public discussion' and a return to issue-based political discussion (219). Others have been more sceptical about phone-ins. Davis and Owen (1999), whose work is US-centred, found that phone-ins tended to reflect existing news agendas. The present writer has argued that the organization of the phone-in format results in less openness than the production rhetoric claims (1997), but, in a detailed study of the 1997 BBC *Election Call* series, in which citizens were invited to question leading politicians, it was found that, although callers to the programmes only had a minority of airtime to themselves (27 per cent, as against 60 per cent for the guest politicians), 69 per cent of TV viewers and 53 per cent of radio listeners agreed with the proposition that 'the callers as a whole asked the type of questions I would want to ask', 69 per cent of TV viewers and 64 per cent of radio listeners agreed that '*Election Call* provided a real democratic voice for the public' and 60 per cent of viewers and 69 per cent of listeners stated that 'the programme(s) made me change my mind about some of the issues in the election' (Coleman, 1999).

Political debate on television has itself become increasingly characterized by the presence of vocal studio audiences. The 1992 presidential debate in the USA, which took the form of an audience-participation talk show, broke the mould of such encounters, and the 1997 UK election was replete with formats enabling citizens to interact with their would-be representatives (Coleman, 1998 and 2000). A particularly attractive version of citizen involvement is the deliberative poll whereby a random sample of a population (be it national or local) is invited to attend a single site for a weekend of deliberation on a specific issue. Before they arrive they are polled on a range of questions related to the issue they will be discussing. They are provided with balanced briefing documents on the issue concerned, including main policy options and arguments for and against them. Participants deliberate for the weekend within two types of setting: small-group discussions led by trained moderators and plenary sessions in which they can question panels of policy experts and politicians. At the end of the weekend they are polled again. After deliberation there have been fascinating changes of opinion by participating groups. For example, in the UK Channel 4's 1994 deliberative poll on crime 57 per cent favoured sending more offenders to prison before deliberating, but only 38 per cent thought that at the end. In the 1995 poll on Europe 51 per cent favoured closer economic links with the EU before and 67 per cent after; 16 per cent favoured replacing the pound by a single European currency before and 28 per cent after. Before the 1996 deliberative poll 51 per cent agreed that the monarchy should remain as it is, but only 39 per cent took that position at the end. Such changes in group opinion are not sought for their predictive value, but for their prescriptive value: this is what a random sample of the population thinks once it has informed itself and deliberated and therefore one might expect the wider population to arrive at similar conclusions given the same conditions. Deliberative polls have proved attractive to TV companies and to audiences, allowing the public to view a microcosm of itself possessing the resources of information and time to communicate that are required for fully engaged citizenship to flourish.

However much the mass media open themselves up to or seek to simulate authentic civic life they remain essentially channels of one-way communication. They are appropriate technologies for a hierarchical and manipulative political order in which sovereignty resides with the state and civil society constitutes a marginal sphere, regarded by political elites as a suitable object for opinion management. As Thelen observes in his excellent study of citizens' letters to their Congressmen during the 1987 Iran–Contra hearings: 'Opinion management has led naturally to the creation of a self-referring group of insiders who see it as their mission to keep public conversation among individuals within limits they have so expertly crafted . . . The ultimate creation of opinion management is a class of people trapped within their narrow world, trapped into promoting and perpetuating that world and the tiny corner of their rich personalities that it permits them to express' (1996: 170). This perception of constraint, confinement and closed communication has left many doubting whether the broadcast media can ever produce much more than entertaining distractions from civic life.

New media — citizenship transformed?

Evaluations of the civic worth of the new digital media have been much divided. Some commentators and activists have attributed to them enormous powers of civic reinvigoration. Morris contends that Jefferson's 'utopian vision of a democracy based on town meetings and direct popular participation is about to become a reality' (1999: 27). Campbell *et al.* reflect that 'MPs are only just beginning to realize the implications for their own way of working. It is not just that the library is empty because researchers are sitting at web-browsers: the physical constraints on information dissemination and the need for physical proximity that created the need for a parliament – an assembly of representatives – may be being challenged by the capabilities of the new information and communication technologies . . . perhaps it is time to consider a virtual parliament' (1999: 41). Riley observes that 'The Internet has brought about a decentralization of power. In the wired world, individuals can now make their own choices as to which authorities and information sources they will accept. This is leading to a greater democratization of knowledge, empowerment of the individual and the potential for more informed interactions between the citizenry and organizations, including government' (2000: 67). Others are much less sanguine, regarding such prophecies as so much utopian hyperbole. Norris, on the basis of her study of new media use during the 1998 US mid-term elections, concludes that 'the Web seems to have been used more often as a means to access traditional news rather than as a radical new source of unmediated information and communication between citizens and their elected leaders' (1999: 89). Wilhelm argues that 'rather than being the antidote to democratic ills . . . new information and communication technologies, as currently designed and used, pose formidable obstacles to achieving a more just and humane social order in the digital age' (2000: 6). On the basis of an extensive content analysis study, Hill and Hughes conclude that 'The Net itself will not be a historical light switch that turns on some fundamentally new age of political participation and grassroots democracy', but that 'people will mould the internet to fit traditional politics' (1998: 186).

What is one to make of such deeply divergent analyses? A simple response would be to say that the optimists are naive and the pessimists full of scholarly wisdom. An alternative reading would be that the optimists do not understand politics or citizenship and therefore make technocratic, deterministic claims for civic transformation which fail to address the complexities of such change. The pessimists, on the other hand, have insufficiently explored the unique functions of the new media and therefore criticize them for failing to improve upon or replace traditional media and models of representation, when it is precisely those functions that are not performed by old media and existing democratic models that point up the promise and innovative scope of the new media.

Rather than test the transformative outcomes of new media technologies, it is more useful to examine them from the perspective of their unique functionality, by considering how they allow citizens to behave and engage in new ways. Whether these new ways are separate from or superior to older ways associated with traditional media is at best a secondary question. In short, it is not argued here that citizens need to stop watching television, reading newspapers or voting for traditional politicians for new activities facilitated by digital media to be regarded as transformative processes.

The new media are having a transformative effect upon civic communication in at least three ways. First, they are opening up to public scrutiny a wealth of hitherto remote information which can enable citizens to engage on a more equal basis with political and other authorities (see Stromer-Galley and Hall Jamieson's Chapter 8 in this book for a consideration of the US experience). Second, they are developing spaces for unmediated public deliberation in which citizens can interact with one another, with other communities and with elites that were once less vulnerable to such direct engagement. Third, they are changing the way that representatives do their jobs because the very nature of the mandate for democratic representation is open to transformation. We shall now examine each of these developments.

Information

The report to the Rome meeting of the EU Information Society Forum (November 1999) was unequivocal about the promise of ICTs. It stated that:

> The new information technologies may, for the first time in the history of industrial societies under liberal regimes, make it possible to recreate the perfect information arena, the *agora* of Ancient Greece, a meeting place where citizens could go to be fully informed and to participate directly, with no intermediary, in the government of the city, exercising all their political rights unconditionally and without restriction. Thanks to digital networks and technologies, every aspect of political, institutional, administrative and judicial life can become truly 'transparent', allowing the citizen to exercise close scrutiny over decision-making processes and

administrative procedures. The interactive nature of the new technologies may also allow the citizen to interact with government at will, using simplified, non-bureaucratic procedures, either to exercise his political rights or to make use of public services.

The following month the e-Europe project was launched, with a commitment to improve European citizens' information rights in ten key areas. Much of this is reminiscent of similar US initiatives earlier in the 1990s, although advocates of e-Europe would claim that it is more citizen-centred than its US precursors.

What does all this amount to for citizens and for the quality of citizenship? Firstly, institutions of governance are becoming more accessible and transparent by digitizing their data and delivering services via the Internet. The UK government is committed to being able to transact all business with citizens electronically by 2008. Public information has traditionally been made available in a general form to a national constituency; digitally transmitted information can be customized for specific users, allowing citizens to access information of personal interest to them. So, rather than searching for general information about income tax or state pensions or NHS hospitals, users of the new media can access instant information about their tax rate, pension entitlement or local hospital. The UK's ambitious me.gov project is designed to provide just such customized information.

Secondly, even if citizens have formal access to information, it is not always clear where to find specific kinds of information, what it means when it is found and how to keep track of updated information. Electronic portals provide a gateway to broad categories of information (institutions, government departments, charities, business news, cultural perspectives) and are designed to guide citizens to levels of information appropriate for their needs. Efficient portals work with intelligent agents which update information, search for alternative sources of information and point users towards knowledge categories that they may not know they needed. (One of the great paradoxes of free information is that people often do not know what they need to know.)

Thirdly, the relative ease and cheapness of transmitting information via the new media offers scope for a much more liberal array of alternative data, interpretations and opinions. For comparatively resourceless citizens, it is much more difficult to challenge information when it emanates from entrenched state and commercial organizations. Of course, the new media are developing their own trusted sources, such as BBC Online, the largest Web site in Europe. Citizens, as consumers of information, will continue to adopt strategies intended to test the worthiness of new information sources, as they have learned to do when using old media.

Deliberation

According to the democratic theorist, Giovanni Sartori (1987), deliberation is a substantive element of effective democracy. But most existing democratic societies have failed to develop open arenas for public deliberation. Indeed, apart from symbolic but obsolete forums such as Speakers' Corner in Hyde Park, London, it is hard to think of a single site specifically dedicated to public discourse. To some extent, the media-generated experiments in creating discursive public spaces – phone-ins, audience-participation debates, deliberative polls – were successful innovations in public participation, but, unlike a Habermasian public sphere, they were controlled by media organizations and were first and foremost media events endeavouring to simulate an authentic public arena.

The inherent interactivity of the new media, in which traditional distinctions between producer and consumer become irrelevant, provides an opportunity to create virtual public spaces in which civic discourse can take place. Experiments in civic deliberation began as bottom-up, citizen-designed projects. In 1995 Steven Clift and other grassroots local activists established MN-Politics, an e-mail list for the public discussion of political and civic life in the US state of Minnesota. Lessons from this highly successful (and still active) project were taken up in Britain by UK Citizens Online Democracy (UKCOD), a project which sought to provide an on-line forum for national debate. Its more successful sister organization, UK Communities Online (UKCO), succeeded in encouraging a network of community-based projects, several of which have now become embedded within their local civic cultures (for examples of other projects in creating micro-publics and reworking the public sphere, see Chapter 4 by Sassi, in this volume).

The problem with much on-line discussion has been its apparent irrelevance to the 'real' world of policy and politics. Much as the practice of deliberation is in itself a civic skill, rational citizens seek outcomes from their participation and meaningful outcomes often depend upon there being a link between the virtual world of open discussion and the physical world of complex political relationships and institutions. Linking discussion to recognized channels of power has not tended to occur and this is why scholars have found so little debate of real value in forums that have been analysed (Davis, 1999; Hill and Hughes, 1998; Wilhelm, 2000). On the other hand, on-line discussions set up by existing institutions of power, such as government consultations, or the 10 Downing Street or White House Web sites, fall prey to the management of public relations experts (Hacker, 1999; Morris, 1999).

There have been some attempts to create open public spaces under the aegis of respected bodies, which have linked citizens to elected representatives. The Hansard Society e-democracy programme has run a series of on-line discussions and consultations linking UK citizens to parliamentary committees conducting inquiries or scrutinizing legislation. Some of these discussions have involved selected groups of citizens with relevant experience or expertise – such as women scientists and engineers, who gave on-line evidence to a House of Lords Science and Technology committee inquiry; e-democracy activists and experts who gave on-line evidence to the House of Commons Public Administration Committee; and several hundred women who had lived with domestic violence, who gave evidence to the All-Party Domestic Violence Group. Other on-line consultations have been opened to any member of the public, such as the Commons Information Committee's investigation into an effective information and communication strategy for the UK parliament. Citizens feel more motivated in taking part in such on-line events because they feel connected to a real source of power. Unlike the government, which has an overriding need to implement its policies, legislatures exist to scrutinize policy, hold executive policy-makers to account and to account for themselves to those who elect them. So, representatives, like citizens, have a strong motive to participate in such events, as long as they are not hijacked by partisan bodies. There is a good deal of experience of successful new-media-based consultations in which local authorities have engaged with local citizens. This trend can be expected to increase in the UK where local councils have new statutory obligations to consult with citizens. The future of on-line deliberation may well be as a 'fifth estate', scrutinizing and engaging with national parliaments and local councils.

Representation

Much of the early thinking about e-democracy came from advocates of direct democracy (Becker and Slaton, 2000; Slaton, 1992; Toffler, 1970). This had two enduring effects: first, e-democracy came to be mainly associated with proposals for electronic voting; second, much e-democratic discourse was disconnected from the established institutions and procedures of representative democracy, which was regarded as an obsolete political tradition soon to be replaced by push-button plebiscites. Serious arguments can indeed be made for the political theory of direct democracy (Budge, 1997) but there is no likelihood that such vast changes in the political organization of society will emanate from purely technocratic roots. If power is to be redistributed as active citizens use the new media, this will involve public engagement with existing structures of power rather than with putative anarchic communities.

However, the nature of representation will change as new media become more pervasive. To begin with MPs will embrace more of the technologies that can make them more efficient. It is hard to imagine a modern representative without a mobile phone or pager. Most now have computers in their constituency and parliamentary offices, even if they have to rely upon assistants to work them. More MPs are setting up Web sites, although it is not clear whether the majority know what to do with them (like most owners of most sites on the Web). They are beginning to use e-mail and this trend will increase rapidly when filtering software improves. (The Hansard e-democracy programme has been working with BT to devise an efficient and secure system which will allow MPs to identify senders of e-mail.) Party Web strategies are still in their infancy, and even in the USA, where the 2000 election was supposed to mark the coming of age for on-line campaigning, on-line strategies are far less important than off-line media activity, and the candidates with the most effective new media campaigns (McCain and Bradley) still failed to defeat the front-runners.

Despite the misplaced emphasis upon e-voting, the first significant election to be run solely via the Internet is still some way off. The California Internet Task Force's *Report on the Feasibility of Internet Voting* concluded that 'At this time [January 2000] it would not be legally, practically or fiscally feasible to develop a comprehensive remote Internet voting system that would completely replace the current paper process used for voter registration, voting and the collection of initiative, referendum and recall petition signatures' (2000: 46). If that is true for California, one can only assume that on-line voting elsewhere is an even more distant prospect – although it may well come about eventually, especially if one looks to developments in digital TV. But the electoral process will still be affected by the new media, as electronic voter information guides become more sophisticated and popular. These guides, which are effectively specialized electoral portals, were key features of the 2000 elections in the USA and are likely to change the way that citizens survey, select and contact parties and candidates as much as television did in the 1960s.

Trusted portals will change citizens' relationship to electoral activity, but citizenship need not stop after the election results have been announced. Whoever can establish publicly trusted gateways to 'peace time' politics will play a key role in transforming the relationship between citizens and their representatives. Such a portal would have paths to issues, parties and each elected representative. Citizens will be able to call up the digitized record of their representative – all speeches made, voting record, excerpts from constituency events and visits further afield – and to contact their representative via cyber-surgeries, on-line issue seminars and on-line community gatherings.

Although direct democracy is not the logical next step, as early e-democrats argued, it is equally unlikely that practices of governance will stay as they were before the digital age. The increase in public information and deliberation will produce a much stronger and more frequently renewable and reviewable mandate from the people to their chosen representatives. There is manifest scope in all this for evolution towards what Barber (1984) has called 'strong democracy' and the present writer refers to as 'strong representation'.

Cautionary notes

The picture painted above is of the new media as forces for civility which could lead to the enrichment of civic culture. But such a development is by no means automatic. Citizenship depends upon equal opportunities to participate in public life. If, as is the case, most citizens lack the machinery of access to the interactivity of the new media, then empowering those with such access will be at the expense of those without, thereby exacerbating unjust disparities. The UK Department of Trade and Industry's (2000) report, *Increasing the Availability and Take-up of ICTs in Deprived Neighbourhoods*, states:

> The development of ICTs provide a once in a lifetime chance for people living in deprived neighbourhoods to reconnect with society in a variety of productive and positive ways. To take advantage of this, Government, acting in partnership with regional and local organisations, the community and voluntary sectors and business, must act quickly to improve access to and uptake of ICTs in deprived neighbourhoods.

A number of policies for achieving this end are outlined (DTI, 2000). It may be that the full civic value of the new media will have to wait for the next stage in the development of the technology, when analogue television is switched off and citizens will be compelled to join the digital age through their televisions. In the UK 98 per cent of households have televisions – even more than have telephones. So, by the second decade of the twenty-first century the digital divide, at least in terms of access, could be eliminated.

If citizenship requires universal access, democracy needs trustworthy channels of information and deliberation if it is to prosper. Populist adventurers, with their plans for push-button plebiscites, seek to reduce the democratic process to a grand version of a tabloid phone poll. Vote.com, the US company led by Dick Morris, promises to deliver citizens' votes to their representatives who, they are warned, would be foolish to ignore the clicks and ticks of those choosing to participate in such polls: 'In short, balance in our system has already begun to swing toward direct democracy and away from representative democracy. Our representatives had our trust and they blew it . . . With the rise of Internet voting . . . the pendulum will continue to swing toward direct popular control' (Morris, 1999: 43). Morris nowhere addresses the question of how his citizens will arrive at their views, whether any standards of public deliberation are required for them to do so or who speaks for the vast majority who are not counted by his polls but are represented, however poorly, by those they elected to save them from 'direct popular control'. Such technopopulist diversions from democracy will not just go away and if other, more responsible, projects do not come to the fore they will surely usurp the e-democratic agenda.

Becoming digital citizens

Citizens of the digital age will need to learn new skills. Good public deliberation amounts to more than an equation between technology and civic space. People need to learn how to argue. After a century which culminated in the anti-eloquence of the US 'shock-jock' and the banal presidential debates of recent years, it is time for skills of speaking, chairing, listening, summarizing and reflecting to be acquired. For healthy democracy they are no less important than arithmetic or geography. Strong representation requires not only better representatives who are more connected to the public who gave them their power, but also citizens who understand how to be democratically represented: how to seek and use the records of their representatives; how to ask meaningful and incisive questions; how to hold their legislators to account; and how to change their minds when the evidence is against them. Anyone can be a cynic who relentlessly decries the inadequacies of 'them up there'. Strong representation involves supporting representatives with knowledge and experience and ensuring that the public is never far enough away from power to allow it to grow corrupt in isolation.

References

Anderson, Benedict (1983) *Imagined Communities: Reflections on the Origin and Spread of Nations.* London: Verso.
Arterton, F. Christopher (1987) *Teledemocracy: Can Technology Protect Democracy?* Newbury Park, CA: Sage.
Barber, B.R. (1984) *Strong Democracy: Participatory Politics for a New Age.* Los Angeles: University of California Press.
Barber, B.R. (1998) *A Place for Us – How to Make Society Civil and Democracy Strong.* New York: Hill & Wang.
Becker, T. and Slaton, D.C. (2000) *The Future of Teledemocracy: Visions and Theories – Action Experiments – Global Practices.* New York: Praeger.
Blumler, Jay G. and Gurevitch, M. (1995) *The Crisis of Public Communication.* London: Routledge.
Budge, Ian (1997) *The New Challenge of Direct Democracy.* Cambridge: Polity.
California Internet Task Force (2000) *Report on the Feasibility of Internet Voting.* http://www.ss.ca.gov/executive/ivote/
Campbell, Anne, Harrop, A. and Thompson, B. (1999) 'Towards the virtual parliament – what computers can do for MPs in parliament in the age of the Internet', in S. Coleman, J. Taylor and W.V. van de Donk (eds), *Parliament in the Age of the Internet.* Oxford: Oxford University Press.
Coleman, Stephen (1997) *Stilled Tongues.* London: Porcupine.
Coleman, Stephen (1998) 'Interactive media and the 1997 UK general election', *Media, Culture & Society*, 20 (4): 687–95.
Coleman, Stephen (1999) *Election Call: A Democratic Public Forum?* London: Hansard Society.
Coleman, S. (ed.) (2000) *New Media and Social Exclusion.* London: Hansard Society.
Coleman, Stephen, Taylor, J. and van de Donk, W. (eds) (1999) *Parliament in the Age of the Internet.* Oxford: Oxford University Press.
Crick, Bernard (1998) *Education for Citizenship and the Teaching of Democracy in Schools: Final Report of the Advisory Group on Citizenship.* London: Qualifications and Curriculum Authority.
Davis, Richard (1999) *The Web of Politics: The Internet's Impact on the American Political System.* Oxford: Oxford University Press.
Davis, R. and Owen, D. (1999) *New Media and American Politics.* London: Routledge.
Department of Trade and Industry (2000) *Increasing the Availability and Take-up of ICTs in Deprived Neighbourhoods.* London: DTI.
Groombridge, Brian (1972) *Television and the People: A Programme for Democratic Participation.* Harmondsworth: Penguin.
Hacker, K. (1999) *The Internet and Politics: there is no Internet Democracy.* http://www.zianet.com/khacker/indem.html
Hill, Kevin A. and Hughes, John E. (1998) *Cyberpolitics: Citizen Activism in the Age of the Internet.* New York: Rowman and Littlefield.
Information Society Forum, www.eurvoice.org
Knauft, Bruce M. (1999) *From Primitive to Precolonial in Melanesia and Anthropology.* Chicago: University of Michigan Press.

McCallum and Readman (1945) *The British General Election of 1945*. London: Frank Cass.

McLuhan, M. (1964) *Understanding Media*. London: Routledge & Kegan Paul.

Morphy, Howard (1992) *Ancestral Connections: Art and an Aboriginal System of Knowledge*. Chicago: University of Chicago Press.

Morris, Dick (1999) *Vote.com: How Big-money Lobbyists and the Media are Losing their Influence, and the Internet is Giving Power Back to the People*. Los Angeles: Renaissance.

Norris, Pippa (1999) 'Who surfs? New technology, old voters and virtual democracy', in Ellaine Kamarck and Joseph S. Nye Jnr. (eds), *democracy.com? – Governance in a Networked World*. New Haven, CT: Hollis.

Riley, Tom (2000) 'The changing face of democracy today', *The Riley Report*. www.rileyis.com/report/jan2000.html

Sartori, G. (1987) *The Theory of Democracy Revisited*. New York, NJ: Steven Bridges Press.

Scannell, Paddy and Cardiff, David (1991) *A Social History of British Broadcasting – Vol I: Serving the Nation, 1922–1939*. Oxford: Basil Blackwell.

Scupham, J. (1967) *Broadcasting and the Community*. London: C.A. Watts.

Slaton, D.C. (1992) *Televote*. New York: Praeger.

Thelen, David (1996) *Becoming Citizens in the Age of Television*. Chicago: University of Chicago Press.

Toffler, Alvin (1970) *Future Shock*. New York: Random House.

Treneman, J. and McQuail, D. (1961) *Television and the Political Image: A Study of the Impact of Television on the 1959 General Election*. London: Methuen.

Wilhelm, Anthony G. (2000) *Democracy in the Digital Age: Challenges to Political Life in Cyberspace*. London: Routledge.

Williams, Raymond (1974) *Television: Technology and Cultural Form*. London: Fontana.

Wright, Tony (1980) *Local Radio and Local Democracy*. Department of Extramural Studies, University of Birmingham.

6 The Transformation of the Political Audience?

Richard Huggins

Introduction

This chapter discusses the attitudes and approaches of young people to democratic political participation, with particular reference to political communication, in order to examine the under-researched notion of the political audience. Starting from the widely discussed idea that certain forms of political practice are in 'crisis', it examines some of the central issues in this debate and thus what might be read as the tensions between modern and postmodern readings of contemporary politics. The argument is contextualized by reference to what are best seen as cultural developments in the social environment of young people (amongst others) – most notably the emergence of media cultures and what have been called 'promotional cultures' (Axford and Huggins, 1997; Wernick, 1991). Media cultures are not simply those in which a high level of communications media and processes are prevalent but in which, as Castells notes, cultural and social expressions and power relationships are mediated by electronic communications (Castells, 1996; but see also, Fiske, 1995; Kellner, 1995; Skovmand and Schroder 1992; Stevenson, 1995). Taking these two developments together I argue that it may be appropriate to talk in terms of a transformation – although exactly how, to what extent and with what outcome is far less clear – when considering how political communications are received, interpreted and given meaning by individuals. The chapter explores the notion of the political audience and discusses some of the implications that follow. The final section of the chapter reports a case study of qualitative data collected during the last British general election campaign in 1997 which focuses on how young people received and interpreted political communications during an election campaign.

The current crisis of democratic politics

There is a current vogue to discuss democratic politics throughout European and North American states as experiencing a crisis in terms of levels of participation and public interest (Blumler and Gurevitch, 1995; Franklin, 1994; Katz, 1996; Esser, 1999). The evidence for such a crisis includes falling levels of participation and electoral turnouts attended by reportedly high levels of citizen disaffection and cynicism with political and public life, and a 'dumbing down' of political communication.

Taken at face value there is a surfeit of data which can be used to consolidate this claim. In the USA a recent survey by the National Association of Secretaries of State discovered that an increasing number of 15–24-year-olds are 'increasingly alienated from the political process' and expressed alarm that voter turnout amongst this group is likely to fall further in the 2000 presidential elections. Indeed voter turnout has fallen amongst this age group in the USA, from 50 per cent in 1972 to 32 per cent in 1996. Worse still, for those behind the survey, the lowest-rated priorities for this group are 'being a good American' and being 'involved in democracy and voting' (National Association of Secretaries of State, 1999: 5–6). Taken with shocking statistics that more young people in the USA know who Bart, Homer and Marge Simpson are than who the Vice-President is, we can truly see how deep the crisis has become.

Such statistics are seen as typical of the motivational crisis afflicting many democratic states. Crucially the young are seen as most vulnerable to such afflictions. In the UK, in keeping with the modernizing motif of the Blair administration and its refrain of 'active citizenship', the creation of the new assembly in Scotland was attended by statements about the need to generate higher levels of participation by young people and a strategy statement aimed at achieving greater voice and empowerment among young people in Scotland.

Young people are seen by many academic and other commentators as being a key indicator group of new social phenomena. Indeed, much discussion of 'young people' and politics revolves around youth as carriers of 'new' political attitudes, practices and behaviours. For example Bryner et al. (1997), in their study of young adults, (defined as individuals born in 1970), position young people in the 'vanguard' of the 'new politics'. They identify a range of significant phenomena, including political attitudes and behaviour that young people display and which can be held to designate the emergence of a new politics. These include the heightened role of commodification and consumption (rather than production) in the constitution of the identity of young people, the role of the media in the framing of social experience and the increased substitution of the workplace as a source of values and norms by the media. Media are seen as the main source of the constitutive elements through which identities are constructed, social relations mediated and peer and youth culture created (Bryner *et al.*, 1997; see also Livingstone, 1998a). Finally, the study notes an increasing move away from party politics to issue-based politics, a 'vehement' anti-racism and commitment to new political programmes such as the green movement (Bryner *et al.*, 1997: 4). Like many commentators, Bryner *et al.* share the creeping pessimism about the developments outlined above and suggest that they are a significant cause of the growing cynicism and apathy about politics and politicians said to be characteristic of the young.

The idea that young people display levels of cynicism, apathy and disengagement with the formal political process that are higher than average is widely held. In the run up to the 1997 British general election considerable attention was devoted to this topic by the political parties, media and polling organizations. Indeed data can be found that appears to support the sense of motivational crisis. A report for Demos in 1995 found that only 6 per cent of people between the ages of 15–34 described themselves as 'very interested in politics' (Wilkinson and Mulgan, 1995). In terms of actual voting behaviour young people do appear to vote proportionately less than other age groups. In the British general election of 1992 only 61 per cent of 18–24-year-olds voted (a figure down by around 10 per cent from 1987), compared to 75 per cent of older age groups. Furthermore young people who had registered to vote were less likely to use their vote than older people (British Election Survey, 1992).

Furthermore the stated intentions to vote among young people in the parliamentary elections of that year were very low. An ICM poll on 24 April 1997, one week before the election, found that only 32 per cent of voters under 25 were certain to vote in the forthcoming election, a figure slightly lower than a MORI poll which showed that only 36 per cent of 18–24-year-olds would vote. On the other hand voting patterns, as opposed to voting intentions, reveal a more politically astute constituency than might be supposed. Throughout the 1960s and 1970s the Labour Party was a long way ahead of the Conservative Party in terms of percentage of the vote polled. Among young people in 1979 the two main parties were neck and neck, each with 40 per cent of the youth vote. In 1983 more young people voted Conservative (43 per cent) than Labour (31 per cent) and in the last two elections Labour has led by only 4 per cent. In 1997 a special survey of 500 students (admittedly a skewed constituency) for the *Sunday Times* (Driscole and Kelly, 1996) found that 75 per cent of this group were registered to vote and pretty much clued up on recent history and seminal events like the 1978–9 'winter of discontent'. However, in the same survey a modal cynicism was apparent, exemplified by a female student who argued 'basically I don't think that they are interested in how well they do their jobs. They're just interested in getting re-elected.'

Suggestions that young people are less engaged with the political process are evidenced not only by voting intention and behaviour, party membership and stated levels of interest, but also in responses to the coverage of election campaigns by British broadcasting organizations. Thus the Independent Television Commission's study of the 1997 campaign, *Election 97*, has noted that young people are the 'least interested' in elections, the least engaged and the group most liable to be 'waverers' in terms of voting intention. In addition this group records the lowest intention to vote at around 65 per cent, and the highest tendency to avoid political communications with 41 per cent of 16–24-year-olds switching channels to avoid election coverage. All of this leads the ITC report to conclude that 'younger people are less interested in elections'. Now, this may be true, but it is also worth noting a NOP survey, compiled shortly after the election, which found that 59 per cent of those under 35 felt that there was scope for change in the British approach to elections and certainly both the ITC study and the findings reported later in this chapter indicate that some of the 'problem' lies with the way in which campaigns are put together by the parties and covered by the broadcasters (Sancho-Aldridge, 1997).

For many this crisis is either a direct or indirect outcome of the increased significance of the mass media, and particularly visual media, such as television, in social and political life. For example, Blumler and Gurevitch (1995) say that it is precisely the role of the media as public communicator that lies at the heart of the crisis. For Franklin (1994) it is more the convergence of promotional culture, media commercialization and an increased reliance on the discourse of advertising that has undermined the democratic validity of the political process. Katz (1996) argues that it is changes in the constitution of both the audience (in terms of its homogeneity and 'mass') and the decline of the public service tradition which is undermining the foundations of liberal democracy.

These developments are part of a pattern of complex causation involving globalization, rapid technological innovation and cultural change (see Axford, Chapter 1 in this volume). For example, Ignatieff argues that the global media, in particular television and television news, is the instrument of a new kind of politics he calls 'species' politics. This new politics is both anti-political, with a highly sentimental and voyeuristic focus on the 'victim', and yet capable of producing an 'internationalization of conscience' exemplified by the Live Aid global media event of 1985

(Ignatieff, 1998: 10), or, perhaps more recently, the global response to the flooding in Mozambique (*Guardian*, 28 March 2000, p. 1).

If Ignatieff alerts us to both the global reach and the ambiguous nature of the media, for others the role of the media in the crisis of politics is less ambiguous. Hart argues that the steady rise of cynicism, citizen ignorance about and care for the political process, all characteristics of politics since the 1960s, have been a direct consequence of increased television coverage and the consequent emphasis of style over content. So much so in fact that he argues that cynicism has become the dominant mind-set in the electorate, implying, paradoxically, a quite widespread understanding of the intricacies of political campaigning, the use of polling statistics, the meaning of soundbites and negative ads (Hart, 1994).

Blumler and Gurevitch (1995) argue much the same in many ways, although they place a significant emphasis on the apparent decline of the public service tradition under the impact of the rapid commercialization and deregulation of the televisual media characteristic of the early to mid-1980s in Europe. Indeed the lament often focuses on the decline of the public service tradition and ethos and this is a powerful motif in the study of political communications. Norris *et al.* (1999) note that television coverage of British general election campaigns 'reflect a high standard of public service' and illustrate this by quoting directly from the BBC producer guidelines which state 'there is an absolute obligation for the BBC's journalism to remain impartial as the people of the UK exercise their right to vote'. Indeed so powerful is this motif that the main commercial broadcasters echo such aims in their guidelines to staff (Norris *et al.*, 1999: 29). It is interesting to note that the public service tradition is a more problematic one than is sometimes acknowledged (Axford and Huggins, 1996) in that the service provided to the public in terms of democracy and participation was always more implied than real. However, many commentators are unable or unwilling to see the deeply ideological components that make up the 'PSB' tradition and overlook the contribution of this ideology to forms of cultural and social control (Ouellette, 1999).

In recent years the emergence of 'new media' forms and practices have excited both optimism and pessimism about the ability of the media to reinvigorate the public sphere and political discourse and communication (Barber, 1997; Barnett, 1998; Boggs and Dirmann, 1999; Coleman *et al.*, 1999; Cubitt, 1999; Davis and Owen 1998; Holmes, 1997). There is considerable discussion about what the nature of the 'new media' are (Livingstone, 1998a; Axford, Chapter 1 of this volume) and care is needed when categorizing media as either 'new' or 'old'. More significant than simple classification are two points. First, that the phrase 'new media' can be taken as a shorthand label for significant shifts in both the technologies and formats of media that have occurred in recent years. Second, that key attention should be given to the emergence of new media technology and formats in view of the centrality of the media in contemporary social life and the shift to media cultures discussed in other chapters in this book.

Because young people conventionally are early users of new media technologies (Livingstone, 1998a), the study of the young and their use of media in relation to the political process is a matter of some practical significance in that they provide a convenient focus at which to study use and impact. Young people are more likely to be both conversant with and literate in media cultures as much of their social life is conducted in media-saturated environments. The use of the term 'media environment' (Livingstone, 1998a) provides a more subtle way of conceptualizing the relationships between media technologies and formats and the human interface with them. It is more appropriate to think of young people as being immersed in a media environment in which they actively interface, (rather than simply watch or view), with various media rather than being simply users or consumers of media products and outputs.

There are then three main points to stress at the end of this section of the chapter. The first is that there has been a significant extension and intensification of the role of the 'media' in the framing, in the Castellsian sense, of social life in general and politics in particular. Second, that this extension has been accompanied by a vigorous discussion about the 'quality' of the political process thus framed by the media. Third, these developments are both consequences of major cultural shifts which may be referred to, in short, as the diffusion of both media and promotional cultures in the widest possible sense. It is pertinent to ask what evidence of such developments can we detect in the attitudes and behaviours of young people to the practice and form of democratic politics? It is also pertinent to attempt to assess what the outcomes of the three developments mentioned above are in relation to the young. The next section of this chapter will focus on the results of a research project which looked at young people's attitudes to political communications in the 1997 British general election campaign.

Young people, participation and the political audience

The notion that 'young people' represent a distinct constituency within the electorate is a relatively recent development that is a consequence of two factors. The first is the emergence in the 1950s of the notion of 'teenagers' as a sociological phenomenon and distinct social group with their own interests, activities and values (Hebdige, 1988). The second is the significance of the passing of the Representation of the People Act of 1969. This act, coming as it did in the wake of considerable political and social activism on the part of young people, saw the electoral franchise widened to accommodate individuals between the ages of 18–21 and both recognized and reinforced the idea that the 'young' constituted a specific potential voting group.

Despite the significance given by the main political parties to 'catching' the young vote there has been a relative lack of studies about young people and politics and in particular on what sense young people make of political communications. The study of youth has tended to focus on the sociology of youth culture and, where it crosses with politics, this political sociology has tended to revolve around the potential for the young to be involved in forms of conflict (Melucci, 1996). Conflictual action can take many forms and focus is often given to different manifestations of youth culture: 'folk devils' and deviance (Brakc, 1980; Cohen, 1972), the sociology of youth culture (Amit-Talai and Wulff, 1995), or youth as a site and celebration of resistance (Redhead, 1997). Much of the literature defines young people as either a problem group, an 'outsider' group inherently in tension with older members of society and the institutions of that society, or a group of people who need some form of policing, be that moral, economic, legal or social (Skelton and Valentine, 1998). The concept of 'youth' is both ambiguous and contested, a factor which complicates much of the study of young people as political actors.

The reported indifference or outright hostility to political participation among the young is not in fact as clear cut as much anecdotal (and some more systematic) evidence suggests. Perhaps this is a matter of being able to read the evidence in a number of ways. For example, it is particularly important to note that there is little agreement over what constitutes a 'young person' in terms of age range. It is also the case that many of the studies of young people and politics which have been done do little more than touch the surface of motivation. The slackening of partisan alignment (Norris, 1997) holds true for all age groups and is probably less marked in the 1990s than in the 1970s. The sharpest decline is evidenced among those in higher education, but again, as Parry *et al.* (1992) point out, we should be careful in drawing inferences about the propensity of the young to participate in politics just from indexes of support for political parties. Students, although more peripatetic than most other parts of the population, are rather more likely to participate in politics than long-term residents, although not always in elections.

The concept of the audience is one of the most central in communications studies and has received considerable attention over the years. However, this attention has often focused on the effects of media on audiences and the ability of media outputs to influence the audience (Livingstone, 1998a; Silverstone, 1990). To some extent this tendency rested on the assumption that the audience was a relatively homogeneous entity and it is also a legacy of the conception of the unified public and hence the unified audience that developed under the 'old media order' (Axford and Huggins, 1996). However, much recent work draws attention to the increased complexity of the audience and stresses the fragmentated, heterogeneous and multiple nature of the media audience (Davis and Owen, 1998). Audience research has increasingly stressed the active role of the audience in creating meaning from the content viewed (Livingstone, 1998b). Audiences may be passive or detached in their relationships to mass media, or they may actively process, interpret and create meaning from media messages (Davis and Owen, 1998).

A focus on the audience allows us to explore some important ideas. For example, as Silverstone (1990), amongst others, notes, the audience is crucial to developing an understanding of social and cultural processes and studying the audience allows us to explore the cultural processes at work in the generation of social meaning. For the purposes of this chapter it is important to underline the stress that some audience research places on the social centrality of the audience in the twentieth century. Thus living in the twenty-first century is strongly influenced or framed by the media and the attendant modes of interactivity and discourse (Castells, 1996). The implications of such ideas for the audience, be that a set of viewers for a particular media form or an audience of an electronic political communication campaign, in terms of, say, democratic participation or citizenship, are considerable. For example, Livingstone argues that our experiences as members of media audiences is crucial to our modes of participation as citizens and our social position is increasingly mediated through our 'audiencehood' (1998b).

Livingstone (1998b: 194) also draws attention to what she calls the 'implied audience', noting that much commentary on audiences makes a number of implicit assumptions about their use of media, without undertaking actual analysis of audience reception. She notes that such audience analysis raises important political questions because the reception of communication is a crucial site of conflict over the definition of social (Livingstone, 1998b). It is crucial to distinguish between the notion that certain *things* – ideas, 'truth', 'reality' – are either communicated or happen to viewers and the idea that the media are part of the way in which the everyday social world of the (young) person is constructed, framed or bounded.

If the ideas outlined above are only partly accurate descriptions of social transformations currently under way they have important implications for many of the central ideas of democratic politics, such as notions of citizenship, political participation and public communication. For example, the liberal democratic ideal of active political citizens may commute to one which emphasizes the active, critical members of an audience, in which strategies of media literacy are privileged over other conventional definitions of political competence and social agency (Kellner, 1995). Furthermore it may be necessary to take greater account of the media as a site for the performance of politics in contemporary society and, indeed, to investigate further the notion that politics and political participation may be viewed as a form of media and public performance (Bell, 1999; Chaney, 1993; McKay, 1998; also Street, Chapter 10 in this volume).

Privileging the concept of the audience should refocus our attention on some of the developments that attend the emergence of media cultures and the discourses that flow from them; it should also remind us that *politics* is as much immersed in these cultural developments as other social process. The aestheticization of everyday life (Featherstone, 1991) – characterized by the saturation of everyday experience with signs and images, through the 'postmodern carnival' of communications – finds reflection in both the conduct and interpretation of electronic political communications and has specific implications for both the conduct of election campaigns and our understanding of them.

For example, the possibility that advertising might be seen as a form of public communication is pertinent here. While this is a problematic notion (Fowles, 1996) it is also one that we could suggest is particularly relevant in promotional and media cultures (Kellner, 1995; Skovmand and Schroder, 1992; Wernick, 1991) in which the discourses of advertising (Cook, 1992) are central. Meijer takes this further, arguing that the performative aspect of advertising can be used to create positive notions of contemporary citizenship. By this she means that we should look at advertising as the act of telling stories that enable a certain interaction with and thus management of 'reality' (Meijer, 1998).

The sheer level of advertising and the immersion of young people within promotional culture means that a serious consideration of the role of advertising in public communication is an important aspect of political study. Advertising is ubiquitous, pervading a number of areas hitherto innocent of such discourses. In 1997 the Church of England attempted to woo the public back to church with a campaign based around the Virgin Mary experiencing the birth of Christ, and the subsequent visit of the Three Wise Men, as a 'bad hair day'. In more recent times the same organization has used an image of Christ based on the popular 1960s poster of Che Guevara, to widen appeal amongst the young. Advertising also demonstrates a pronounced ability to mix various language and sign codes with playful ease. Sometimes the traffic is two-way: political advertising borrows heavily from product advertising and product advertising borrows from the discourse of politics. The most striking examples in the 1997 British general election campaign were the Tango (soft drink) ads on television and the Tesco (supermarket) newspapers ads ('Demon Pies'), both of which traded on well-known political communications techniques.

Now, clearly, many will only see further evidence of dumbing down. But we should note two points. First, with the advent of media cultures and the framing of social life by the media, a serious discussion about the possibilities of advertising as public communication is needed. Second, the responses of young people to certain types of political advertising demonstrates both the potential and the importance of such a discussion and this idea is taken up later in the chapter.

Such ideas raise interesting variations on the nature of political communication, and its reception. For example, it is likely that the growing trend for popular and political culture to blend will continue and the way in which the main political parties attempt to capture the youth vote will depend increasingly on their ability to exploit such trends.

But, as van Zoonen (1998) notes, exploiting the interface between popular culture and political communication is a dangerous and difficult strategy for the parties whose attempts to attract the attention of the young do not always work. Attempts to do so are numerous, with politicians frequently making appearances on television programmes that are either directly for the young or have the type of audience and credibility that the politicians wish to exploit. So, in the UK, Neil Kinnock appeared on the television comedy *Drop the Dead Donkey* and Tony Blair has appeared almost everywhere. In the USA Bill Clinton and even George Bush appeared on MTV. Politicians also attempt to court the young through the medium of popular music, either directly by making recordings themselves – for example, David Steel's 1983 pop song 'I Feel Liberal Alright' – or more often indirectly through association, for example Harold Wilson's much publicized meeting with The Beatles in the 1960s. In the 1990s Tony Blair has attempted to exploit this technique as fully as possible, appearing at *Q* magazine events, being photographed at the 1996 Labour Conference with the head of Creation Records and offering encouragement for performers from the then current 'Brit-pop' success, such as Oasis. Attempts to appear cool even extend to the adoption of D.Ream's 'Things can Only Get Better' as an election anthem.

In these ways politicians demonstrate both their extraordinary desire for public exposure and their concern to capture the youth vote. But this is a potentially dangerous tactic amounting to what has been termed 'limousine democracy'. Politicians who use this strategy in an attempt to harvest the youth vote run the risk of appearing insincere and, even worse, patronizing. As we shall see, such tactics also encourage accusations of 'Americanization', which attracts much academic and non-academic criticism. Although political parties have identified the young as a group they wish to capture and have made special attempts to do so, their efforts seem to have been less successful than they would hope.

Not only have the parties failed to attract an influx of support among the young but they have been less than successful in affecting the number of young people who are not even registered to vote. Of the 40 per cent or 2.08 million who did not vote in the British general election of 1992, more than 1 million had disappeared from the electoral register altogether by 1997, leading Charter 88 to argue that apathy, disappointment and a hangover from the poll tax were to blame.

So critical had the situation become that a campaign directed specifically at getting young people between the ages of 18–24 on to the electoral role was launched in the UK. The 'Rock the Vote' campaign was launched in February 1996 at the Ministry of Sound club in London with a mixture of political support and support from different entertainment and business interests. Drawing heavily on a campaign of the same name in the USA, begun in 1990, the UK 'Rock the Vote' campaign has been a high-profile, media-based one. The campaign has utilized the full range of media channels – cinema, radio, television and publications – to promote its message and has organized a range of events to promote the campaign, including rock concerts, 'cyber elections', a 'Rock the Vote' nationwide tour and a range of poster launches and informational events. All of this has involved the active participation of a number of pop groups (including Radiohead, Suede and Supergrass), comedians (including Eddie Izzard, Ben Elton and Jo Brand) and other high-profile public figures (such as the athlete Linford Christie). As we shall see below some of the materials produced in this campaign elicit very strong responses from young people and the campaign has claimed that 400,000 people between the ages of 18–24 registered to vote as a direct result of exposure to the campaign.

So in the ways outlined above the political communication of a contemporary election campaign has become populated with both modern and postmodern figures, reliant on the modes and discourses of the culture industries and heavy with the discourse of advertising. It is appropriate to ask, how do young people experience all this?

Young people and the 1997 British general election campaign

The following discussion draws on conversations with groups of young people held in Oxford over four weeks beginning on 7 April 1997 and concluding on 29 April, two days before polling in the general election. The study focused on the way in which young people (in this case 18–26-year-olds) receive, understand and interpret political communications within the context of an election campaign. The study was a qualitative investigation that attempted to focus on the reception end of the processes of political communication, and in particular on political marketing. Rather than conduct a content analysis of the messages sent to the political audience, this study explored the complex processes of reception and meaning given to political messages by young people. The study wanted to examine if young people – who are fully immersed in media cultures and probably the most media literate members of our society – respond in ways that demonstrate some of the points discussed in the first section of this chapter, for example apathy, disengagement, cynicism and ignorance. Consequently the findings are organized under a set of antinomies which are engaged–disengaged, context sensitive–context free, image–content and negative–positive.

The study involved three discussion groups of different social categories of 'young people': an undergraduate group, a group of employed and non-employed graduates, and a group of employed and non-employed non-graduates. Each group contained both men and women and all the members were recruited from the general locality of Oxford. All participants were asked to complete a short questionnaire to provide biographical details and background information. This recorded age, sex, educational background and occupation. The questionnaire also asked them to record how often they read a newspaper, watched television in general and television news and current affairs programmes in particular. Responses to the questions regarding use of media differed little across the groups. Most did not read a newspaper on a daily basis, nor did they watch television news regularly, and their viewing of current affairs programmes was most often noted as 'hardly ever', a finding which has parallels with other studies (Barnhurst, 1998). These responses pose one key question for future study, and that is from where do young people get their political information?

The groups were shown a wide range of materials. In week one, before the official campaign had begun, the groups were shown non-political advertisements, to see what they thought of advertising as a genre, and campaign ads from previous UK general elections and US presidential elections. The groups were also shown more examples of political advertising in this week, including postcards from the Ministry of Sound (a British music co-operative) 'Use Your Vote' campaign and materials from the 'Zero Tolerance Campaign' sponsored by Oxford City Council's Safer Cities Project and designed to raise awareness about domestic violence against women in the city.

In the subsequent weeks materials from the 1997 British general election campaign were shown, including all the parliamentary election broadcasts of the three main political parties and some of the broadcasts by minor parties. On a particular point of note, in the final week of the campaign participants were shown the final broadcasts by the Labour Party (Monday, 28 April) and the Conservative Party (Tuesday, 29 April) as they were broadcast at 6.55 p.m. These broadcasts were shown directly to the groups as they went out to the rest of the nation and had not been seen by anyone involved in the study before their transmission. These broadcasts yielded some of the most interesting insights of the study. In addition to PEBs (party election broadcasts) the groups were shown a range of election literature, posters, handbills, manifestos, promotional material and newspaper advertisements.

The findings

Engaged–disengaged

A key concern of the crisis thesis is the extent to which citizens are disengaged from the political process, and this study found that levels of disengagement were high or apparently so. Almost without exception, participants expressed themselves less than caught up in the election campaign itself although almost all of them indicated that they did intend to vote. Among these there was no great enthusiasm for any of the political parties, but some mild excitement was felt by those who were voting for the first time. One non-graduate male said that 'I didn't vote last time (1992) but I will this time, I just don't know which way I'll vote yet'. Despite the prevalence of a low intensity of partisan identification, most group members who were inclined to vote for a particular party at the beginning of the campaign stuck to that intention. However, there was a tendency to echo the sentiments of a female, first-time voter that 'all the parties look pretty much like each other'.

In more general terms the members of the groups demonstrated low levels of engagement in politics, reporting that they rarely held conversations about politics, except 'now and again in pubs' (non-graduate male) or 'occasionally at home with friends' (female, graduate). Few people watched television news 'regularly', while for most, newspapers were seen as providers of entertainment rather than information in general. The political pages of newspapers were rarely perused (Barnhurst, 1998). Now clearly this sort of attitude towards politics could be seen to be direct evidence for the thesis that the young are disengaged from the political process. However, it emerged that what participants meant by 'politics' was mainstream party politics. Further discussion revealed that these young people did talk about a range of social issues, such as 'the environment', 'chemicals and their relation to illnesses like breast cancer', 'the treatment of animals' and 'the rights and wrongs of motorway building', and some confessed feeling quite strongly about these issues. These responses provide some evidence that there may well be a 'new politics' waiting to be tapped.

Interestingly, some individuals, especially among the graduate group, expressed a desire to be more engaged, as though this was experienced as some kind of moral imperative. Curiously, however, group members were less clear how this could be achieved because even in an information-rich election campaign, as a female graduate said, 'there's too much useless bumph and hot air going around at the moment'. Now of course it is difficult to know how serious such desires are, but these reflections do raise questions about the ways in which intelligent, articulate and ambitious young people sublimate apparently conflicting demands on their time, and on their emotional and intellectual energies. Furthermore, underlying this 'wanting to be more interested' motif is the sense that what group members really meant was that they are actually waiting to be stimulated, and, moreover, that they expect to be importuned by the sellers of political products. If this is the case (and, as I argue later, it is not as straightforward as this), it has some interesting and potentially radical implications for political allegiance and the marketing of political brands, because it suggests that the future basis of partisan choice may well be on grounds of consumer preference rather than on habits of the heart.

As a subtext to the previous comments, much was made across both the graduate and non-graduate groups of the extent to which they found the election campaign itself, and coverage of it, boring. Group participants seemed to mean a number of things by the term boring. First, that election campaigns were intrinsically yawn inducing. However, there was not a marked sense that they felt thus, and generally respondents meant that the sheer weight of media coverage was numbing. One graduate male said that 'the media is full of election politics. I skip all the stuff on this. There's a need to switch off from it all', while another, female non-graduate said 'there's just too much of it. I tend to stay away from newspapers at election times'. No group members suggested that there was too little in the way of election coverage in the media. A further sense of the term boring suggests that although the participants did not think of themselves as being members of a discrete category of 'young people', some of them found the campaign boring because it was 'for the older generation – they like it, but usually I can't relate to it' (male non-graduate). What this says about the youth-friendly campaigning indulged in by New Labour especially, is hard to say, and it would seem to modify the point raised earlier, to the effect that young people are empty vessels waiting to be filled by the right sort of campaign.

Context sensitive–context free

As we have seen, one of the concerns about the quality of political communication and, indeed, democracy itself is the extent to which processes of 'Americanization' can be said to have permeated, in this case, British politics (Brants, 1998). Interestingly, in all the groups there seemed to be a marked antipathy to what they saw as the Americanization of British politics and campaign style. A male graduate described American-style political advertising as 'too shallow, it really gets my goat', while many tended to dismiss those aspects of the party election broadcasts which they did not like as 'too American'. Their complaints in this regard seem to equate Americanization with both the emphasis on personality over policy and the triumph of image over content in political communications. Some people in each group also mentioned the ways in which American political ads (shown in the first session) compressed difficult issues to the point where they became meaningless. The 30-second spot typical of televised political commercials in US campaigns did not go down well with most of the people in these groups, although they were often taken with the verve and inventiveness of these offerings. To some extent this is a little surprising given the generally low esteem in which the British genre is held. 'Far too long', 'incredibly boring' and 'this is when I go out to make the coffee' are typical of the responses to the not so venerable institution of the PEB. Taking these apparently contradictory sentiments together, it is hard to see how political marketers can win. The antipathetic response to US advertisements per se and to the perceived Americanization of British campaigning may be less a matter of cultural resistance (after all a considerable range of other Amercian cultural products are consumed with alacrity), although there are some traces of this, and due more to the inability to relate to the context in which such messages are being trafficked. When the groups were shown some of the classic American ads of the last 30 years or so, including the little girl and the bomb spot from the Johnson–Goldwater contest and the bear in the woods clip from Reagan's campaign in 1984, they could not empathize at all, and were reduced (if that is the right word) to making aesthetic judgements, not least about the production values. Even the elegaic and formulaic pastiche of Bill Clinton's Arkansas–Kennedy boyhood left them cold, although the President and his alleged peccadillos were well known to them. On the other hand, Hugh Hudson's 'Kinnock – the movie', which was the centrepiece of Labour's 1987 PEB effort, evoked strong, even passionate responses: 'I personally detest Kinnock' and 'he is obviously a passionate man, I found it very moving'. And on a slightly different tack, most of the group members applauded the Liberal Democrats' use of Punch and Judy to caricature the adversarial style of Labour–Conservative rivalry, despite the fact that it was clearly a form of knocking copy. They were happy to endorse it because it was funny, and also because it was apposite, a fitting depiction of a political style with which they were familiar. It was also an effective use of characters straight out of childhood, woven into the fabric of national culture. The responses to the Conservatives' first PEB, which put a futuristic gloss on life under a Labour government, elicited a range of sentiments. The most pronounced, however, was that it was not particularly credible in face of 'the world as it is now and as it will probably continue' (undergraduate). It was also considered to be 'negative', a usage to which I return below, and to have been weakened by poor acting.

Image–content

It is in this area that the most ambivalence is observed. In general this ambivalence appears as a powerful, if perhaps residual, nostalgia for a style of politics and political campaigning (face-to-face encounters between voters and candidates, detailed debating of issues, other forms of dialogical communication) and the cool and detached style of the theatre critic (Adatto, 1988). In this respect there were quite marked differences between the groups. The student group were by far the most laid-back, deconstructing every offering from the parties and making judgements about the production values in and aesthetic qualities of the PEBs and poster advertisements, but seeing these aspects of the marketing mix as an integral part of the communication process. The graduate group couched their responses in like vein, but were more inclined to see a party's attempts to use the medium of television effectively as some sort of artifice. Even then there is a twist to the basic ambivalence. Artifice may be frowned upon, but where it is used (as in employing actors to play ordinary members of the public) it ought to be done well, that is professionally. On some occasions when a 'real' political actor appeared in a PEB (for example, Jimmy Goldsmith for the Referendum Party, the First Speaker for the Greens and the Party Leader of the Natural Law Party), the response throughout all the groups was almost vitriolic. Goldsmith, whose terminal illness was not public knowledge at this time, was described as 'manic', 'like a Vincent Price character', 'something from a Hammer Horror movie'. Irony of ironies, he was also accused of being unconvincing because he was too passionate. Geoffrey Clements for the Natural Law Party impressed as 'a staid-looking man in a suit, talking gibberish' (male, graduate), while the unfortunate First Speaker for the Greens suffered from looking 'too Green' (female non-graduate) and 'amateurish' (from several people), both of which detracted from her message.

Sincerity by itself, then, is no guarantee of a good reception; it must be presented properly. Goldsmith obviously broke some implicit code of what is acceptable and the force of his message was dissipated as a result. John Major on the other hand was unable to shake off the Spitting Image persona which had clung to him throughout his premiership. To all of the members of all the groups he was and remained uniformly 'grey'. Several people actually said that they realized that their perception of him was entirely mediated by his latex *alter ego*, and still they could not colour him anew. Here we seem to have some corroboration of the extent to which it is possible to enfold both positive and negative images of politicians in the collective consciousness (Axford *et al.*, 1992).

The Referendum Party broadcast by Jimmy Goldsmith moved some participants, notably in the non-graduate group, to opine that the approach adopted by the party was 'simply not good television'. This judgement turned not just on the apocalyptic style of Goldsmith's address, but on the device of using a 'talking head' to get the message across. Major's heartfelt, but more reasoned, discourse on Europe in the second Conservative PEB was seen by a majority of the participants as worthy, but soporific – 'you just had to drift off' (female graduate). And yet, time and again, members of the groups insisted that they wanted to know more about 'what the parties stand for', and to be told about these things in a direct and no-nonsense way. This appears to stop short of being told about party policy at length and through the medium of a semi-presentable and reasonably articulate politician. Major's performance was likened by one group member as being 'worse than watching paint dry'. Some measure of what might be an acceptable blend of straight talking and entertainment values was the first PEB run by the Liberal Democrats, which featured various and apparently 'real' people – in the NHS, in education and so on – asking questions of, and being given answers by, the Liberal Democrat leader, Paddy Ashdown. This was generally liked because it was lively, involved real people with real jobs and said things that ordinary people might reasonably be expected to ask about public policy and a party's intentions in that regard. Even then, participants were quite willing to draw attention to production faults, especially to continuity, to wonder how many of the 'real' people were party activists and to conjecture whether Ashdown had actually been present when the questions were being put.

The focus on party leaders occasioned some concern across the groups, being seen as further evidence of the Americanization of politics and a deliberate shift to a presidential style of campaigning. Most concern was expressed about the Labour Party in this respect, with one female graduate worrying that 'maybe it's alright during an election, but you can't govern the country like this'. Generally, criticism was reserved for the manner in which and the effectiveness with which leaders were handled, rather than with the principle of the thing. The attempts by the Liberal Democrats in their second PEB to gloss Paddy Ashdown as a man of action and a thoroughly nice guy provoked exactly the sort of responses that the party (and its predecessors) must have dreaded over the years, from the query 'OK, its nice, but would we want to be governed by these people' (male non-graduate) to the rather more elliptical, but still dismissive, 'it's like an advert for Pedigree Chum' (undergraduate). Molly Dineen's fly-on-the wall portrait of Tony Blair produced generally favourable reactions from the non-graduate group, but much more critical responses from both the graduate and the undergraduate groups. The ordinary blokishness of it encouraged some people to see Blair as more than 'slimy', 'superficial' and 'calculating', all epithets which had been used about him in various sessions, but not sufficiently to lose the 'plastic' label with which he had also been tagged. 'I thought he was going to burst into tears', said a member of the graduate group, and this was not an expression of approbation. 'It looked fake', said another member of the same group, adding, 'but then they're all fake'. However, most seemed to think that the personalization of the campaign was an inevitable part of modern electronic electioneering

But on general flakiness, the last Labour PEB scored highest of all. In their responses to it group members demonstrated not only that they are perfectly capable of mustering a 'knowing savviness' in the face of the delirium of communications, but that they also discern and understand the highly self-referential world of politics and political promotion. Capra's *It's a Wonderful Life* put to work in the service of New Labour cast actor Pete Postlethwaite as the angel and (as several people pointed out) a minor actor best known on television for appearing in insurance commercials as Jimmy Stewart in Brixton, or maybe Birkenhead. The responses to it can only be described as both gleeful and outraged. 'Can they seriously believe that this sort of thing will influence people?' (male, non-graduate). Well, no, said others in each of the groups, since it was 'a deliberate counter-weight to the first Tory PEB, which was also OTT' (female non-graduate). Deliberate parody (if such was intended) was seen as acceptable and not at all negative. This is a response of a highly sophisticated kind to a political communication working on many levels. These are responses in keeping with the idea of politics as a postmodern carnival – fake, but funny for all that. 'How would we have known it was not serious' asked a member of the graduate group? 'Put Mel Smith or Mr Bean in the driving seat of the taxi', replied a colleague.

Negative–positive

Negative copy came in for a great deal of criticism, but everyone who used the term employed it in a very specific way. 'Negative', as used by members of the groups, meant not stating your own position, not saying it like it is, or how you (as a party or candidate) would like it to be. More specifically it means failing to tell voters what your policies are. Being nasty to opponents, even being economical with the truth, was acceptable provided that you observed the injunction to put forward your case. Presumably this is why, when asked what the political parties should do at election times, a goodly number of group members said things like 'list policies' and 'spend more on literature and manifestos'. From a constituency which had already declared its reluctance to follow news and tune in to 'boring' PEBs, the prescription to spend more on documents which are bought by nobody except the political cognoscenti and their rivals, might seem ludicrous or hypocritical, but this kind of sentiment, along with the claim that a dialogical politics is more authentic than a mediated one, is repeated as a sort of mantra. Their experience and their general demeanour suggests that they are likely neither to be engaged by such a shift, nor are they significantly impoverished by its absence.

Interestingly, the political communications which engaged all of the groups most (but especially the graduates and undergraduates) were those from 'unconventional' sources. Of particular note were the 'zero tolerance' posters and the visually powerful ads from the Ministry of

Sound. After the groups had been shown these posters there was always a long and intense discussion about what they meant, who they were aimed at and how effective they were. Although some people in the non-graduate group were unsure about their provenance (i.e. whether they were in fact racist or sexist rather than opposing these things), for the most part the messages were clear and the Labour bias in the ads accepted. Expressions of approbation like 'clever', 'bold', 'aimed at youth' and 'striking use of images' were common. The much larger and more expensive poster campaign waged by the mainstream parties had little purchase on the imagination of participants. Blair's 'Demon Eyes' was generally felt to be funny, and legitimate knockabout, as was the picture of a puppet Tony Blair on Chancellor Kohl's knee. Clearly they are not just making aesthetic judgements here as there was a general sense that both these images had some purchase on a contested reality and were about proper issues – trust in politicians and Britain's place in Europe. Group members expressed themselves mostly unaware of the rest of the poster campaign, although one person in the non-graduate group said the A4 trunk road was 'an ocean of yellow [Liberal Democratic] posters'. The Green's steal from Friends of the Earth was well received, apart from the unfortunate First Speaker, but they had little to say about the censorship of the Pro-Life Alliance's broadcast.

Conclusion

Taken simply at face value the young people in our focus groups seem to value positive political marketing, with a high information content. This discourse is low on negativity and is not obsessed with image. Looked at more closely, their nostalgia for seemingly more authentic styles of political communication disguises a more complex pattern of reception in which aesthetic values vie with instrumental ones and both carry received moral overtones. While they are detached from the routines of politics and political communications, they are not unduly cynical. Rather they are savvy about the communications genres in which political discourse is now framed, and while they are not politically informed in the conventional sense, they are certainly not at sea in an ocean of Baudrillardian hypertechnology (Baudrillard, 1983). Their savvy responses to political marketing of a quite sophisticated kind may be facilitated by their general lack of commitment to any one political creed or vehicle. Certainly there is a sense that their relative detachment from mainstream politics, their ideological rootlessness, turns politics rather more into a facet of lifestyle, something to be taken up and, perhaps, put down at will. In a sense they constitute lifestyles in search of a politics. If this sounds as though it is morally weightless, it should be noted that it is nowhere fully realized – witness the ambivalence over aspects of political marketing and the nostalgia for a form of dialogical politics they are unlikely to have experienced. What is very noticeable is the extent to which their responses to political and media events are occasioned by the media's own construction and deconstruction of them. Although it was not covered, Princess Diana's death and funeral are prime examples of this where the wider public is concerned, which may suggest that the alleged gap between young people and the rest is less wide in this respect than some have cautioned. So are they victims of the three-minute culture of politics or postmodern characters still in search of a script? As we have seen, a number of commentators bemoan the negative impact of mediatized culture upon civic participation and social capital (Putnam, 1995). The sense is that the young people in these discussion groups are quite skilled in negotiating the postmodern terrain which is the electronic campaign. Their distance from mainstream politics does not leave them exhausted of normative values, but it does raise questions about whether their enthusiasms, however fleeting, can be accommodated by such modernist forms.

This chapter has argued that when considering the location of young people within the political system it may be useful to conceptualize this group as constituting a political audience rather than a more conventional notion of political constituency. Clearly such a reading will be problematic for many of the commentators referred to here and at best such a shift may be attended by ambiguous outcomes and uncertain potential. But whether we like it or not this may be a useful way of conceiving of young people and politics (and, indeed, in time all voters and citizens) and the demeanour of this group within a highly mediated public sphere and society.

References

Adatto, K. (1988) *Sound-Bite Democracy*. Joan Shorenstein-Barone Centre: Harvard University Press.

Amit-Talai, A. and Wulff, H. (1995) *Youth Cultures: A Cross-Cultural Perspective*. London: Routledge.

Axford, B., Madgwick, P. and Turner, J. (1992) 'Image management, stunts and dirty tricks – the marketing of political brands in television campaigns', *Media, Culture and Society*, 14 (4): 637–53.

Axford, B. and Huggins, R. (1996) 'Media without boundaries: fear and loathing on the road to Eurotrash or transformation in the European cultural economy?', *Innovation: the European Journal of Social Science*, 9 (2): 175–84.

Axford, B. and Huggins, R. (1997) 'Anti-politics or the triumph of postmodern populism in promotional cultures?', *Javnost*, 4 (3): 5–27.

Barber, B. (1997) 'The new telecommunications technology: endless frontier or the end of democracy?', *Constellations*, 4 (2): 208–28.

Barnett, S. (1998) 'New media, old problems: new technology and the political process', *European Journal of Communication*, 12 (2): 193–218.

Barnhurst, K. (1998) 'Politics in the fine meshes: young citizens, power and media', *Media, Culture and Society*, 20 (2): 201–18.

Baudrillard, J. (1983) *Simulations*. New York: Semiotext(e).

Bell, V. (1999) *Perfomativity and Belonging*. London: Sage.

Blumler, J. and Gurevitch, M. (1995) *The Crisis of Public Communication*. London: Routledge.

Boggs, C. and Dirman, T. (1999) 'The myth of electronic populism: talk radio and the decline of the public sphere', *Democracy and Nature*, 5 (1): 65–94.

Brake, M. (1980) *The Sociology of Youth Culture and of Youth Subcultures: Sex and Drugs and Rock 'n' Roll*. London: Routledge and Kegan Paul.

Brants, K. (1998) 'Who's afraid of infotainment?', *European Journal of Communication*, 13 (3): 315–35.

ESRC (1992) *British Election Survey*. ESRC Archive, University of Essex.

Bryner, J., Ferri, E. and Shepherd, P. (1997) *Twenty-Something in the 1990s*. Aldershot: Ashgate.

Castells, E. (1996) *The Rise of the Network Society*. Oxford: Blackwell.

Chaney, D. (1993) *Fictions of Collective Life: Public Drama in Late Modern Culture*. London: Routledge.

Cohen, S. (1972) *Moral Panics and Folk Devils*. London: MacGibbon and Kee.

Coleman, S., Taylor, J. and van de Donk, W. (1999) *Parliament in the Age of the Internet*. Oxford: Oxford University Press.

Cook, G. (1992) *The Discourse of Advertising*. London: Routledge.

Cubitt, S. (1999) 'Virilo and new media', *Theory, Culture and Society*, 16 (5–6): 127–42.

Dauncey, H. and Hare, G. (1999) 'French youth talk radio: the free market and free speech', *Media, Culture and Society*, 21 (1): 93–108.

Davis, R. and Owen, D. (1998) *New Media and American Politics*. Oxford: Oxford University Press.

Driscole, M. and Kelly, F. (1996) 'Party People', *Sunday Times*, 18th February (News Review Section) p. 3.

Esser, F. (1999) 'Tabloidization of news', *European Journal of Communication*, 14 (3): 291–324.

Featherstone, M. (1991) *Consumer Culture and Postmodernism*. London: Sage.

Fiske, John (1995) *Media Matters: Everyday Culture and Political Change*. Minneapolis: University of Minnesota Press.

Fowles, J. (1996) *Advertising and Popular Culture*. Thousand Oaks, CA: Sage.

Franklin, B. (1994) *Packaging Politics Political Communications in Britain's Media Democracy*. London: Edward Arnold.

Hart, R. (1994) *Seducing America: How Television Charms the Modern Voter*. New York: Oxford University Press.

Hebdige, D. (1988) *Hiding in the Light: On Images and Things*. London: Routledge.

Holmes, D. (ed.) (1997) *Virtual Politics: Identity and Community in Cyberspace*. London: Sage.

Ignatieff, M. (1998) *The Warrior's Honor : Ethnic War and the Modern*. London: Chatto & Windus.

Johnston, R. and Pattie, C. (1997) 'Fluctuating party identification in Great Britain: patterns revealed by four years of longitudinal study', *Politics*, 17 (2): 67–77.

Katz, E. (1996) 'And deliver us from segmentation', *Annals of the American Academy of Political and Social Science*, 546 (July): 22–33.

Kellner, D. (1995) *Media Cultures: Cultural Studies, Identity and Politics between the Modern and the Postmodern*. London: Routledge.

Livingstone, S. (1998a) 'Mediate childhoods: a comparative approach to young people's changing media environment in Europe', *European Journal of Communication*, 13 (4): 435–56.

Livingstone, S. (1998b) 'Audience research at the crossroads: the implied audience and cultural theory', *European Journal of Cultural Studies*, 1 (2): 193–217.

McKay, G. (1998) *DIY Culture: Party and Protest in Nineties Britain*. London: Verso.

Marliere, P. (1998) 'The rules of the journalistic field: Pierre Bourdieu's contribution to the sociology of the media', *European Journal of Communication*, 13 (2): 219–34.

Meijer, I. (1998) 'Advertising citizenship: an essay on the performative power of consumer culture', *Media, Culture and Society*, 20 (2): 235–49.

Melucci, A. (1996) *Challenging Codes: Collective Action in the Information Age*. Cambridge: Cambridge University Press.

National Association of Secretaries of State (1999) *New Millennium Project – Phase I, A Nationwide Study of 15–24 Year Old Youth*. Washington: The Tarrance Group/Lake, Snell, Perry and Associates, Inc.

Norris, P. (1997) *Electoral Change Since 1945*. Oxford: Blackwell.

Norris, P., Curtice, J., Sanders, D., Scammell, M. and Semetko, H. (1999) *On Message: Communicating the Campaign*. London: Sage.

Ouellette, L. (1999) 'TV viewing as good citizenship? Political rationality, enlightened democracy and PBS', *Cultural Studies*, 13 (1): 62–90.

Parry, G., Moyser, G. and Day, N. (1992) *Political Participation and Democracy in Britain*. Cambridge: Cambridge University Press.

Putnam, R. (1995) 'Tuning in, tuning out: the strange disappearance of social capital in America', *Political Science*, December, 28 (4): 664–83.

Redhead, S. (ed.) (1997) *The Clubcultures Reader: Readings in Popular Cultural Studies*. Oxford: Blackwell.

Sancho-Aldridge, J. (1997) *Election 97: Viewers' Responses to the Television Coverage*. ITC Research Publication, London: ITC.

Silverstone, R. (1990) 'Television and everyday life: towards an anthropology of the television audience', in Ferguson, M. (ed.), *Public Communication: The New Imperatives*. London: Sage.

Skelton, T. and Valentine, G. (1998) *Cool Places: Geographies of Youth Cultures*. London: Routledge.

Skovmand, Michael and Schroder, Kim Christian (1992) *Media Cultures: Reappraising Transnational Media*. London: Routledge.

Stevenson, N. (1995) *Understanding Media Cultures: Social Theory and Mass Communication*. London: Sage.

van Zoonen, L. (1998) 'A day at the zoo: political communication, pigs and popular culture', *Media, Culture and Society*, 20 (2): 179–81.

Wernick, Andrew (1991) *Promotional Culture*. London: Sage.

Wihelm, A. (1998) 'Virtual sounding boards: how deliberative is on-line political discussion?', *Information, Communication and Society*, 1 (3): 313–38.

Wilkinson, H. and Mulgan, G. (1995) *Freedom's Children*. London: Demos.

7 The Transformation of Governance?

Ken Newton

Mankind in general judge more by their eyes than their hands; for all can see the appearance, but few can touch the reality. Everyone sees what you seem to be, but few discover what you are. (Machiavelli, *The Prince*)

Have the mass media transformed modern government? Many claim they have. They argue that the mass media are no longer the humble carriers of news, but have become enormously influential players in the political game with independent powers of their own. They can destroy or prolong political careers; they can bring down governments or protect them from criticism. They shape public opinion, set the political agenda and determine the content of public policy. They have changed the role and nature of institutions of government, and they have even undermined democracy itself. According to this view the modern media are no longer the 'fourth estate' that informs the public and acts as 'watch-dog of the constitution'. They have become a kind of fifth column with great but hidden political power and little accountability.

Others are alarmed not by the mass media but by the powers they give to governments and political elites. According to this view, politicians can use the technical capacities of the mass media for their own purposes. Advised by teams of public relations consultants, spin doctors, media managers, opinion pollsters, publicity directors and information officers, politicians use all the tricks of mass communications technology to influence political events and public opinion in a hidden and possibly undemocratic manner. The result, it is said, is that modern politicians can control the very language of political discussion, control the flow of news and information and manipulate political opinion.

It is often difficult to know what to make of these claims. Many of them are plausible, but also contradictory. For example, some claim that the media hold politicians more accountable for their deeds and words, while others argue that politicians are now well equipped by the new media to manipulate and deceive the voters. Some claim that the mass media undermine government leaders and shorten their political lives by subjecting them to continuous criticism, but others hold that politicians can use all the tricks of media management to help them stay in power.

One theory argues that televising parliaments makes them better able to perform their democratic role; another that it has undermined the democratic functions of parliaments. Some believe that the mass media give all shades of opinion a voice in affairs, others are no less certain that the mass media encourage hyper-democracy and government overload.

This chapter will examine a set of conflicting claims about the media's capacity to transform modern government. It will deliberately consider a wide assortment of theories, starting with the most specific and working up to the most general. The first section will briefly review the ways in which central government in the UK has reorganized its communications operations in response to the challenges and opportunities of the new media. The second section will deal with individual level effects on government leaders – have they been able to exploit the propaganda potential of the mass media to project the desired image, or are they, on the contrary, the victims of the pitiless glare of media attention and criticism? The third will consider the impact of televising parliament – mass media effects on a central institution of government. The fourth will concentrate on policies and policy content – how successful are the public relations campaigns of governments? The fifth will consider media effects on the nature and processes of government – transparency, secrecy and the nature of leadership. And the last will deal with the democratic system as a whole – the role of the media in producing hyper-pluralism and government overload. The chapter will concentrate on the UK, but will take sidelong glances at other countries every now and again to get a comparative perspective.

The internal organization of the government communications machinery

Ramsay MacDonald created the job of Press Secretary to the Prime Minister in 1931, and from the very start it had a centralizing effect on government. Its first incumbent claimed he was not just spokesman for the Prime Minister, but was 'required to act for the government as a whole in all matters of a general character'. The press and information offices of central government – the prime minister and all the Whitehall departments – became larger and more elaborate over the next fifty years, particularly during the war (Ogilvy-Webb, 1965), but it was in the 1980s, under Thatcher and her Press Secretary, Bernard Ingham, that the system became much more centralized, expensive and powerful than before. Ingham defined his job as the conductor of the government's communications orchestra, and to do this he created a centralized organization that covered the whole of Downing Street, Whitehall and Westminster.

Ingham used the weekly Meeting of Information Officers (MIO) as the centre of his efforts. Before Ingham took control, the 22 most senior information and press officers in central government attended the MIO but it was not an important body. The press secretaries of Heath and Wilson did not even bother to attend. Ingham turned it into a clearing-house controlling and co-ordinating all information flowing from government to the outside world. He required advance information about all press releases, announcements and media engagements for clearance at the MIO. He insisted that all MIO members owed loyalty and allegiance to him (and hence to the Prime Minister), not to their own departments or ministers, and he took control of the recruiting and training of the government's elite corps of press officers so that they developed the proper loyalty. Under Ingham's iron rule the MIO became the shadow cabinet for government press officers (Cockerell *et al.*, 1984; Franklin, 1994: 82–95).

Whitehall press departments were directly linked by computer network to the No. 10 Press Office so that it was able to consolidate its control of information. In its turn, the Downing Street Office was hooked up to journalists, news desks and news agencies by means of the Electronic News Delivery Service (ENDS), so that press releases, neatly pre-packaged and ready for use, could be distributed easily and efficiently to all those interested. ENDS issues about 7000 government press releases a year and many other forms of news and information in the form of leaflets, booklets, special articles, advance notices of meetings and speeches, publications lists and information sheets.

In 1989 Thatcher made Bernard Ingham the head of the Government Information Service (GIS), which had an annual budget of close to £200 million and a total staff of 1200 press officers, journalists, radio producers, film-makers and editors. At this point Ingham was head of the now highly centralized communications organization of central government. In effect, he became the country's Minister of Information. One journalist referred to him as 'the real Deputy Prime Minister' (Franklin, 1994: 85).

The top priority attached by government to public relations and media management expressed itself clearly in hard financial terms. In 1948–9, central government's main department concerned with the co-ordination and procurement of publicity services, the Central Office of Information (COI), spent £4.1 million. Fifteen years later in 1963–4 this had doubled to £8.3 million (Ogilvy-Webb, 1965: 207). Fifteen years after that in 1980 the total was only a little short of £50 million. Between 1980 and 1987, however, the figure jumped to £150 million.

However, the COI did not handle all central government publicity expenditure and the grand total for all departments and ministries came to nearly £200 million in 1988–9 (National Audit Office, 1989: 5). In constant prices the COI's publicity expenditure rose from £60 million in 1982–3 to £80 million in 1985–6 and £151 million in 1988–9 (Cobb, 1989; National Audit Office, 1989: 5). The real advertising value of this was substantially higher, because with so much money to spend the COI was able to negotiate substantial discounts.

In 1988 the government was the nation's third largest advertiser. By 1989–90 it was the largest and spending was rising fast (Scammell, 1991). In 1987–8 the COI paid for over 30,000 TV advertising spots, over 9000 newspaper advertisements and 100 publicity campaigns. It also produced 1800 publications, more than 140 films, videos and commercials, and participated in 140 exhibitions (Franklin, 1994: 100).

Under Major the Thatcher/Ingham publicity machine declined, but it was reinstated under Blair by Peter Mandelson and Alastair Campbell (Blair's Press Officer) in an even more powerful and centralized form than before. A daily 9 a.m. meeting attended by all important communications staff and chaired by Mandelson ensured that all core executive officers and departments were 'on message' and that all major ministerial press releases, speeches, interviews and public appearances were cleared through the No. 10 Press Office. In this way the timing and content of media activity is strategically planned and organized. A 24-hour media monitoring service enables the government to respond to the news almost instantaneously. Interviews and media appearances by any given minister are planned, and may be delayed or cancelled if they interfere with the overall strategy or the plans for media-management that day.

Moreover, public relations are no longer something to be wheeled in after politicians have settled public policy. On the contrary, the need to communicate and 'sell' government policy is now an integral part of the whole policy-making process, and public relations and media people are brought in at the very earliest design stages of the process (Mountfield Report, 1977). According to some, this amounts to 'government by propaganda' (Franklin, 1997: 8).

The first conclusion to draw, therefore, is that post-war history, particularly under Thatcher and Blair, shows that the new media have had a direct impact on the organization of central government's public relations machinery. It is now larger, more centralized, more efficient, more responsive, more thoroughly planned, more carefully thought out and enormously more expensive than ever before. In this sense the new media have undoubtedly transformed central government's public relations operations and, thereby, the organization and process of central government itself. The point, however, is not just to show how central government has responded internally to new circumstances, but what difference the new media make, if any, to what government does in the wider world. This is the subject of the rest of the chapter.

Mass media effects on government leaders

Shortening political careers – the pitiless glare of publicity

According to some observers, the modern mass media have shortened the lives of governments and their leaders by turning on them the constant glare of critical publicity and by exposing their human frailty to the world at large (see, for example, Ranney, 1983: 147–50). We see close-ups of Nixon sweating in the debates with Kennedy, Ford hitting his head as he leaves a helicopter, Bush fainting at a banquet in Japan, Thatcher losing her poise in a TV discussion about the battleship *Belgrano*, Carter collapsing in a fun run and Clinton being devious about his relationship with Monica Lewinsky (see Meyrowitz, 1995: 133). The mass media demystify not only by presenting 'Shelley plain', but also by over-exposing him as well. Nothing the contemporary politician ever does or says escapes public attention, and since the camera does not lie, least of all the TV camera with its reputation for presenting people as they really are, politicians cannot hide their real selves any longer. On television, Nixon looked shifty, Alec Douglas-Home seemed incompetent, Wilson appeared to be sly, Heath was stiff and ill at ease, Thatcher was hectoring and Major lived up to his *Spitting Image* greyness. Modern politicians can no longer withstand the enormous pressures of critical media attention for long; like football managers, they are often fired after a short period without success.

What is the evidence for the theory that the modern media cut short political careers? It is certainly true that the success of some politicians has been limited because of unfriendly media or because they have not been able to exploit the media to project the right image. This is true of Douglas-Home, Heath, Foot and Kinnock in the UK, and of Dukakis, Ferraro, Mondale, Ford and eventually Bush in the USA.

At the same time it is no less true that some leading European politicians in the last two decades have had unusually long political

careers – particularly Thatcher, Kohl and Mitterand. John Major sur-
vived a long time by post-war standards, much of it in the face of strong
media criticism. In Spain the Socialist party of Gonzales lasted from
1982 to 1996, and in Australia Fraser, Hawke and Keating dominated
the office of Prime Minister from 1975 to 1996. In the USA both Reagan
and Clinton have been re-elected for a second term. In Canada Trudeau
served for 13 years as Prime Minister, and Mulroney for nine. In case
this is thought to be anecdotal evidence, Budge and Keman (1990: 162)
find little variation in government duration in twenty Western states
between 1950 and 1983.

Lengthening political careers – the power of image making

Some writers claim that the mass media do not shorten political careers,
but on the contrary provide leaders with the capacity to manage the
media, manipulate public opinion, project the desired image and thereby
prolong their period in office. Perhaps Thatcher is the prime example of
a modern politician who was able to survive for a long time because she
was able to exploit the media's potential to create an image for herself
and support for her policies. It is worth considering her case more
closely.

In her early years as a minister and then as prime minister she was not
a naturally gifted public speaker or performer, and no match for her
opponents, Foot and Kinnock. Her manner was school-marmish, her
intonation odd, her style hard and her personality often unsympathetic.
She was unpromising material for a great, beloved and long-lasting
leader of her country. But this takes no account of the power of public
relations. To compensate, her public performances were prepared down
to the last detail and tirelessly rehearsed. She was trained to change her
voice, her accent and her speaking style. She was coached to speak at the
right pace, with the right gestures and timing. Her body language was
videoed, studied and changed. Her clothing, hair, make-up and appearance were planned, her speeches crafted by a team of professional
writers and advisers. She was set up to deliver soundbites in the right
place at the right time. Her public relations team, lavishly funded and
highly trained, used the latest methods to create the desired image. She
was photographed as a caring human being cuddling a newborn calf,
walking a King Charles spaniel on the beach and eating fish and chips.
As a tough world leader and defender of her nation she was pictured in
a tank turret, steely gaze focused on the enemies of the nation.

Her appearances at public occasions followed the manner of her carefully stage-managed 'royal visits' to the last day of the Conservative Party conferences – designed to present her in the best possible light to adoring audiences. Whenever she was on-stage she was in the limelight, and whenever she was off-stage a large team of public relations specialists worked to get her the best possible publicity and discredit her enemies. Thatcher had one unfortunate encounter in the 1983 campaign when she was questioned in a polite and persistent way about the sinking of the battleship *Belgrano*. She lost her cool and her image was scratched. After that she never again faced the public in an election campaign when the media were watching, appearing only in set piece occasions with an audience handpicked to treat her with admiration and reverence. Conditions for her media interviews were negotiated in advance, including the physical setting, the lighting, the matters to be discussed and the timing of the broadcast. She usually appeared alone, and had the last word.

Thatcher had the huge advantage of a national press that was not merely Conservative but ardently Thatcherite. She was served by Bernard Ingham, one of the most astute and supremely effective press officers of his time. The system of lobby correspondents worked to the inestimable advantage of the government. Never before in the UK, and quite possibly not in any other democratic country, have circumstances so strongly favoured the public relations efforts of a government leader; rarely can any politician in a democracy – or Hollywood film star or commercial product, for that matter – have had so many people spend so much time, effort and money on nurturing their public image.

Table 1 compares Thatcher's popularity ratings with British prime ministers since 1945. The figures show that she was the most unpopular with the exception only of Heath, before her, and of Major after. Even in her most popular period (1979–83) her ratings were below most postwar prime ministers in Britain. The figures in Table 1 measure her *political* ratings as leader of the government. Other figures about her *personal* ratings as an individual also show that the electorate in general did not see her as her public relations team wished. Between 1986 and 1988, for example, the Gallup poll shows that most members of the public saw her as tough (68–75 per cent), determined (66–75 per cent), sticking to principles (60–64 per cent), shrewd (45–52 per cent), and decisive (42–54 per cent), but they also saw her as uncaring (88–94 per cent), personally dislikeable (90–95 per cent), and unlikely to listen to reason (90–94 per cent). Over the same period, Neil Kinnock's ratings were almost the opposite – more caring, likeable and reasonable but lacking in determination, shrewdness, toughness and principles (Gallup poll, 8–12 October 1988).

TABLE 7.1   *Satisfaction with Thatcher as a Prime Minister*

Dates	Prime Minister	Average satisfaction score (%)	Low	High
1945–51	Attlee	47	37	66
1951–55	Churchill	52	48	56
1955–57	Eden	55	41	70
1957–63	Macmillan	51	30	79
1963–64	Douglas-Home	45	41	48
1964–66	Wilson	59	48	66
1966–70	Wilson	41	27	69
1970–74	Heath	37	31	45
1974–76	Wilson	46	40	43
1976–79	Callaghan	46	33	59
1979–83	Thatcher	40	25	52
1983–87	Thatcher	39	28	53
1987–90	Thatcher	38	23	52
1990–92	Major	51	46	59
1992–97	Major	24	16	36
1997–98	Blair	72	62	83

Note: The question asked was 'Are you satisfied or dissatisfied with . . . as Prime Minister?'
Sources: Gallup, *Political and Economic Index*, Report No. 418, July 1995: 10 (1945–1997), and Gallup monthly reports thereafter.

A Gallup poll in August 1987 also shows that the largest opinion group saw Thatcher as out of touch with the working class and ordinary people (70 per cent), talking a lot but not doing much (44 per cent), dividing the country (68 per cent), having destructive rather than constructive ideas (41 per cent), thinking a lot of herself (78 per cent), knowing little about the cost of living (57 per cent), a snob who talks down to people (56 per cent) and as not coming over well (43 per cent). In the same year 60 per cent said they disliked her personality and 63 per cent that they disliked her policies. By comparison 37 per cent said they disliked Kinnock's personality and 53 per cent disliked his policies (Gallup poll, 11–16 February 1987: 8). In 1987, 53 per cent of the public said they did not favour the Britain Thatcher was trying to create, and 49 per cent were unfavourable towards the 'Thatcher revolution' (Gallup poll, November and December 1987). In 1989 the largest single group of respondents said that they did not like her but did respect her (38 per cent), whereas 25 per cent liked and respected her and 29 per cent neither liked nor respected her (Gallup poll, December 1989).

The point of these opinion poll figures is to show that, in spite of their best efforts and well before she lost power, Thatcher's image-makers did not meet with great success. Their power to manipulate public opinion and thereby to transform government was strictly limited.

Media impact on institutions: televising parliament

The decision to televise the German parliament was made partly on the grounds that it would help to legitimize it (Schatz, 1992: 234). Euro MPs made the same calculation about televising their parliament (O'Donnell, 1992: 254). In the UK, proceedings of the House of Lords were first televised as an experiment in 1983, but the practice was soon made permanent. The Commons followed suit in 1988, one of the last parliaments in the democratic world to do so. The change was vehemently supported and opposed in both the Lords and Commons for a long list of reasons.

Those against argued that it would show parliament in its worst light; would give a misleading impression of the real work and business of the two chambers; that members would 'grandstand' to attract attention; that it would discourage much needed reforms of procedures; that it would undermine the influence of the government by giving equal attention to the opposition; that it would undermine the influence of backbenchers by limelighting frontbenchers; that it would inevitably require editing and therefore censorship; that it would change the intimate, debating-chamber nature of the Commons; that speeches would be made to please and amuse voters; that debates would become party set-pieces; and that it would degrade the whole nature and purpose of parliament. In short, televising parliament would irreversibly change the nature and content of British government and politics, and undoubtedly for the worse.

Those favouring the reform argued the opposite case with the same fervour: that it was a natural extension of basic democratic rights and principles; that it would improve the quality of debate; that it would inform and educate the public; that it would promote procedural reforms; that it would encourage rational debate and discussion; that MPs would behave better in front of the cameras; that more members would attend debate; that it would help improve the image and reputation of parliament and its members; that it would educate the general public in the importance of debate between political enemies; and that it would help politicians present themselves as they are, rather than through the eyes of hostile or biased journalists. In short, televising parliament would irreversibly change the nature and content of British government and politics, and undoubtedly for the better.

In the event, televising parliament seems to have had rather little impact. A survey of the Lords (Watts, 1997: 155–6) strongly supports Lord Gilmour who said 'I don't think that television has had any effect on this place whatsoever'. The impact on the Commons may have been greater (Hetherington, 1985), at least as far as the internal workings of the House are concerned. MPs may try to give longer speeches and try harder to get in on Question Time. Frontbenchers may now be more visible to the general public, and backbenchers and third parties less so. But there is little evidence or argument to suggest much impact on the way the general public perceives politics, or in the way that governments behave. On the contrary, William Hague's reputation as a good performer during parliamentary Question Time has done little to salvage his reputation as a politician on the national stage. Summing up the overall impact of televising parliament, Watts (1997: 173) comments that it is difficult to see what all the fuss was all about.

The new media system and government policy

Government public relations campaigns in the 1980s and the early 1990s were conducted in a political environment that was strongly favourable to their success. Quite apart from the lobby system and an overwhelmingly supportive national press, some people even felt that the independence of the BBC and ITV had been weakened by government attacks on them. The Labour opposition was weak, ineffective and divided for long periods in the 1980s. There was a general, low-key and ill-defined feeling in the country that something radical had to be done to prevent economic decline and social problems. The government could justify its policies by pointing to three successive mandates won in general elections. In its enthusiasm for publicity and information, it sometimes seemed to cross the thin line dividing legitimate public information from party political propaganda, and to have used large amounts of public money to promote its own private ends. Seldom can any Western democratic government have had such a favourable setting in which to practice the gentle arts of public persuasion.

In trying to evaluate government success in this respect it is necessary to exercise great caution, for it is exceedingly difficult and perhaps impossible to measure the effects of public relations campaigns. Carefully planned and expensive publicity could be matched by disappointing public opinion figures, but approval might have been even lower without efforts to improve them. Conversely, publicity campaigns might be accompanied by correspondingly high opinion poll ratings, although there might be no connection between them, only coincidence. Nevertheless it is worth comparing the campaigns and their results to see if there is even a rough equivalence between effort and outcomes.

Privatization

Privatization in the form of the sale of public sector assets and companies was a key part of Conservative government policy in the 1980s and 1990s. Both the Thatcher and Major governments put a huge amount of time, effort and money into campaigns to persuade the public to buy shares, and to convince people that the policies were good ones in the first place.

Table 2 shows the advertising costs and the public approval/ disapproval ratings for each sell-off. Public approval varies from one case to another, but nonetheless there is a tendency for approval ratings for any given privatization to decline over time, and for the rating of each successive measure to be lower than the previous one. But the most important point to emerge from Table 2 is that not one single privatization secured majority approval. In fact, at no point between 1983 and 1994 was the *highest* support for any given measure greater than its *lowest* unpopularity score. Although more than £240 million was spent on advertising, and probably much more, privatization started off as an unpopular policy and became progressively more unpopular over time. The most expensive advertising campaign, for water and electricity, is associated with the lowest approval ratings.

TABLE 7.2   *Advertising costs and public approval of privatization*

	Costs	Public approval		Public disapproval		Dates
		High	Low	High	Low	
British Telecom	£25m	42	26	59	43	10/83–12/94
British Aerospace	£2.3m					
Britoil	£3.5m					
Trustee Savings Bank	£10m					
British Gas	£40m	36	24	59	41	5/85–12/94
British Airways	£11m					
Rolls Royce	£4m					
British Airports Authority	£5.7m					
British Petroleum	£23m					
Water	£40m	22	10	83	62	8/88–12/94
Electricity	£76m	38	17	73	47	3/88–12/94
Coal Board	?	36	31	56	51	8/88–3/91
Steel	?	43	35	50	45	8/88–7/98
British Rail	?	40	11	75	49	8/88–5/94
Post Office	?	15	11	77	74	5/94–10/94

Sources: Expenditure figures from Franklin, 1994: 103; opinion poll figures from *Gallup Political and Economic Index*.

The poll tax

The poll tax has often been described as the flagship of the Thatcher government, and it certainly went to considerable trouble and expense to persuade the British public that it was a good thing. In 1986, even before legislation was passed, the government printed and distributed 70,000 copies of a leaflet, *Paying for Local Government: Proposals for Change*. Immediately after the 1987 election, 53,000 copies of a 12-page leaflet were distributed comparing the failings and injustices of the old rates with the merits of the poll tax. In early 1989 an expensively printed and illustrated 20-page leaflet, *You and the Community Charge Your Step by Step Guide* replaced this. Some felt strongly that this publication transgressed the thin line between public information and party political propaganda. Meanwhile specialist leaflets were aimed at students and businesses, and others dealt with particular aspects of the poll tax such as tax rebates and appeals.

In the spring of 1989 a large-scale publicity campaign was started involving the distribution of 23 million leaflets, *The Community Charge (the So-Called 'Poll Tax': How it Will Work for You)*, costing £1.8 million. Simultaneously, 'ready for use' press releases were faxed to local news desks across the country. This was followed by an Ogilvy and Mather advertising campaign, 'How to Pay Less', costing £3.1 million and covering television, local and national press and magazines. In 1990 every business – one and a half million of them – was sent literature about the Uniform Business Rate. Throughout the whole period the government issued a long string of press releases designed to shape public opinion in its favour and counter-act adverse publicity (Golding and Deacon, 1994: 48–70).

Thatcher staked her own reputation on the new tax, and obliged her ministers to do likewise, saying often that if it were properly presented, the general public would soon realize its merits. Local government ministers went to the regions on public relations tours. The national and local press, and local radio, were targeted with press releases, videos and tape recordings. Indeed, the full weight of Mrs Thatcher's authority and government, the concerted efforts of the government's public relations machinery and the considerable resources of the public purse were brought to bear to persuade the citizens of the UK that the poll tax was what the country needed.

According to the MORI poll the number who approved of the poll tax stayed constant at around 25 per cent between 1987 and 1990, but the number opposing it rose from 45 per cent to 76 per cent. At the peak of the campaign, when the legislation was passed, 71 per cent of the population thought the poll tax was 'a bad idea'; in 1990 54 per cent described themselves as 'very strongly opposed to the poll tax', and another 22 per cent said they were 'fairly strongly opposed'. Six per cent were 'very strongly' and 16 per cent 'fairly strongly in favour'. The government worked especially hard to get the public to accept its positive sounding name for the tax – the 'Community Charge' – but failed. It was popularly known as the 'poll tax' – something both anachronistic and politically unacceptable. The implementation of the tax provoked widespread social unrest, protest and even violence. Once enacted, the public blamed central government for high poll tax levels, whereas it had insisted all along that these were the entire responsibility of local authorities. When the tax was eventually abolished, two thirds thought it had been a bad idea and that it was right to get rid of it. Seven per cent thought it a good idea worth keeping (Butler, Adonis and Travers, 1994: 260).

Privatization, the poll tax and Thatcher's personal image are not special or unusual examples of unsuccessful government public relations campaigns in the 1980s and early 1990s. They are part of a wider picture showing that the electorate remained fairly impervious to the appeals of the Thatcherite project as a whole. At the end of the era the electorate was no more enthusiastic than at the beginning about family and Victorian values, conservative morality, the relative merit of low inflation over high unemployment, cutting taxation and services, rolling back the frontiers of the state, the individual blame attached to those in poverty, the importance of self-reliance, or the pride the nation could take in itself. Reviewing the polling evidence up to 1988, Crewe (1989: 44) concludes that 'The electorate, in other words, is hardly suffused with Thatcherite values on either the economic or the moral plane. Not surprisingly, therefore, it has consistently opposed a raft of specifically Thatcherite policies and decisions . . . Conservative success remains a puzzle. Voters oppose the Government on the vast array of its specific policy initiatives.' (For an American example suggesting the same general conclusion about government public relations, see Brown and Vincent, 1995.)

It is true that the popularity of the policy initiatives might have been even lower without government campaigns, but they are unlikely to have been much lower given the minimum or 'core' support for almost any policy promoted by the government. However, support could have been substantially higher than it was. In short, the evidence for successful government public relations is not impressive. This is not government transformed by the new media, but politics pretty much as usual.

Constraining policy options

The mass media can broaden political horizons by drawing examples of political debates, policies, practices and outcomes from all over the world. They could turn us all into amateur comparativists, drawing on their huge knowledge of world trends and practices, to help their audiences understand the wide range of policy options employed in other countries. In fact, the mass media are more usually parochial, concentrating on local or national issues, and presenting them within the framework set up by government and opposition politicians.

Policies that might attract widespread but diffuse support are likely to be rejected if small and intense minorities can gain publicity. Policies that might in previous eras have been allowed to grow and develop slowly over a period of time may now be dropped quickly because of initial opposition. The speed with which the Blair government moved against genetically modified food in response to strong media pressure – perhaps reporting public opinion, perhaps not – is a good example of a policy born in the morning, criticized at noon and killed off by the evening. Other policy options may be ruled out even before the start of the policy-making day because the media flags strong popular opposition in advance. Both tax increases and war may be in this category, although judging by the Gulf War and NATO bombing of the former Yugoslavia, it is not aerial war but war on the ground with troop casualties that is now generally out of the question.

These last speculations suggest that the new media may have effects on public policy, in that they speed up the policy making process, either by revealing strong public preferences on a matter, or by creating these preferences in the first place. At the same time the evidence lends little support to the idea that governments can manipulate public opinion. On the contrary, neither the media nor the government seems able to shift public opinion once it is decided.

Transforming the political process – open government versus secrecy and blandness?

One of the effects of modern political reporting, especially television, is said to be the opening up of debate to the public and pressuring politicians to forsake their smoke-filled rooms for the public arenas of the television studios and press briefings (Ornstein, 1983). In this way politicians may be held by the media to be more accountable and accessible to the general public. In the same way, the constant glare of publicity combined with a permanent record of who said what and when means that politicians can no longer say different things to different audiences, or deny the words that are recorded for posterity. The prime example is George Bush's statement, 'Read my lips: no more taxes' – words that were brought back many times by the media to haunt him. So, do the modern media open government to public inspection and help to keep politicians honest?

The answer seems to be 'generally not'. Governments and politicians seem to have responded to the new accountability and openness with even more bland and harmless statements. Political speeches are increasingly saturated by warm words and weasel words. Much is left to inference and implication, and so far as possible policy positions are not stated clearly. In other words, the mass media now make it more difficult for governments to be fork-tongued or two-faced, but this simply encourages them to be vague, cautious and non-committal. Deterred from dishonesty they resort to blandness. The potential impact of the media, therefore, has tended to be neutralized by politicians acting in the time-honoured fashion of politicians the world over. However, this seems to have a further set of effects on the style if not the content of modern government.

Media politics are populist politics (Franklin, 1994: 5). The thrust of political marketing is to find out what the average or median voter wants and to use the mass media to sell it back to as many as possible (Maarek, 1995). This encourages governments to follow short-term strategies, and discourages them from speaking painful or complex truths (Entman, 1989: 126). The result is a form of bland populism in which government and politics drift towards safe ideological ground, but looks and appearance count for more than ideology and policy. Austin Ranney (1983: 103) calls this 'nice guy' politics. Packaging, presentation, dress, manner and style are more important than beliefs and principles. Policy statements are of the motherhood and apple-pie kind. Politicians tend to play the 'percentage game', committing them to as little as possible and waiting for the opposition to make mistakes. Negative campaigning is preferred. As a rule it is easier to make political enemies than friends among the voters, and therefore the less said about many issues the better. Interviews with politicians become increasingly meaningless as they stall, avoid answering questions, throw the question back or make prepared statements in answer to whatever question is asked. Valence politics and valence elections (where parties tend towards the same policies and are distinguished mainly by style, image and competence) become more frequent. Examples of the modern media populism include Blair, Clinton and Schroeder. They look the part and are steeped in the media-management and image-making skills, while holding the centre ground, displaying a polished blandness and a strong propensity for ideological caution.

If the modern media push conventional politics towards bland populism, they also thrive on drama, personality and outrage – whatever sells papers and gets people to turn on the television news. Therefore, the mass media help to create bland populism, and then for the sake of audience and circulation figures, help to create extreme populism as well. The more mainstream political life is dominated by the safe and the conventional, the more the media will search out – create if necessary – the politically outrageous, the dangerous and the unusual. Le Pen, Berlusconi and Perot have all capitalized on their flamboyance and outspokenness, using the media's insatiable appetite for the unconventional and unusual to gain publicity. They are the analogues of the Benetton advertising campaign, which deliberately created controversy by bucking advertising fashion for glossy niceness.

Because they need corruption, scandal, incompetence, sex and drama the media try to expose public figures if there is a good story to be had. This is likely to be difficult in the case of the bland populists, whose image is wholesome and clean, and there is generally more potential in the rogues and outsiders of politics, the extreme populists, who are more likely to have skeletons in their cupboards. Journalists will do their best to expose these to a scandalized and fascinated public. The extreme populists are, therefore, likely to rise and fall fairly quickly, to reach heights of notoriety rather than power and to make more of a mark on the news than on government. Nevertheless, unconventional populism is unlikely to be wholly ineffectual for it may help to shift the agenda and introduce new ideas that will be taken up in a more acceptable form by conventional politicians. In politics the moderates invariably disown the extremists, but keep a close watch on them to see what they can steal.

Finally, the more polished, bland and populist government leaders become, the more political space opens up for 'real-people politicians' who are not clean cut, photogenic and smooth. Their appeal lies precisely in the fact that they are human beings, warts and all. They are likely to play supporting rather than prime ministerial or presidential roles on the political stage. In the UK, John Prescott, Anne Widdicombe, Ken Livingstone, Kenneth Clarke, Frank Dobson, Tony Banks and Mo Mowlem are examples. All are accomplished at playing the media game, but none have quite the right combination of appearance and style to rise to the very top of the political ladder in the world of image-driven media politics.

The mass media, democracy and ungovernability

According to Ranney (1983: 154) 'the glare of television's attention has helped significantly to weaken the ability of presidents and congressmen to govern'. This is because vested and special interests in society can use the media to gain publicity for their own demands, so escalating pressures from all sides on government. News and current affairs programmes are saturated with special interests, pressure groups, spokesmen and advocates of every conceivable kind, all trying to gain publicity, make their case, win public support and influence government policy. The public arena is packed with competing and conflicting interests, all pleading their own special case and all making their demands on government. The media are pleased to give them a political voice – they fill media time and space with new ideas, new voices and new ideas – and therefore help escalate the number and diversity of political demands on government. In short the mass media help to create ungovernability, overload and hyper-democracy.

It is difficult to know how to evaluate or test this claim. On the one hand, the crisis of ungovernability and overload, though predicted twenty years ago, has not yet overwhelmed any Western democracy to the point of collapse (Kaase and Newton, 1995). All governments have problems, some have many problems, a few have severe problems, but none has run into system-threatening crisis like the Soviet Union, or been forced to peaceful transformation like South Africa. It may be that the modern media have helped to make government more difficult, but it is a simple empirical fact that they have not made any Western state ungovernable or overloaded to the point of collapse.

Media research shows why this is the case. The popular press in the UK often excludes, ignores, or undermines and devalues some political voices (see, for example, Curran, 1986; Hollingsworth, 1986; Snoddy, 1992). In the 1970s and especially the 1980s the mass circulation tabloids, and even some of the broadsheets, focused on a narrow conservative political agenda in support of the government (Newton, 1995: 168). Minority and unconventional views were often ignored or ridiculed – loony-lefties, peaceniks, gays and lesbians, pacifists, anti-road demonstrators, rent-a-crowd troublemakers, ethnic minorities, or sometimes well-intentioned but misguided people. Even the TV news, required to be fair and balanced, has been criticized for its caution and conservatism (Glasgow University Media Group, 1976; see also Harrison, 1985).

Research also suggests that news reports often give most space to government statements or spokesmen, even to the extent of relying heavily on government press releases. For simplicity's sake much political discussion is reduced to only two sides, usually the government and the opposition. The rest of the political spectrum is largely overlooked and ignored in mainstream reporting. As Gurevitch and Blumler (1990: 282) put it: 'Instead of promoting a "market place of ideas", in which all points of view are given adequate play, media neutrality can tend to privilege dominant, mainstream positions.'

Summary and conclusions

It is clear that new media systems have had an enormous impact on the structure of central government in the UK. First, since the war, and especially under Thatcher and Blair, the government's media and information organizations have been totally reorganized to create a single, expensive, centralized, rapid-response operation. Second, public relations considerations are no longer brought in at the end of the policy-making process but at its very beginning. Third, the need to manage the news and to exploit its publicity potential has added to the forces encouraging the centralization of government under the prime minister and the No. 10 Press Office.

The highest priority attached by the Thatcher and Blair governments to media management has led some people to fear government by manipulation, image-making and spin doctoring – the '1984' propaganda scenario. It is too early to draw conclusions about the Blair government, but analysis of the Thatcher decade throws up rather little evidence to support this view. In spite of highly favourable circumstances and enormous quantities of skill, time and cash, government success in creating a favourable image for Thatcher was modest. Success in selling government policies was scarcely more impressive. It is true that public opinion might have been even more opposed without the campaigns, but it is unlikely to have been much lower than it actually was, given the minimum or 'core' support for the policies, with or without government propaganda. There was plenty of room for support to have been much higher than it was. This is not government transformed by the new media, but politics pretty much as usual.

Similarly and probably for the same reasons, the mass media have neither prolonged nor shortened political careers. Some politicians have been able to exploit the possibilities of the media, and in doing so may well have lengthened their political careers and improved their success. Others have not been able to do this. The difference between success and failure in this respect seems to be due to the gifts of the politicians, their public relations advisors and the political circumstances they operate in, not to the nature of the modern media themselves.

The evidence suggests that neither the mass media nor politicians and all their media experts can hope to make much of a dent in public opinion once it has made its mind up about a matter. For this reason, televising parliament had little effect on public opinion about the institution and rather little internal impact on the two Houses. Public opinion was never so interested in parliament that a little bit of television was going to make any difference. Nor do the mass media appear to have encouraged trends towards hyper-democracy, ungovern-ability or government overload. On the contrary the media seem to favour the political centre and its leaders, and to treat most unorthodox or radical opinion as a sideshow not to be taken seriously. If anything, the mass media in the UK have acted as a force against hyper-democracy and overload.

This diverse list of minimal media effects suggests caution in dealing with what are often sweeping generalizations about how the media have transformed modern government. Some of these generalizations are a form of crisis-mongering, some are long-term predictions based on short-term trends and in many cases there is an equally plausible but contradictory generalization to be made.

Yet the new media system *has* had an impact on government, though probably on form and appearance more than content. The enormous potential of the new media, combined with the drive towards political marketing has caused the emergence of a form of bland populism, as personified by Clinton, Blair and Schroeder. With the right looks and image, they represent the emerging attempt to market safe politics to median voters – photogenic, 'nice-guy' politics with a strong emphasis on packaging, appearance, caution and centre-ground policies. Such clean-cut valence politics, however, is likely to breed its own reaction, not least because the media have an insatiable appetite for scandal and drama. The more bland populists come to dominate the highest levels of government, the more extreme populists – flamboyant radicals, national-ists, racists, and advocates of strong minority opinion (such as Berlus-coni, Le Pen and Perot) – will rise and fall. The bland and extreme populists will feed off each other; the extremists introducing new issues and solutions, the bland following at a safe distance with their own watered-down versions of the policies, as the median voter demands.

As the quotation from Machiavelli at the start of this chapter suggests, looks and appearance have always been important in politics and modern bland populism simply gives a new media twist to the old theme. The question is whether the new mass media will ever help to create government and politics in which appearances are invariably more important than reality, and form becomes content.

References

Brown, W.J. and Vincent, R.C. (1995) 'Trading arms for hostages? How the government and the print media "spin" portrayals of the United States policy towards Iran', *Political Communication*, 12 (1): 65–79.

Budge, I. and Keman, H. (1990) *Parties and Democracy: Coalition Formation and Government Functioning in Twenty States*. Oxford: Oxford University Press.

Butler, D., Adonis, A. and Travers, T. (1994) *Failure in British Government: The Politics of the Poll Tax*. Oxford: Oxford University Press.

Cobb, R. (1989) 'Behind big brother', *PR Week*, 13 February: 14–15.

Cockerell, M., Hennessy, P. and Walker, D. (1984) *Sources Close to the Prime Minister: Inside the Hidden World of the News Manipulators*. Basingstoke, Hants.: Macmillan.

Crewe, I. (1989) 'Has the electorate become Thatcherite?', in R. Skidelsky (ed.), *Thatcherism*. Oxford: Blackwell.

Curran, J., Ecclestone, J., Oakley, G. and Richardson, A. (eds) (1986) *Bending Reality: The State of the Media*. London: Pluto Press.

Entman, R.M. (1989) *Democracy Without Citizens: Media and the Decay of American Politics*. New York: Oxford University Press.

Glasgow University Media Group (1976) *Bad News*. London: Routledge.

Golding, Peter and Deacon, David (1994) *Taxation and Representation: The Media, Political Communication and the Poll Tax*. London: John Libbey.

Gurevitch, M. and Blumler, J.G. (1990) 'Political communication systems and democratic values', in J. Lichentberg (ed.), *Democracy and the Mass Media*. Cambridge: Cambridge University Press.

Franklin, B. (1994) *Packaging Politics: Political Communications in Britain's Media Democracy*. London: Edward Arnold.

Franklin, B. (1997) *Newszak and News Media*. London: Arnold.

Harrison, M. (1985) *TV News: Whose Bias?* Hermitage, Berks.: Policy Journals.

Hetherington, A. (1985) *News, Newspapers and Television*. London: Macmillan.

Hollingsworth, M. (1986) *The Press and Political Dissent*. London: Pluto Press.

Kaase, M. and Newton, K. (1995) *Beliefs in Government*. Oxford: Oxford University Press.

Maarek, P.J. (1995) *Political Marketing and Communication*. London: John Libby.

Meyrowitz, J. (1995) 'How television changes the political drama', in P.C. Wasburn (ed.), *Research in Political Sociology Volume 7: Mass Media and Politics*. Greenwich, CT: Jai Press.

Mountfield Report (1977) *Report on the Working Group of the Government Information Service*. Cabinet Office, London: HMSO.

National Audit Office (1989) *Publicity Services for Government Departments*. London: HMSO.

Newton, K. (1995) 'The mass media: fourth estate or fifth column?', in R. Ryper and L. Robins (eds), *Governing the UK in the 1990s*. Basingstoke: Macmillan. pp. 155–75.

O'Donnell, T. (1992) 'Europe on the move: the travelling Parliament', in B. Franklin (ed.), *Televising Democracies*. London: Routledge. pp. 254–69.

Ogilvy-Webb, Marjorie (1965) *The Government Explains: A Study of the Information Services*. London: Allen and Unwin.

Ornstein, N. (1983) 'The open Congress meets the President', in A. King (ed.), *Both Ends of the Avenue*. Washington, DC: American Enterprise Institute.

Ranney, A. (1983) *Channel of Power: The Impact of Television on American Politics*. New York: Basic Books.

Scammell, M. (1991) 'Political advertising and the broadcasting revolution', *Political Quarterly*, 61 (2): 200–15.

Schatz, H. (1992) 'Televising the Bundestag', in B. Franklin (ed.), *Televising Democracies*. Routledge: London.

Snoddy, R. (1992) *The Good, The Bad and the Unacceptable*. London: Faber and Faber.

Watts, D. (1997) *Political Communications Today*. Manchester: Manchester University Press.

8 The Transformation of Political Leadership?

Jennifer Stromer-Galley and Kathleen Hall Jamieson

The power of the presidents of the USA is largely rhetorical. They can recommend legislation and sign or veto it but not pass it; they can call for a declaration of war but cannot enact it. Lyndon Johnson put it more bluntly. ' "Power?" he asked. "The only power I've got is nuclear . . . and I can't use that" ' (Sidey, 1978: 260). Johnson, a master of the art of interpersonal persuasion, would have agreed, however, with Harry Truman, who observed: 'the principal power that the President has is to bring people in and try to persuade them to do what they ought to do without persuasion. That's what the powers of the President amount to' (Truman, 1949: 247).

In this chapter we explore the ways in which leadership is influenced by and influences the media environment. Specifically we will argue that the power of a president who can communicate directly to the American people is enhanced. As direct channels of communication between leaders and citizens are opened by C-SPAN, satellite transmission and the Internet, and as public respect for news as a mediator drops, the president's power to set the agenda is magnified. When media norms emphasize the simple over the complex, conflict over consensus and scandal over substance, they make it less likely that a leader will engage in the sorts of discourse conducive to good government. However, public disdain for the press minimizes the ability it once had to set agendas and establish the standards by which we assess those in power.

The power of unmediated access

Even in a highly mediated environment, presidents can use television to speak directly to the American people. 'Television does, however, provide the leader with one advantage that can be crucial,' writes Nixon, 'particularly in a crisis situation. It enables him to go directly to the people . . . to make his case to them without the intervention of reporters and commentators. He can do it only occasionally' (Nixon, 1982: 343).

Direct address

The balanced budget debate of 1995–6 illustrates the power the president can exert when he gains direct access to the nation's airwaves and cable channels. At the end of 1995 and again at the start of 1996, the US federal government ground to a halt as the Republican majority in the Senate and House of Representatives struggled with the Clinton administration over the terms of a balanced budget agreement. In the middle of the year, Clinton left the balanced budget rhetoric to the Republicans. Behind the scenes, he was uncertain how to respond to their plan (Morris, 1997). Should he wait until after both chambers had passed a balanced budget? Should he veto any balanced budget initiative they passed? With encouragement from Dick Morris, advisor from Clinton's days as Governor of Arkansas, he decided to offer a balanced budget proposal of his own. In a rare move, Vice-President Gore lobbied the national television networks for airtime for the President to deliver a five-minute address in which he proposed a new balanced budget plan. With a hint of reluctance, the networks granted the request.

Clinton's decision and Gore's move to gain network airtime made Clinton's balanced budget proposal a media event that would serve to shape the legislative agenda. Clinton's public address served as a starting point for the balanced budget debate that would culminate in a national crisis by the end of the year. Even at this early stage of the process, all the parties were using the news media to advance their own interests. Clinton, however, gained the upper-hand by making his balanced budget proposal a media event. The newspapers made his proposal front-page news and the broadcast news covered Clinton's televised appearance.

The address Clinton gave positioned him above the conflict. He acknowledged that the Democrats and Republicans had fundamentally different ideas about how to balance the budget. 'But this debate must go beyond partisanship. It must be about what's good for America, and which approach is more likely to bring prosperity and security to our people over the long run', Clinton explained, placing himself above the partisan bickering. He spoke to both Democrats and Republicans from above, more like a father figure rather than another participant in the debate. Clinton put himself above the petty, obstructionist bickering when he stated:

There are those who have suggested that it might actually benefit one side or the other politically if we had gridlock and ended this fiscal year without a budget. But that would be bad for our country, and we have to do everything we can to avoid it. If we'll just do what's best for our children, our future and our nation, and forget about who gets the political advantage, we won't go wrong.

When the networks agree to carry a president's statement live, they cede control to the president. Occasionally the sense that they have been conned is palpable, as it was when a 1983 news conference by Ronald Reagan on the drop in unemployment was interrupted by Nancy Reagan, complete with cake, who had arrived on the scene to celebrate her husband's birthday coincidentally before a live national television audience. The drama of the cake, the cake-cutting and the seemingly surprised chief executive displaced the questions of reporters about the claimed drop in joblessness and held the cameras and the live national coverage. 'We were used,' griped a network reporter (*Washington Post*, 1983: 1).

The power of nationally televised speeches as well as the ability to shape the media agenda led Clinton to observe that:

> even a President without a majority mandate coming in, if the President has a disciplined, aggressive agenda that is clearly in the interest of the majority of the American people – I think you can create new political capital all the time, because you have access to the people through the communications network. (Blumenthal, 1994: 33)

An examination of the major addresses to the nation from Harry Truman through Ronald Reagan justified Clinton's conclusion. On average, such a speech added six points to the president's approval rating (Brace and Hinckley, 1992: 53).

Expanded opportunities for direct address

Satellite

Satellite technology has increased the ability of a leader to speak directly to the public. Access to satellites makes it possible for a leader to bypass the national media. So, for example, in 1992 and 1996 both Democrats and Republicans made their presidential and vice presidential candidates available for satellite interviews with local newscasters. In the primaries of 1992, a study by the Freedom Forum Media Studies Center found that one in ten local news stations were accepting video news releases

from candidates and the number of stations doing direct satellite interviews with candidates had doubled over 1988.

The Internet

The Internet allows politicians to circumvent journalists by creating a
direct line of communication to their constituents that is unfiltered and
unrestricted by the norms and structural constraints of traditional print
and broadcast journalism. Although in the 24-hour news climate events
are more heavily defined by journalists in their never-exhausted quest to
get the story, on the Internet politicians can communicate with citizens
outside of the journalism environment. Politicians now have at their
disposal Web sites, e-mail and on-line forums to generate a direct line of
communication to citizens.

As a result, the Internet is a direct channel of contact between leaders
and the led. The number of users is small but growing. In 1996 about 12
per cent of the voting age citizenry or 21 million Americans reported
that they had gathered political information from the Internet; for 3 per
cent, the Internet was the main conduit of political material (Pew Study,
1996). 'The new venues,' wrote *Washington Post* reporter Howard
Kurtz, 'will give ordinary folks the ability to search voting records,
election returns, exit polls, speech and position papers, enabling them to
cut through the political fog by downloading the facts for themselves'
(Kurtz, 1995: B1). A citizen can express her views in the form of e-mail,
in discussion groups, in chat rooms or electronic bulletin boards.

All the US senators and most of the representatives have official Web
sites. However, few have fully engaged this new technology to communicate with their constituents. For example, Arlen Specter (R.PA), a
veteran member of the Senate, did not update his Web site in a three-
month period. In September 1998, when the President admitted he had
an affair with Monica Lewinsky, only a handful of senators mentioned
their views on the President's admission on their Web sites. Most federal
politicians' sites ignored the impeachment controversy. By contrast, the
House Judiciary Committee's Web site was updated almost daily during
the impeachment debate in the House and the trial in the Senate. A
citizen interested in staying abreast of the latest manoeuverings in the
impeachment saga could turn to it to verify information in the press or
to secure information not there.

A second potential outcome of the Internet is transformation of time
and space constraints. In traditional form, broadcast and print journalism are restricted to short, linear communication moments. Because of

the time constraints, detailed analysis of legislation and of the institutional or social effects of political decisions is unlikely in broadcast news.

Although they have much greater flexibility in printing stories that can delve deeper into a political story, newspapers still have space limits. By contrast, the Web is a non-linear medium. Through hyperlinking, a story can tie to additional sources for readers to peruse at their convenience. The advent of hyperlinking further shifts control to citizens who can choose what to explore and what to ignore. An on-line report about health care legislation can lead to the representatives' Web sites who sponsored the bill, to the Library of Congress's THOMAS, a searchable Web site that houses current and past legislation, to another Web site that details the history of health care reform in the USA, which then links to a Web site in Canada that compares the US system to the Canadian system.

The wealth of data stored on the Internet coupled with access to Congressional deliberation through C-SPAN make it possible for average citizens to have as much access to information as political elites. The impeachment proceedings are a case in point. Any viewer in the USA with access to cable could watch the impeachment deliberations of the House Judiciary Committee, as well as the full debate on the floor of the House.

The distribution of the Starr Report is indicative of the changes produced by Internet access. The report was released on the Internet at approximately the same time as it was made available to the Senate, the House and journalists. People flooded the Internet to read and download the report for themselves. 'The downloads were slow, the error messages were many, but in the first experiment in electronic communication between the United States Government and its citizens on a massive scale, millions of persevering Internet users were devouring the Starr report yesterday within hours of its release', noted a report in the *New York Times* (Harmon, 1998). The newspaper characterized the release of the Starr report and the subsequent influx of messages on electronic message boards as an 'unprecedented kind of electronic town hall meeting'.

In response to the Starr Report, citizens contacted their senators and representatives at unprecedented levels. Although legislators received much of their correspondence via telephone and postal mail, electronic mail was also a major conduit for citizens' opinions. Senator Mike DeWine's (R.Ohio) press secretary reported that the senator had received approximately 6700 e-mail messages over a four day period after the release of the report. The volume of e-mail traffic was so heavy that the managers of the Senate Internet server sent a message to each office stating: 'We are currently experiencing Internet e-mail delays due to extremely high volumes of mail' (Wertheimer and Abramson, 1998). The release of the Starr Report reveals that people are interested in having direct access to documents important to civic life. Armed with that information, they acted by contacting their elected representatives.

The interactivity of the Internet also transforms the relationship between the leader and the led. Hyperlinking offers a control over the mediated experience that surpasses 500 channels of cable or 30 pages of news print. In this environment, citizens have control over the information to which they are exposed (Landow, 1993; Lanham, 1992). This environment is information rich, dense and growing. Citizens can educate and set agendas themselves rather than having journalists set agendas and filter information for them.

The Internet also facilitates human communication by e-mail and in real-time chat and Web boards. People can discuss laterally with each other and vertically with political leaders. Some are doing just that. Gurak (1997) conducted a rhetorical study of two protest movements, one against the Clinton administration's Clipper Chip and the other against Lotus's Marketplace. Using e-mail, privacy activists were able to stop Lotus from gathering private information about users for market research through Marketplace, and stopped the Clinton administration from advocating the Clipper Chip, a content-blocking device. Activists communicated with each other and organized the protest solely over e-mail and on-line chat forums. They also used e-mail to write letters and petition corporate executives and White House officials.

The Internet has also helped people communicate their opinion about the political situation to Washington. The recent creation of Move On, a Web-based organization focused on pressuring the House and Senate to not impeach Clinton or remove him from office, exemplifies uses of the Internet for political mobilization. Although public opinion polls typically communicate citizens' views back to politicians, sometimes polls published in major newspapers and magazines are not enough. Throughout the Clinton/Lewinsky scandal, for example, polls indicated that popular support was with the president. When Drudge ran his report on the Internet and the mainstream media reported on the new investigation, the president's popularity in the polls dropped. However, by 30 January, a CBS News poll indicated that the President's job approval rating was at 73 per cent (Berke, 1998: A1) and by summer 1999, had not dropped below 60 per cent since – even after he was impeached by the House. Nonetheless, legislators have ignored public opinion and continued the process of impeachment.

Joan Blades and Wes Boyd, owners of Berkeley Systems, a computer company, created Move On to stop legislators from continuing forward with impeachment. At its inception, the Web site logged 300 petitioners the first day and 25,000 by the end of the first week (Moffett, 1999). Boyd stated that if the Web-based initiative were successful 'it's going to mean representives [*sic*] are going to have to be more responsive to their constituents' (Kennedy, 1998: 44). After the elections in November, they began fund-raising to give challengers money for their campaigns in 2000 against legislators who voted for impeachment. By January 1999 they had raised $12.8 million.

Direct democracy

At the same time as the Internet is increasing the citizen's access to the dialogue of democracy in the USA, the climate of governance itself is being altered by moves toward direct legislation. Citizens are demanding and winning more opportunities for direct democracy, transforming the roles of leadership and altering the political landscape. Although the US government was established as a republic, an indirect form of democracy, direct democracy has been debated since colonial times (Cronin, 1989). On one side, direct democracy, through ballot initiatives or referenda, has been praised for permitting citizens to participate more actively in the democratic process. On the other, it has been seen as the harbinger of hyper-democracy to be used by wealthy, self-interested groups who can inflame voters into decisions they would, on reflection, regret (Cronin, 1989). This new form of governance has led some to speculate that 'democracy by initiative' could be the 'new form of twenty-first-century governance', or the fourth branch of government (California Commission on Campaign Finance, 1992).

Referendum voting has its roots in the western half of the USA. A century ago, South Dakota voters were the first to cast their ballot to restructure their government (O'Toole, 1998). Today, 24 states' voters use ballot initiatives to pass legislation. California has led the march to direct democracy. In the past decade, the citizens of California 'have used this power to write, circulate, debate and directly adopt many of the state's important laws'. In 1978, California voters passed Proposition 13, the 'tax revolt' initiative, which cut local property taxes reducing local government revenues. This proposition thrust ballot initiatives into the national political spotlight (Bowler and Donovan, 1998).

Since then voters in California have addressed issues from insurance regulation to campaign financing. The number of initiatives has 'jumped fivefold' in California since the 1960s (Democracy by Initiative, 1992: 1) with 72 of 224 balloted initiatives approved in an 80-year period

(Democracy by Initiative, 1992: 55). Tolbert (1998) argues that citizen's distrust of government, which has steadily increased since the 1950s, leads citizens to enact political reforms such as increased ballot initiatives that change the process of governance. A national poll conducted in 1994 indicated that 64 per cent of those asked favoured conducting national referenda and giving equal weight between referenda and legislation passed by Congress (Americans Talk Issues, 1994).

The move towards direct democracy parallels that at the turn of the twentieth century. Tolbert (1998: 171) explains that: 'each era is marked by a rise in the use of direct democracy, the adoption of a significant number of reforms, preference for procedural over substantive policies, and the pervasive distrust of representative government's institutions'. Missing from her comparison is the rise of new mediated-communication technologies at the turn of the century and today. A century ago, newspapers disseminated information across the nation and the world faster than before. This communication technology led one scholar to sing its praise: 'the new communication has spread like morning light over the world, awakening, enlightening, enlarging, and filling with expectation' (Cooley, 1909: 89). By contrast, Walter Lippman condemned the expanded role of newspapers. He explained that:

> The press . . . has come to be regarded as an organ of direct democracy, charged on a much wider scale, and from day to day, with the function often attributed to the initiative, referendum, and recall. The Court of Public Opinion, open day and night, is to lay down the law for everything all the time. (1922: 363)

He concluded that 'it is not workable' (*ibid.*). Newspapers, he argued, were unable to fully characterize the event they covered, which lead to distortion, misrepresentation and falsehoods. The faulty decisions made on deficient information had legislative consequences. For Lippman, not direct democracy but experts working to gather facts could make good legislative decisions.

The move toward referenda and direct democracy forecasts increased citizen involvement in the legislative process. Citizens have the opportunity to sidestep the mediation of news through direct access to legislative documents on the Internet.

Mediated access

The relationship between citizens and a president in the USA has been mediated since the inception of the republic. Newspapers gave way to radio and then to television as the channel through which the public came to understand its elected leaders. In recent times, the influence of television news is demonstrable. For example, experiments show that 'Issues and events highlighted by television news become especially influential as criteria for evaluating public officials' (Iyengar, 1992). Scholars label this process *priming*. At the same time, the public's sense of which issues matter is shaped in part by the prominence given these issues in the news (Iyengar, Peters and Kinder, 1982; Portess and McCombs, 1991). This function is known as *agenda setting*.

Leaders have always been conscious of the constraints placed on them by a mediated communication environment. Thompson (1995: 135) explains that political figures from the beginning of political time have had to 'construct their self-images and to control their self-presentation'. Some in power have even contended that the importance of television as a mediator has transformed the kind of person able to be elected to public office. After leaving the White House, for example, Lyndon Johnson noted of the media:

> All of politics has changed because of you. You've broken all the machines and ties between us in Congress and the big city machines. You've given us a new kind of people. . . . They're your creations. Your puppets. No machine could ever create a Teddy Kennedy. Only you guys. [Kennedy's] all yours. Your product. (Halberstam, 1979: 6)

That view was shared by Richard Nixon who noted that 'Television today has transformed the ways in which national leadership is exercised and has substantially changed the kind of person who can hope to be elected to a position of leadership . . . The premium today is on snappy one-liners' (Nixon, 1982: 342).

Presidents recognize the power of media. As Richard Nixon observed: 'The media are far more powerful than the president in creating public awareness and shaping public opinion, for the simple reason that the media always have the last word' (Nixon, 1978: 355). '[P]residents make no rhetorical decision (perhaps not even very many policy decisions) without gauging likely media responses to that decision', notes Hart (1987: 129).

The relationship between a president and the press can be described as a contest over control: reporters complain that the president is trying to manipulate them; presidents respond that press coverage ignores the substance of the president's agenda and actions. So, for example, Gerald Ford grumbled that 'Every time I stumbled or bumped my head or fell in the snow, reporters zeroed in on that to the exclusion of almost everything else' (Ford, 1979: 343). In 1979 Jimmy Carter wished that 'you all as people who relay Washington events to the world (would) . . .

take a look at the substantive questions I have to face as a president and quit dealing almost exclusively with personalities'.

Good policy-making; bad media

Media norms are often antithetical to traditional notions of good leadership. To elicit media coverage, politicians simplify their messages, cast their positions in stark contrast to others and reduce multi-sided issues to two-sided ones. So, for example, as the military build-up to the Gulf War was escalating, President George Bush told a reporter, 'I've got it boiled down very clearly to good and evil' (Walsh, 1990: 1).

While a simplifying, dramatic, categorical rhetoric is more news-worthy than a more complex nuanced one, this is not a form of rhetoric conducive to the reasoned discussion of alternative points of view. Those politically involved elites in search of a complex discourse will, as a result, find many of the stories in news disappointing. Yet, as Murray Edelman notes, those who pay little attention to politics 'want symbols and not information, dramatic in outline, devoid of detail and of the realistic recognition of uncertainties and of opposing considerations' (1974: 157). News caters to such consumers.

The balanced budget debate illustrated the extent to which confrontation attracts more media attention than compromise. In the USA the mediated environment restricts the ability for leaders to compromise. Leaders who change a position in response to new evidence or a changed situation are likely to be labelled inconsistent at best, hypocritical at worst.

The price of compromise is evident in headlines in the debate over the balanced budget: 'Budget battle has come down to a game of chicken' (Toner, 1995); 'GOP freshmen find a mission in budget battle' (Gugliotta, 1995). One metaphor was the staring contest: who was going to 'blink' first (Devroy and Pianin, November 1995a; Dewar, 1995; Toner, 1995) and who was 'staring' whom 'down' (Gugliotta, 1995). Others described the debate in terms of who was the most 'macho' (Dewar, 1996). Much attention was paid to who was 'battling' whom (Edsall, 1995; Gray, 1995) with the new Republican representatives characterized as being like the Confederate soldiers during the Civil War (Gugliotta, 1995).

The coverage of the balanced budget impasse focused on the crisis itself rather than on the Democratic and Republican solutions. Reporters emphasized the who rather than the what or the why of the debate. The coverage focused on spectacle rather than substance. As Edelman (1988) argues, politics is a constructed spectacle. The media draw attention to the drama and the actors involved in the play rather than to the complex social environment and institutional structures that move the world in mysterious and mostly uncontrollable ways. Throughout the budget crisis, the leaders used the media, and were in turn used by the media, to play up certain elements of the 'crisis' and play down others. The news focused on the dramatic, conflict-driven, emotional event. The details of the process, the successful negotiations, the resolutions were played down.

Scandal displaces substance

Although politicians mould their materials to the media, and the media often cover them, reporters have discretion in what they choose to play up or down (Semetko *et al.*, 1991). Their choices are dictated by a set of identifiable norms which produce news that is event driven, dramatic, conflict-oriented, novel and focused on individuals (Jamieson and Campbell, 1997). A paradigmatic example is the Clinton–Lewinsky scandal of 1998–9. For more than a year the press heavily covered both the revelations about the married president's relationship with a young employee in her twenties and his attempts to mislead the courts, his family and friends, and the nation about it. Since the news hole is limited, this preoccupation with the scandal pushed more mundane events to later pages or out of the news entirely.

A case in point is the 'Patient Bill of Rights' that Clinton proposed on 10 March 1998 in a speech to the American Medical Association. Under that proposal, health maintenance organizations (HMOs) would have been required to protect the medical privacy of patients, guarantee access to health care specialists, provide payment to emergency rooms and ensure that patients had the right to an appeal when coverage was denied.

On 1 April Democrats in the House and Senate sponsored legislation containing the Clinton guarantees. In May a reporter for the *New York Times* noted public anger at HMOs and a response by Senate and House candidates who were concentrating on patient rights as a campaign issue in the 1998 elections. In July Republicans offered a plan of their own. Under that plan, which contained many of the same provisions as the Democrats' proposal, citizens would have been barred from suing HMOs that denied them coverage. On 10 October the 'Patient Bill of Rights' legislation died in the Senate.

Here was a matter of consequence to a sizeable portion of the US public that had elicited a great deal of political discourse. The President had offered a plan as had Democrats and Republicans. Debates had occurred in the House and Senate and among medical insurers and health care providers. But that activity was largely lost in the press's preoccupation with the Clinton–Lewinsky affair. The *New York Times*, for example, carried only five stories about the legislation in March, a month in which it ran 220 articles about the Clinton scandal. In October, when the Senate debated the legislation, *The Times* carried five articles on it and over 450 on the Clinton–Lewinsky controversy. The volume of stories on the Clinton scandal, a dramatic, individual-focused, conflict-filled event, overwhelmed coverage of the legislative events.

Effects on leaders

The climate and conditions of leadership are changing as the media environment changes. The advent of the 24-hour news cycle increases the pressure on reporters and leaders. The Cable News Network (CNN) signalled the beginning of this trend. Before CNN, viewers turned on an all-news radio station or waited for the evening news or morning newspaper to learn about the latest events. Now, people can turn to the Internet for the *New York Times* on-line, CNN on-line, or turn on the television for CNN or MSNBC to find the news any minute of the day.

Round-the-clock access affects leaders as well as citizens and reporters. So, for example, in August 1989, President George Bush contemplated ways to respond to the threat to US hostages in Lebanon while 'watching CNN'. Marlin Fitzwater, the president's press secretary, noted 'CNN has opened up a whole new communications system between governments in terms of immediacy and directness. In many cases, it's the first communication we have' (Wittemore, 1990: 302).

Instant information 24 hours a day from around the globe can impel action where it otherwise would not exist. Pictures have always been powerful. The 1984 famine in Ethiopia was widely reported in newspapers in late 1983 and early 1984. In late October and early November 1984 efforts to assist the starving people of that country were mobilized when network news carried its first pictures from the refugee camps. Round-the-clock news speeded the transmission of pictures. After the Persian Gulf War, President George Bush 'was determined not to be drawn into Iraq's internal battles, confident that the blows he had dealt

Saddam Hussein would prompt his overthrow. Instead, Saddam attacked the Kurds and pictures of their misery were so affecting that Bush felt forced to intervene to protect them' (MacNeil, 1995: 123).

Effects on confidence in news

The continuous rotation of news also increases the likelihood that news outlets will carry inaccurate, incomplete or false stories. 'The problem nowadays,' writes former White House correspondent James Naughton, 'is that we're expected to make the right calls on the run. . . . Many journalists now spend valuable time scanning the Web and surfing cable channels to be sure they're not belated in disclosing what someone else just reported, breathlessly, using sources whose identity we'll never know' (Naughton, 1998).

The Clinton–Lewinsky scandal is a case in point. The sexual harassment lawsuit filed against President Clinton in 1997 by Paula Jones, a former Arkansas state aid, prompted *Newsweek* reporter, Michael Isikoff, to search for other alleged instances of sexual misconduct by the President. Isikoff received a tip on 13 January 1998 that Kenneth Starr, the Whitewater independent investigator, had begun investigating perjury and obstruction of justice charges in connection with the Jones sexual harassment lawsuit. Isikoff found that Starr had established a sting operation on a former White House intern who had indicated on tape to her friend and co-worker, Linda Tripp, that she had had a sexual relationship with the President. When Isikoff informed his editors of this story, they decided to delay publishing the piece because they felt there was insufficient information on Monica Lewinsky and on the specifics of this new Starr investigation.

Matt Drudge, author of an on-line gossip column, The Drudge Report, found out about *Newsweek*'s decision and released the story himself on Sunday, 19 January, on his Web site under the title, 'A White House intern carried on a sexual affair with the President of the United States!'. Drudge, in effect, 'scooped' *Newsweek*. It responded by dispatching reporters to the 24-hour-a-day cable stations. The information flow after Drudge's report was a deluge. According to Ricchiardi (1998: 30), who wrote an analysis of coverage during the first weeks of the Clinton/Lewinsky crisis: 'Americans found themselves besieged by an unprecedented rush of information. If the *Guinness Book of Records* recorded media stampedes, the Clinton crisis would be in first place, knocking out O.J. Simpson and the death of Princess Diana for massive, round-the-clock, soap-opera coverage'.

In the weeks that followed, several news venues ran stories with little corroboration, leading to corrections and retractions. On 26 January the *Dallas Morning News* reported that someone in the White House had witnessed the President and Lewinsky in a 'compromising situation' (Jackson, 1998). The story ran both on their Web site and in the early edition of the newspaper. The *Dallas* report was re-reported in several media outlets around the country. The report was factually false. The anonymous source who originally provided the information retracted his statement. Two days after the story ran, the *News* explained that it now had another source who confirmed the story, but that the original source 'felt compelled to withdraw his confirmation of the initial story because of the time pressure and because those elements of the story he had initially outlined were incorrect' (Leubsdorf and Jackson, 1998: 1A). The newspaper had failed to follow the standard rule of requiring two independent sources to corroborate the story. Even after gaining a second source, the *News* still reported information that never proved true. In another example, a *New York Post* headline proclaimed that Lewinsky had stated on Tripp's tape that 'The big creep told me to lie'. No evidence surfaced to verify such a statement.

In the 24-hour news cycle, journalists can release stories at any hour of the day. The newspaper or CNN reporter with the story wins the competition to get the story first. The *Wall Street Journal* ran a story on its Web site 4 February 1998 saying that a White House steward had testified to the federal grand jury that he witnessed Clinton and Lewinsky alone in the study near the Oval Office. The newspaper did not check with the White House or the steward's lawyer before putting the story on the Web site. On 9 February *The Journal* retracted the story when it learned that the steward's testimony did not include those details (Ricchiardi, 1998). A second outcome of this 24-hour-a-day cycle is an expanded definition of journalist. Matt Drudge and Arianna Huffington played important roles in spreading unsubstantiated information. Because of the Internet's low cost and ease of use, it provides the opportunity for anyone to create a Web site. Drudge seized that opportunity to create his on-line column, The Drudge Report. Drudge, who has no formal journalism experience, devotes his Web site to political and social gossip. When he struck gold with Isikoff's story, he became famous overnight and the national network FOX gave him his own television talk-show. He also appeared on several political talk-shows, including *Meet the Press*. There, NBC Washington bureau chief Tim Russert moderated the conversation between Drudge and *Newsweek*'s Isikoff. On the show, Drudge revealed that he knew that another White

House staffer was going to come forward with her own story of sexual relations with the President. That claim, which went unchallenged by Russert, proved inaccurate.

Another novice columnist, Arianna Huffington, appeared on the CNBC's 24-hour cable news show, *Equal Time*, to explain that she believed Clinton had had sex with the widow of an ambassador whose burial in Arlington National Cemetery had elicited controversy. She confessed, however, that she did not have proof. Nonetheless, the show carried the unsubstantiated rumour.

In the era when three major television networks and a morning or evening paper were the primary sources for news, members of the media elite, such as Walter Cronkite, had more sway both with citizens and leaders. So, for example, President Johnson knew he had lost public support of the Vietnam War when Cronkite, anchor for the CBS network news, opined: 'It is increasingly clear to this reporter that the only rational way out [of the conflict] . . . will be to negotiate, not as victors but as an honorable people who lived up to their pledge to defend democracy and did the best they could.' After this declaration, Johnson continued to defend his policies but shifted his rhetoric to that of unification. Cronkite's message changed Johnson's rhetoric toward the political offensive in Vietnam. 'It was the first time in American history that a war had been declared over by an anchorman', wrote Halberstam. 'Lyndon Johnson watched and told his press secretary, George Christian, that it was a turning point, that if he had lost Walter Cronkite, he had lost Mr. Average Citizen' (Halberstam, 1979: 514). Today, it is unclear who are the media elite and none has the influence that Cronkite had in the 1960s.

In a bow to the influence that once belonged to the press and a sign that that influence is a memory, on the weekend after his August 1998 confession that he had misled the public and his family about his relationship with Lewinsky, Clinton went for a widely publicized boating outing with Cronkite. The message was not lost on the press. 'Not only did he choose to align himself with a figure of larger-than life rectitude,' noted Michael Wolff, 'but he chose one who provided a marked contrast to the present day faces who deliver the news. . . . Cronkite, the last and greatest figure of an all-powerful network-news media that offered not only information but temperament, credibility, heroism even, proffered a cheerful wave and a sage smile as his sloop moved out of the Vineyard harbor past the press jackals on the shore' (Wolff, 1998: 34).

In this changed environment, the press has lost the respect that enlarged its power to contest with the president over the national agenda. Forty-eight per cent of the public believes that the media play a negative role in society; 46 per cent trust the media less than they did five years ago; 79 per cent think the media rearrange and distort the facts to make a better story; 71 per cent believe legitimate news outlets are sinking to the level of tabloids with gossip and unsubstantiated stories; 45 per cent regard the press with indifference, 22 per cent with respect, 20 per cent with disgust, 6 per cent with admiration (Wolff, 1998: 32–4).

The effects are evident in the inability of the press to set the agenda on the Clinton–Lewinsky scandal or to prime it as a matter of importance in assessing Clinton's performance as president. From January 1998, when the scandal broke, to January 1999, in the wake of Clinton's impeachment by the House and trial in the Senate, public approval of Clinton's performance in office did not drop below 60 per cent. That finding is remarkable in the face of a consistent assumption by reporters for much of that time that the affair with Lewinsky and Clinton's cover-up of it would spell the end of his presidency with the public.

Conclusion

The kind of leadership that has characterized the USA in the past places the citizen in the position of spectator and the press in the role of mediator. Both conditions are changing. With the emergence of new communication technologies, we see a shift in the relationship between citizens and leaders and leaders and media. Leaders are losing their legislative prerogatives as citizens demand more opportunities for referenda and direct democracy. Citizens can achieve the status of media elite as they gain direct access to primary sources of news through C-SPAN and the Internet. For those who take advantage of the changed climate, the result may be a more active citizenry.

Meanwhile, with public respect for the media at an all-time low and with increasing channels for direct communication with the citizenry, leaders can more readily set the national agenda than they once could. An optimist might argue that this changed climate will help leaders realize the ideal articulated by historian James MacGregor Burns when he wrote that leadership should 'engage followers, not merely to activate them, to commingle needs and aspirations and goals in a common enterprise, and in the process to make better citizens of both leaders and followers' (Burns, 1978).

References

Americans Talk Issues (1994) *Improving democracy in America*. Washington, DC: Americans Talk Issues Foundation.

Berke, Richard L. (1998) 'Gleeful democrats assail ads by GOP on Clinton scandle', *New York Times*, 29 October.

Blumenthal, Sidney (1994) 'The Education of a President', *The New Yorker*, 24 January.

Bowler, Shaun and Donovan, Todd (1998) *Demanding Choices: Opinion, Voting, and Direct Democracy*. Ann Arbor, MI: University of Michigan Press.

Brace, Paul and Hinckley, Barbara (1992) *Follow the Leader: Opinion Polls and Modern Presidents*. New York: Basic Books.

Burns, James MacGregor (1978) *Leadership*. New York: Harper and Row.

California Commission on Campaign Financing, Democracy by Initiative: Shaping the Fourth Branch of Government (1992). Report and Recommendations. Aspen: Aspen Institute.

Cooley, Charles Horton (1909) *Social Organization: A Study of the Larger Mind*. New York: Scribner.

Cronin, Thomas E. (1989) *Direct Democracy: The Politics of Initiative, Referendum and Recall*. Cambridge, MA: Harvard University Press.

Devroy, Ann and Pianin, Eric (1995a) 'Clinton offers a balanced budget plan; preserving education, controlling Medicare are priorities in 10-year program', *Washington Post*, 14 June: A01.

Devroy, Ann and Pianin, Eric (1995b) 'Clinton, Republican hill leaders fail to reach agreement on debt extension', *Washington Post*, 2 November: A01.

Dewar, Helen (1995) 'Neither side has developed an exit strategy; In the old days, opponents could just split the difference; neither side included an escape hatch', *Washington Post*, 16 November: A25.

Dewar, Helen (1996) 'Dole's stand risks riling conservatives; Hard-liners blast bill to open government', *Washington Post*, 4 January: A01.

Edelman, Murray (1974) 'The Politics of persuasion', in J.D. Barber (ed.), *Choosing the President*. Englewood Cliffs, NJ: Prentice Hall.

Edelman, Murray (1988) *Constructing the Political Spectacle*. Chicago, IL: University of Illinois Press.

Edsall, Thomas B. (1995) 'Polls bolster both sides in bitter fight over balanced Budget', *Washington Post*, 25 December: A12.

Ford, Gerald (1979) *A Time to Heal: The Autobiography of Gerald R. Ford*. New York: Harper and Row.

Gray, Jerry (1995) 'Battle over the budget: The overview; Gingrich returns to firmer stand on budget accord', *New York Times*, 29 December: A1.

Gugliotta, Guy (1995) 'GOP freshmen find a mission in budget battle', *Washington Post*, 24 December: A01.

Gurak, Laura (1997) *Persuasion and Privacy in Cyberspace: The Online Protests over Lotus Marketplace and Clipper Chip*. New Haven, CT: Yale.

Halberstam, David (1979) *The Powers that Be*. New York: Alfred A. Knopf.

Harmon, Amy (1998) 'Tangled Web tangles up the World Wide Web', *New York Times*, 12 September: 1A.

Hart, Roderick P. (1987) *The Sound of Leadership: Presidential Communication in the Modern Age.* Chicago: University of Chicago Press.

Iyengar, Shanto (1992) *Is Anyone Responsible?* Chicago: University of Chicago Press.

Iyengar, Shanto, Peters, Mark D. and Kinder, Donald (1982) 'Experimental demonstrations of the "not-so-minimal" consequences of television news programs', *American Political Science Review,* 76 (3): 848–58.

Jackson, David (1998) 'Source affirms Clinton affair, attorneys say: White House officials report no record of incident made', *Dallas Morning News,* 26 January: 1A.

Jamieson, Kathleen Hall (1992) *Dirty politics: Deception, Distraction, and Democracy.* New York: Oxford University Press.

Jamieson, Kathleen Hall and Campbell, Karlyn Kohrs (1997) *The Interplay of Influence: News, Advertising, Politics, and the Mass Media* 4th edn. Belmont, NY: Wadsworth.

Jordan, Hamilton (1982) *Crisis: The Last Year of the Carter Presidency.* New York: G.P. Putnam's Sons.

Kennedy, Hellen (1998) 'Put a plug in it, net petitioners tell lawmakers', *New York Daily News,* 2 October: 44.

Kuttner, Robert (1995) 'Unkindest Cuts', *Washington Post,* 15 June: A21.

Kurtz, Howard (1995) 'Webs of Political Intrigue: candidates, media looking for internet Constituents', *Washington Post,* 13 November.

Landow, George P. (1992) *Hypertext: The Convergence of Contemporary Critical Theory and Technology.* Baltimore, MA: Johns Hopkins University Press.

Lanham, Richard A. (1993) *The Electronic Word: Democracy, Technology, and The Arts.* Chicago: University of Chicago Press.

Leubsdorf, Carl P. and Jackson, David (1998) 'Intermediary talks with Starr's staff: Witness or witnesses fear subpoena about seeing Clinton and Lewinsky, source says; ex-official: News' story essentially correct', *Dallas Morning News,* 28 January: 1A.

Lippman, Walter (1922). *Public Opinion.* New York: Harcourt, Brace & Co.

MacNeil, Robert (1995) 'The flickering images that may drive presidents', *Media Studies Journal,* Winter.

McLean, Iain (1989) *Democracy and New Technology,* Cambridge: Polity Press.

Moffett, Dan (1999) 'Internet push to move on; Impeachment foes pledging Millions', *Arizona Republic,* 25 January: A8.

Morris, Dick (1997) *Behind the Oval Office: Winning the Presidency in the Nineties.* New York: Random House.

Naughton, James (1998) 'This Just In! and This!', *New York Times* On the Web, 1 February.

Nixon, Richard (1978) *Memoirs.* New York: Grossett and Dunlap.

Nixon, Richard (1982) *Leaders.* New York: Warner Books.

O'Toole, James (1998) 'Tool of democracy brings change', *Pittsburgh Post-Gazette,* 3 May: B8.

Pew Research Center For People and the Press (1996) 'Campaign '96 gets lower grades from Voters'. (November 15) http://www.people-press.org/contact.htm

Portess, David L. and McCombs, Maxwell (eds) (1991) *Agenda Setting: Readings on Media, Public Opinion, and Policymaking.* Hillsdale, NJ: Lawrence Erlbaum Associates.

Ricchiardi, Sherry (1998) 'Standards are the first casualty', *American Journalism Review*, March: 12–16. 30.

Semetko, H.A., Blumler, J.G., Gurevitch, M., Weaver, D.H., Barkin, S. and Wilhoit, G.C. (1991) *The Formation of Campaign Agendas: A Comparative Analysis of Party and Media Roles in Recent American and British elections.* Hillsdale, NJ: Lawrence Erlbaum Associates.

Sidey, Hugh (1978) *A Very Personal Presidency.* New York: Atheneum.

Thompson, John B. (1995) *The Media and Modernity: A Social Theory of the Media.* Stanford, CA: Stanford University Press.

Tolbert, Caroline J. (1998) 'Changing rules for state legislatures: direct democracy and governance policies', in Shaun Bowler, Todd Donovan and Caroline J. Tolbert (eds), *Citizens as Legislators: Direct Democracy in the United States.* Columbus, OH: Ohio State University Press. pp. 171–90.

Toner, Robin (1995) 'Budget battle has come down to a game of chicken', *New York Times*, 12 November: A36.

Truman, Harry S. (1949) *Public Papers of the Presidents of the United States.* Washington, DC: US Government Printing Office.

Walsh, Kenneth T. (1990–91) 'Commander in Chief', *U.S. News and World Report*, 31 December–7 January: 24.

Washington Post (1983) '72 Years: President stages Birthday Drama', 18 February: PA1.

Welch, William M. and Page, Susan (1995) 'Clinton: no to GOP offer; Says plan to reopen offices "unacceptable" ', *USA Today*, 16 November: 1A.

Wertheimer, Linda and Abramson, Larry (1998) All Things Considered (Congress e-mail), 16 September. Washington, DC: National Public Radio, Inc.

Wittemore, Hank (1990) *CNN: The Inside Story.* New York: Little, Brown.

Wolff, Michael (1998) 'Bad news for the media elite', *New York*, 23 November.

9 Virtual Hype? The Transformation of Political Parties?

Dominic Wring and Ivan Horrocks

New media and the 'crises' of democracy

The proposition that the so-called 'new' media pose both opportunities and threats for democracy has a relatively long and well-established history (Arterton, 1987; Barber, 1984; Donk and Tops, 1992; Friedland, 1996; Horrocks and Pratchett, 1995; Laudon, 1977; Lowi, 1975; Lyon, 1988). These technologies offer the promise of an information-rich society in which citizens have access to a wide range of materials from a variety of sources. In this scenario every issue is extensively debated amongst the public and policy-makers through interactive media. Participation in the political process is thus greatly increased. However, the same 'new' media may also threaten to undermine democracy. They may do this by compounding existing biases in the distribution of knowledge and information; by fragmenting discourse between increasingly differentiated policy areas; and by reducing participation to a distanced and marginalized vote that occurs as a 'knee-jerk' reaction to a limited number of 'soundbite' options.

Despite, and perhaps because of, the ambiguous yet profound consequences for democracy that accompany the ongoing development of new media, interest in exploiting these technologies for democratic purposes has continued to grow. Of particular interest to commentators is one specific characteristic of these technologies, namely their interactivity. It is this feature which holds the potential for the development of political practices and, therefore, new forms of 'electronic' democracy. And it is this interactivity which advocates of the concept have consistently touted as offering the potential to reinvigorate and/or reinvent public debate and accountability (Barber, 1984; Becker, 1981, 1993; Elgin, 1993; Varley, 1991; Varn, 1993). It is not surprising, therefore, that when initial interest in electronic democracy emerged in the USA in the 1970s it was linked with an increasing concern with the 'health' of the American political system (Arterton, 1987; Elgin, 1993). As a consequence, advocates of the technology have been keen to promote the relationship between new media and the supposed reinvention and/or renewal of democracy.

Since the early 1990s rapid advances in the capacities and capabilities of the new media combined with concern over the apparent crisis of political legitimacy throughout the developed world has further heightened interest in electronic democracy. The upshot of this has been the development of a range of projects that can be considered as promoting some variants and/or features of technologically enhanced politics. For example, in their book *Cyberdemocracy* the authors present case studies of civic networking from several different countries (Tsagarousianou, Tambini and Bryan, 1998). A further series of case studies of similar developments from the UK, The Netherlands and Denmark is also featured in Hoff, Horrocks and Tops (2000).

The crisis of democracy thesis, and its specific concern with political participation, has several important dimensions. One of the most fundamental relates to the apparent decline of the political party. The particular role media technologies have played and could play in reinventing this particular feature of democracies is the focus of this chapter. But, before considering this matter, it is necessary to assess what it is about the so-called 'new' media that is new and constitutes a break with the past (see Axford, Chapter 1 in this volume). What distinguishes these forms from previous developments in information and communication technologies? Will their impact be felt equally throughout the polity or more pronounced within certain arenas and/or specific sets of political relationships? Having addressed these questions and explored the emergence and impact of electronic democracy it will be argued that the new media should not always be construed as a radical departure from previous practices. More profitably, they can be viewed as representing the latest in a long line of technological developments that have been utilized by political parties in order to improve their effectiveness and efficiency. In addition to this, claims about the supposedly democratic properties of the new media need to be taken with a great deal of caution. For, as will be seen, the undoubted opportunities are accompanied by a range of threats, primarily associated with centralization, exclusion and control.

Defining the 'new media'

One of the most comprehensive attempts to identify and codify the technologies involved in democratic politics was developed by Abramson *et al.*, 1988. Whilst the typology they produced is still relevant, it has, as the authors themselves acknowledge, some limitations: 'Given the pace of technological change, any attempt to provide a timely list of the new media [technology] is doomed to a short life' (Abramson *et al.*, 1988: 4). They did however identify six properties that characterize the new media and their particular relevance to political activity:

1. They explode all previous limits on the volume of information that can be exchanged.
2. They make it possible to exchange information without regard, for all practical purposes, to real time and space.
3. They increase the control the consumers have over what messages are received and when.
4. They increase the control senders have over which audiences receive which messages.
5. They decentralize control over mass communication.
6. They bring two way or interactive capacities to television. (Abramson *et al.*, 1988: 4–5)

This typology is helpful in that it both defines the broad range of those new media that may have an impact upon democracy and indicates ways in which they can influence politics. But this is only one aspect of the definition of new media. Also significant is the need to distinguish between the properties and potential influences of different technologies. Here it is useful to draw on Laudon's pioneering classification of new media. Three families of technologies are identified. These are:

1 *Data transformation technologies* such as the computer which 'serves as a tool for the collection, storage, manipulation and retrieval of very large sets of information'.
2 *Mass-participation technologies* such as the traditional broadcast media (radio and television) 'which function to transmit information from one central source to thousands or millions of persons'.
3 *Interactive technologies* 'which allow for horizontal communications flows among individuals and organized groups'. (Laudon, 1977: 14–16)

Over two decades after its publication, one of the most significant features of this work remains the author's attempt to analyse the relationship between each technology, its 'modes of organization' and the resulting democratic implications. Laudon argues that the three differing families can be characterized by the way they work or, more specifically, who has access to the information potential and who controls its flow. In turn the mode of organization tends to favour a particular model of politics. Thus, data transformation technologies are typically organized around experts and lead to managerial or technocratic forms of democracy. For their part, mass-participation technologies encourage plebiscitarian modes of organization that can, in turn, encourage populism. Finally, interactive technologies advantage organized sub-groups and tend to deliver an implicitly pluralist system. Ultimately though for Laudon the democratic potential of new media is conditioned by public access and control or, more bluntly, 'who benefits and who loses influence, who decides to participate in what decision, when and how' (1977: 19).

Elements of the three types of technology are present in most advanced democracies. Nevertheless, it is not only the existence of such forms but their relative influence in the policy process that is significant. Furthermore, different political cultures could foster distinctive balances between the alternative types of technology and will, as a result, exploit their democratic potential in differing ways. Thus, pluralist systems are more likely to welcome interactive technologies into the policy process. In contrast more technocratic polities tend to concentrate the same processes around the technologies of data transformation. These contrasts between different political cultures and systems in their development and appropriation of new media technologies emerge as one of the main features of much recent case study research in this field (Hoff, Horrocks and Tops, 2000; Tsargarousianou, Tambini and Bryan, 1998).

The old 'new' media: their historical impact on British party politics

Before looking at the relationship between new media and the crises of contemporary democracy, it is useful to assess the historical response of the political party to earlier examples of each of the three technological families identified by Laudon. The British system is offered as a case study primarily because of its unbroken tradition of democratic elections throughout the twentieth century. In these circumstances, technology has tended to be integrated into the democratic process through parties' pursuit of votes during election campaigns.

Mass-participation technologies

During the 1880 general election William Ewart Gladstone conducted a punishing round of stump meetings at which he spoke to thousands of Scottish voters. These events, collectively known as the Midlothian campaign, have since entered into political folklore (Hanham, 1958). Whilst there were unusually large numbers of people able to hear the Liberal leader, it was the presence of and consideration given to those reporters present which guaranteed that the theatre of Gladstone's oratory would be recorded for posterity. The speeches can be seen as an early example of the modern 'media event'. Since then the relationship between politicians and journalists has become ever more complex and interrelated. In 1910 the Conservative Party appointed an official to co-ordinate the party's press relations (Cockett, 1994). Within a decade Labour had done the same (Wring, 1996). Both organizations began to invest resources in cultivating and maintaining a good public image through the mass participatory medium of the press.

With their pro-business stance, the Conservatives enjoyed favourable coverage in the largely privately owned British national and regional newspapers throughout the early part and, indeed, most of the rest of the twentieth century. By contrast, Labour, with their close ties to the trade union movement, received a hostile press in most of the same titles. This encouraged many in the party to consider publishing their own newspapers. The inter-war period saw the launch of several local Labour papers. Many did not survive. The last major party newspaper, the national *Labour Weekly*, was closed down in 1987 on the grounds of cost. It had served as an independent-minded forum for intra-party debate. Its successors have proved to be more favourable to the leader-ship position.

Besides newspapers, the parties' early attempts to promote themselves to a wider audience centred on outdoor advertising forms such as the poster. Originally of the crude bill-sticker type, campaigners began to recruit commercial artists and designers to help them produce arresting visual propaganda. Through this work, parties began to build relation-ships with professionals working in the marketing industries. These partnerships helped forge links between politicians and advertising executives. New and more experimental publicity initiatives followed, including elementary attempts at developing brand identities through logos, badges and other novelties (Wring, 1997).

Film excited both major parties and each investigated how their organizations might capitalize from its usage. It was, in its way, the inter-war period's equivalent of 'virtual reality'. For the first time audiences were able to see motion pictures which were a sensation previous generations could barely have imagined. Politicians sought to reach voters with appearances on the newsreel services provided by the cinemas between featured presentations. The Conservatives sought to further exploit the new medium by forming the Conservative Film Association. Led by Sir Albert Clavering, the CFA successfully cultivated influential contacts in the industry like Alexander Korda and Michael Balcon. These and others helped the party develop and maintain a programme of film propaganda.

During the three general election campaigns of 1929, 1931 and 1935, a fleet of Conservative cinema vans were dispatched to tour the provinces. The vehicles and the presentations that accompanied them received an enthusiastic response from audiences, although it was probably Stanley Baldwin that the crowds were more curious to see. Labour was less keen on film, principally on the grounds of cost. Tapes were however produced, distributed and exhibited by party members and supporters around the country. Sympathetic filmmakers, such as Paul Rotha and members of the Co-operative Film movement, did try and help Labour, but their efforts were ultimately frustrated by the onset of World War II.

Apart from cinema, sound broadcasting was the other major new medium of the inter-war period in the UK. From the beginnings of the BBC in the early 1920s to the rise of mass television 30 years later, radio provided the major source of political coverage. In 1924 it aired the first political advertisements in the form of party election broadcasts by the three main party leaders. Like President Roosevelt with his fireside chats to the American people, the Conservative politician Stanley Baldwin was adjudged to have the best and thus most persuasive radio manner. Unlike Gladstone in 1880, politicians did not now have to rely on editorializing and could speak direct to the public with this valuable and intimate medium. Unlike their rivals in print journalism, broadcasters found themselves subject to strict regulatory codes.

Parties auditioned and employed the services of professional broadcasters to help them present their case. Labour used veteran writer J.B. Priestley, whilst the Conservatives relied on the so-called 'radio doctor' Charles Hill, a general practitioner and health journalist who later became a government minister with responsibility for the Ministry of Information. The success of sound broadcasting, combined with the restrictions on the BBC service, led some Labour strategists to suggest the party advertise on Radio Luxembourg during the 1930s. A new and increasingly popular commercial light entertainment station, Luxembourg would have reached several thousand British listeners (Wring, 1997). Despite the rise of mass television, radio has continued to be an important political medium in the UK. This is partly because the numerous channels enable parties to target more effectively niche audiences among specific population sub-groups. During the 1960s some political organizations sought to exploit the potential of the then hugely popular and unlicensed pirate radio stations. On several occasions these new independent broadcasters, in many cases broadcasting from ships moored off the British coast, were involved in protracted disputes concerning their supposed interference in politics. Particular concerns were expressed over certain politicians' illegal purchase of airtime to promote their candidatures.

Undoubtedly the challenge of television forced parties to rethink their approach to political communication. Experimentation with this technology in the 1930s resulted in only a select number of wealthy British homes having access to the new medium. Between the general elections of 1955 and 1959 households with television sets leapt from around 30 per cent to 70 per cent. This rapid growth forced a rethink on the part of current affairs programmers with the infant Independent Television News pressurizing the rival BBC service to abandon its traditionally deferential, patrician reporting. The old 14-day rule, whereby TV reporters were unable to comment on any matter likely to come up in parliament over any subsequent two-week period, was swept away. Harold Macmillan and Harold Wilson were two early beneficiaries of the new visual broadcasting. Significantly, a number of younger politicians launched their careers through behind the scenes work advising on the respective merits of television. Two of the most prominent, Tony Benn and John Profumo, later became cabinet members.

The late twentieth century has witnessed considerable fragmentation of the visual media. The rise of video, satellite and cable television offers a clear challenge to party organizations. The USA is now home to several dedicated political channels. Developments of this kind in Europe are in the experimentation stage. Some parties have, like their American counterparts, invested heavily in video technology. During the British general election of 1997 the businessman James Goldsmith launched and sustained a campaign on behalf of his own Referendum Party. Millions of households received a tape cassette featuring a discussion of government policy on the European Union. Interestingly, despite his money and technology, Goldsmith felt obliged to underline his political sincerity by formally launching a party, recruiting several thousand members and contesting most of the constituencies.

Satellite and cable television offered another obvious vehicle for those who get a buzz from elections and electioneering. These enable those with capital, if not labour-intensive organizations, the opportunity to launch a potentially credible and effective campaign in any given contest. Added to these developments, changing patterns of media ownership and regulation in certain European countries have already had an impact on some party systems. In the Italian elections of 1994, businessman Silvio Berlusconi and his recently formed Forza Italia party famously won power with the help of sympathetic coverage on the party leader's own popular not to mention populist television station (Statham, 1996).

Interactive technologies

Aside from facilitating the evolution of various media forms, technology played a major role in the development of other kinds of communication during the early twentieth century. The invention of the car afforded parties an obvious means with which to publicize their case and activities. In 1945, Clement Attlee's wife drove the Labour leader around the country in the family's own vehicle. The car was also used to transport supporters to the polls. Similarly, the rail network helped parties to disseminate their propaganda and enabled politicians to visit several parts of the country in whistle-stop rail tours. Some parties even invested in air transport as a means of communicating their message. During the 1920s the German Social Democrats used planes to drop leaflets on voters in disparate parts of the country (Wring, 1997). Cumulatively the effect of all these major transportation developments was to make countries more accessible. Paradoxically, perhaps they also provided for a greater degree of control and co-ordination from central headquarters, in this case based in the capital London. The local caucus-based party Ostrogorski (1908) wrote about at the turn of the century was looking all the more obsolete with the onset of rail and other forms of communications.

The earliest recorded political use of the telephone occurred in London in 1927 when Streatham Conservative Association used the new medium to canvass voters. Labour agents were quick to see the possible application of the technology to aid with organizational development in the 1930s (Swaddle, 1990). The novelty, in the form of a line 'Call Brum 1411', proved to be a short-lived feature of the journal *Labour Organiser* presumably because it was underused (Wring, 1997). Affordability was not the only reason why some technological developments were not adopted. Some organizers were hostile and suspicious of innovations and were reluctant to change the tried and tested methods. Even young agents such as the future Labour MP John Cartwright raised objections. Still in his twenties, Cartwright attacked a colleague for modestly proposing that technology might improve canvassing: 'At this rate, by

1964 organizers will have been replaced by some sort of cross between Frankenstein and Orwell's Thought Police' (Wring, 1997).

In spite of this early, inter-war usage by parties it is perhaps surprising that the telephone did not really feature in a politically significant way until the 1980s. Then it became an integral part of by-election strategy, playing a prominent role in the keenly fought Brecon and Radnor campaign of 1985 (Swaddle, 1989). Since then anecdotal evidence suggests telecanvassing formed a major part of the Conservatives' ultimately successful efforts during the 1992 general election. This was particularly helpful for a party seeking to best organize its declining and ageing membership. In that campaign and the most recent national elections, parties have also sought to exploit the telephone as a means of fundraising.

The political uses of direct mail date back to the earlier part of the century. In 1924, for instance, the Northampton MP Margaret Bondfield sent potential voters a personalized handwritten style address designed to cultivate and reinforce the link between elector and elected. Other Labour strategists considered how they might best target sections of the public. Mailings were an obvious mechanism for this. In East Anglia one party organizer sent special appeals to teachers in the hope they might support Labour following attacks on 'progressive' educators by Conservative-inclined newspapers such as the *Daily Mail* (Wring, 1997).

It was during the run-up to the 1950 general election that direct mailings became a really significant feature in campaign terms. The technique formed an integral part of the Conservatives' attempts to re-establish themselves as contenders for government. Opinion-formers and other community notables were contacted and cultivated with letters and mailings on various topics of interest to them. The 1980s saw the launch of more capital intensive forms of direct mail. The Social Democratic Party (SDP), launched in 1981, used this medium to recruit members and develop a highly successful fundraising base to fund and sustain an organization. The techniques closely mirrored those of commercial firms. The Conservatives also relied heavily on mailshots, targeting those people who had bought shares as a result of the government's mid-1980s programme of privatizations (McLean, 1989). These campaigns involved massive mailings to several million potential voters.

Data transformation technologies

The arrival of the computer age has offered a new challenge to parties. Initially, during the early 1980s, the use of information technology was restricted to isolated party organizers using rudimentary machines like the Commodore Pet. Thereafter computers began to be integrated into campaign work. The introduction of new and more efficient database systems enabled more effective targeting of prospective supporters. This obviously fulfils a persuasive as well as a fundraising role. Parties have been keen to capitalize on IT, setting up groups such as Computing for Labour. In the 1987 general election the party used the Telecom Gold on-line system to communicate with candidates. More recently database operations have been extended to other areas of campaign work. Prior to the 1997 general election Labour organized its own Excalibur system. This allowed the party to gather huge quantities of information in order to rebut their opponents' accusations more effectively. Faxes were regularly used to inform parliamentary candidates of policy so that they were 'on-message'. Since then the Conservatives have developed their own Broadsword database.

Aside from their function as a communicative medium, computer software allows users to build models and manipulate large datasets. This was not a facility available to the Conservatives when the party set up its own Public Opinion Research Department in 1948 to study popular attitudes towards politics. Clearly the ability to compute statistics has been invaluable to parties seeking to draw out meanings from their often large-scale programmes of polling. During the late 1980s and 1990s parties have been keen to use the services of major London-based market research agencies as well as American political opinion analysts like Richard Wirthlin and Stanley Greenberg. Increasingly this research has involved not only the investigation of voters according to demographic background but also psychographic profiling.

ICTs and democratic politics

Computers, or more appropriately Information and Communication Technologies (ICTs) are central to any notion of 'electronic democracy'. The interactive nature of these technologies creates the potential, it is claimed, for an enriched kind of politics. This is because, as Laudon's typology illustrates, the new 'new' media contain a potent *mix* of the three properties outlined in the discussion above of the older media: data transformation, mass participation and interactivity.

Since the early days of the Internet and the rapid growth of Usenet and Newsgroups throughout the 1980s and 1990s, there has been growing recognition of the potential the new ICTs offer for mass participation, communication and marketing. Some argue that the Internet can and will provide ordinary people with a greater political voice. This view is particularly popular in the USA. In the USA, citizens and groups suspicious of federal agencies and/or other influential elites, together with techno-enthusiasts such as Newt Gingrich, Alvin Toffler and Howard Rheingold, have heavily promoted the idea of electronic mass participation (see, for instance, Toffler, 1980). These and other powerful voices have been supported by Net-age publications, including the successful *Wired* magazine, that regularly produces features highlighting the supposed advent of a new electronic age of direct democracy.

In Europe, and the UK in particular, the euphoria about the democratic potential of the Internet has not matched that seen in the USA. Nevertheless, during the mid-1990s political parties have moved to establish a presence in cyberspace with the development of Web sites. Influenced by the work of certain MPs and think-tanks like Demos, 'New' Labour has moved to exploit the potential of the Internet both while in opposition and now in government (Demos, 1994; Mulgan, 1994). The party set up a Web site in October 1994 and all other major political parties had followed suit by September 1996 (Ward and Gibson, 1998). The impetus for much of this development was, of course, electoral and designed in preparation for a campaign fought in 1997. And although it appears that ICTs had minimal impact on this, the first British 'Internet' election triggered speculation about their future potential role as mass participation technologies (Ward and Gibson, 1998).

If the speculation about the reach of ICTs echoes earlier debates over the efficacy of each new media following its introduction, there are also parallels with the historical struggles by governments and elites to mediate, regulate and police (in other words 'control') the output of radio and television. The Internet, most obviously, is in essence a global medium and so differs from the traditional terrestrial radio and television. Granted, the rise of satellite and cable services transgresses the once-defined geographical and thus governmental boundaries, but they still tend to be subject to licensing laws and advertising tariffs. The Internet is different. It is a network of networks, a vast disaggregated system with no overall control structure. Theoretically it raises the prospect that a 'borderless' world will create the conditions for trans-state parties, as well as trans-national social movements. Those that do exist, such as the federal Party of European Socialists, do so in the context of a supra-national parliament and not because of ICTs. That said, it should be noted that pressure and special interest groups, particularly of the environmental persuasion, have had success in promoting themselves to a wider and more cosmopolitan audience courtesy of cyberspace.

Turning to interactive forms, it is clear that direct mail and other traditional terrestrial techniques will remain important for disseminating campaign material for the foreseeable future. With more households gaining access to the Net, the role of the medium in taking on such functions looks set to increase. Furthermore, the continuing rapid development of technologies which enhance the interactivity inherent in new media afford political parties the opportunity to either engage in remote, real-time, one-to-mass or mass-to-one communication with a variety of constituencies. Though these types of on-line activity are well established, British political parties appear less willing to utilize them than their continental European and North American counterparts. In a number of countries, particularly in northern Europe, parties from both the Left and the Right have set up bulletin board systems (BBSs) and chat-room facilities which allow members to debate issues on-line with other party members, the party hierarchy and elected representatives (Lofgren, 2000). These systems operate in addition to e-mail systems that are now an accepted channel for communication in most of these pioneering organizations. These are 'closed' systems for the use of members and party officials. This particular dimension of electronic democracy is proving a potentially rich vein of research (Barnett, 1997; Coleman, 1999; Smith, 1998; Ward and Gibson, 1998).

It is perhaps in the arena of data transformation technologies that the greatest challenge and opportunity for parties exists. The increasing power and flexibility of software, allied with exponential growth in the power of computers, enables ever-more sophisticated data-mining and data-matching capabilities. In turn, this makes it theoretically possible to build up individual preference and behaviour profiles to a level of sophistication unheard of even a decade ago. Potentially these developments challenge notions of the right to privacy and raise issues of data protection and other civil rights questions. Of additional relevance to political parties is the ongoing development of Web technologies such as 'cookies'. While it has always been the case that users of the Internet have left a 'footprint' or 'data shadow' which allowed others to see basic information on a user's movements, the invention of new surveillance technologies more easily and comprehensively facilitates the harvesting of such information. As the authors of a 1998 review of Web security concluded, the advent of cookies means: 'a high volume server can track a significant amount of information about a user's browsing habits. Multiple servers in collaboration can build up even more information. Many targeted advertising companies share information about user profiles and build massive databases containing users and their data shadows' (Rubin and Geer 1998: 39).

The impact of ICTs on parties

The historical assessment of the link between technological develop-ments and politics in the UK has shown how innovations have tended to coincide with important electoral contests. Modern party organizations are, however, increasingly looking to introduce novel approaches between – and thus in time for – major campaigns. It is also significant that new technologies are not only being integrated to enhance voter persuasion but to provide ever-more sophisticated profiles of individual voters. This direction of developments clearly mirrors – and borrows heavily from – the ongoing development of highly sophisticated techno-logically based marketing practices now widely used by all major retail chains in the UK.

The decline of party organization revisited

A central theme of the literature on the organization of party politics has identified and sought to analyse the apparent decline of mass parties. This has variously been attributed to changing patterns of socialization, political activism and, most pertinently, mediation. The emerging parties have been characterized as more professional organizations (Panebianco, 1988). Critical to this transformation has been the recruitment and installation of new media-conscious personnel. The potential of these staff to alter the nature of the bureaucracy through the introduction of more technologically sophisticated systems has been a feature of the American party system for some time. In the UK and elsewhere it is already apparent that developments of this kind are beginning to follow a similar pattern. Where once there was a premium on interpersonal contact and motivating the voluntary wing of party activists and suppor-ters, now the organizational emphasis of most parties appears to be on mobilizing its support amongst selected opinion forming media.

A serious consequence of parties' attempts to cope with changing media systems and ever more sophisticated ICTs is the increased demand for finances. Fortunately, for those seeking to cope with this emerging, more capital-intensive form of politics, new technologies can aid fundraising. Cynics have discussed the possibility of a largely passive, 'credit card' membership party. In addition, critics have also objected to the emergence of a hierarchy of rich sponsors enjoying privileged access to those whose parties they patronize. Thus public disquiet in the UK has followed revelations surrounding the political donations made by wealthy business people like Lord David Sainsbury, Bernie Ecclestone and Michael Ashcroft.

New media possess the potential to facilitate changes in the nature of intra-party democracies. Direct mail has, in certain circumstances, been adopted to encourage wider participation in key decisions. During the 1994 race for the Labour leadership, all those belonging to the party were directly enfranchized and given a vote in the contest. More contentiously under Tony Blair's leadership, some party members were able to participate in referendums over plans to re-write the party constitution in 1995, and all had the chance to endorse the draft Labour manifesto for the 1997 general election. Critics have attacked these procedures as one-sided exercises and essentially affirmative ballots. The key decisions, already taken by the leadership, would have already been disseminated by the so-called 'spin doctors', courtesy of those traditional media sympathetic to the party and thus disproportionately read by its members (Wring, 1998a).

The use of the referendum has underlined the growing prominence of direct, plebiscitary forms of participation in the making of certain decisions which were hitherto the preserve of leaderships or representative party fora. Arguably the use of such procedures is motivated by a desire to further centralize power within leaderships rather than emancipate members (Lipow, 1996). In the case of the British Labour Party this desire to control the party has resulted in a radical reconfiguring of the organization's democratic structures. These changes have been characterized as control freakery, with, for example, the standard issue of pagers to all Labour MPs to enable the leadership to contact them round the clock to ensure they are aware of the government's position and thus 'on-message'.

The increased use of database systems to manage membership lists and other functions raises issues about democratic accountability within these organizations. Following Labour's victory in 1997, some members expressed doubts about the way in which the organization was using its computerized Excalibur system. Critics such as MEP Hugh Kerr believed the technology, developed to rebut opponents' claims, would now be used to monitor and police the party's own elected representatives. Having spoken out publicly about this and other matters, Kerr was subsequently expelled by Labour.

Party publications and other communications can be used to promote a specific agenda and thus bias debate on controversial internal matters. This can involve the selected use of the organization's own polling findings to reinforce the leadership's position. The question of who controls and enjoys access to this database information and other materials was raised during the internal committee elections of the governing Labour Party in 1998. Allegations were made surrounding the conduct of this ballot of the membership (Wring, 1998b). The faction supporting candidates favoured by the leadership was said to have targeted members with the aid of a telecanvassing agency. This, it was claimed, was a service not available to their less well-funded rivals. Ironically, in this case these efforts proved counter-productive and the critics of the leadership effectively won the election. Though it was not a major factor in this campaign the advent of other new media, notably the Web, raises the possibility of similarly well organized groups within parties mobilizing support for candidates, policies or other positions in opposition to the hierarchy. Nevertheless it is still, as Michels (1949) originally argued, leaderships and their acolytes who tend to enjoy overwhelming advantages in any intra-party dispute.

The possibility for new media to favour one or other group within a party could manifest itself in a number of ways. A consequence of the growing use of ICTs will be to selectively encourage participation and thus increase the potential influence of the so-called 'information rich' to the detriment of the 'information poor', that is those people without the same skills or material resources to access certain communication sources (Golding, 1990). Long seen as the domain of the formally educated, parties may also become the preserves of a technically literate not to mention wealthy elite. This is, of course, an added and important dimension to the wider discussion about the future and nature of democracy.

Effects on party systems

It is too early to determine what long-term impact, if any, the emergence of new media like ICTs will have on the party system in countries like Britain. Historically a combination of factors has encouraged the emergence of new parties. These have tended to be socio-economic not technological in nature. The Conservatives' once-dominant electoral position cannot be explained solely in terms of their ability to adopt and exploit new media. Yet their ability to use technology in the form of direct mail did give them a useful advantage over their rivals. Similarly the rise of the Social Democratic Party in the early 1980s was in part sustained by a healthy funding base reinforced by a well-orchestrated direct marketing campaign.

The party system in the UK, like other Western states, has on the whole been quite resolute. The arrival of the World Wide Web does, on a superficial level, afford competitive minor and fringe parties some degree of parity. Political organizations' ability to present themselves on the Web is only limited by their ability or willingness to design informative pages. In the 1997 general election several fringe parties gained a prominent and, in many cases, equal billing with the major competitors on many of the most popular and impartial Web sites covering the campaign. An obvious consequence of this development is that users have an opportunity to access information about organizations not previously available to them. In 1992 very few prospective voters would have been able to read the manifesto of small parties. By 1997 any casual Web user was able to examine literature from these and an array of other organizations. Some of these, notably the Irish republican group Sinn Fein or far-right British National Party, who had previously experienced media censorship could now effectively evade restrictions courtesy of the Internet.

The Web raises limited possibilities for technically literate new parties to present a challenge to existing systems. But experience has shown organizations like the SDP have done so primarily through traditional media exposure and even then with limited success. Furthermore, those such as the Natural Law Party and Referendum Party who have sought to exploit the potential of new technologies have done so with the help of considerable financial resources. It is not accidental that the increased reliance of parties on all kinds of media has resulted in the need for greater funding sources. With this has come controversy and suspicion arising out of debates as to the character and motivations of certain donors. Public concern over party funding irregularities in the UK resulted in the launch of a government-sponsored inquiry, led by Lord Neill, in to all aspects of the matter. The use of ICTs and the expense incurred may force politicians to revisit some very old questions about the funding of their own organizations and election campaigns.

Conclusion

The synthesis of information processing and communication technologies, and the increasing potential for interactivity that this convergence brings with it, are the defining features of new media. It is widely suggested that these could have a profound impact on democratic practice. In short, the new media may offer the potential for an 'electronic' democracy that will supposedly reinvigorate and reinvent democratic practices. This, it is argued, offers the potential for tackling the so-called 'crises' of democracy or, more specifically, the problems of growing political cynicism coupled with declining levels of voter turnout and participation.

Yet the potential for new media technologies to deliver particular democratic outcomes is far from conclusive. At a practical level it is clear, for example, that new technologies can have differing impacts which depend upon a number of complex and interrelated factors pertaining to the political culture in which they emerge and the model of democracy integral to that particular system. On a more philosophical note, the nostrum, immortalized by Bacon, that knowledge equals power raises questions about whether technologies such as ICTs are inherently democratic. Do the new media, with their ability to collect, store, process and transmit information, facilitate and enhance or limit and regress debate? In other words, new media offers the potential for both liberation and control.

Another criticism that can be made relates to the underlying techno-logical determinism of proponents of electronic democracy. This often informs descriptive as well as prescriptive discussions of the topic. But, like any technology, the new media are political artefacts. Rather than seeing them as autonomous developments it is important to recognize that the design, application and environment that new media create are prescribed by policy choices and are thus political choices. Nevertheless, though technology per se may not 'cause' any particular political developments, it can facilitate them. This applies both in the sense that it enables changes to take place that would otherwise not have been possible (for example, plebiscites in geographically spread areas in real time) and in that it enhances (or exaggerates) other effects. Rather than asking whether the new media have had an impact on democracy, it is perhaps more useful to ask what forms this has taken and how it will continue.

In the UK the historical response of political parties to different kinds of new media has been patchy and partial. Mass-participation and interactive forms of technology have been appropriated and used by organizations. There is evidence to suggest that both have played some part in the internal debates of parties, not to mention the external communication campaigns geared to influencing voters. Yet the notion that the electronic will necessitate the democratic needs to be taken with caution. Where it has been used for organizational purposes, the major political parties' usage of new and indeed other existing media forms has invariably been to bolster one particular opinion – the leadership viewpoint. If the case for mass-participation and interactive technologies transforming the nature of political parties may have been overstated the other key form, data transformation, could have a substantial impact. Computerization combined with developments in opinion research methods raises some intriguing political opportunities as well as threats. Ever-more sophisticated kinds of data manipulation pose interesting questions for parties and those that lead them.

References

Abramson, J.B., Arterton, F.C. and Orren, G.R. (1988) *The Electronic Commonwealth*. New York: Basic Books Inc.
Arterton, F.C. (1987) Teledemocracy: *Can Technology Protect Democracy?* New York: Sage.
Barber, B. (1984) *Strong Democracy: Participatory Politics for a New Age.* Berkeley, CA: University of California Press.
Barnett, S. (1997) 'New media, old problems: new technology and the political process', *European Journal of Communication*, 12 (2): 193–218.
Becker, T. (1981) 'Teledemocracy', *The Futurist*, December: 6–9.
Becker, T. (1993) 'Teledemocracy: gathering momentum in state and local governance', *Spectrum: the Journal of State Government*, 66 (2): 14–20.
Coleman, S. (1999) 'Westminster in the information age', *Parliamentary Affairs*, 52 (3): 371–87.
Crocket, R. (1994) *The Conservative Party and the Press: 1900–45*. London: Andre Deutsch.
Demos (1994) 'Liberation technology', *Demos Quarterly*, 4.
Donk, W.B.J. van de and Tops, P.W. (1992) 'Informatization and democracy: Orwell or Athens?', *Informatization and the Public Sector*, 2: 169–96.
Elgin, D. (1993) 'Revitalizing democracy through electronic town meetings', *Spectrum: the Journal of State Government*, 66 (2): 6–13.
Friedland, L.A. (1996) 'Electronic democracy and new citizenship', *Media Culture and Society*, 18 (2): 185–212.
Golding, P. (1990) 'Political communication and citizenship: the media and democracy in an inegalitarian social order', in M. Ferguson (ed.), *Public Communication: the New Imperatives*. London: Sage.
Hanham, H. (1958) *Elections and Party Management: Politics in the Time of Disraeli and Gladstone*. Brighton, Sussex: Harvester.
Hoff, J., Horrocks, I. and Tops, P. (2000) *Democratic Governance and New Technology: Technologically Mediated Innovations in Political Practice in Western Europe*. London: Routledge.
Horrocks, I. and Pratchett, L. (1995) 'Electronic democracy: themes and issues', in J. Lovenduski and J. Stanyer (eds), *Contemporary Political Studies 1995*. Belfast: PSA.
Laudon, K. (1977) *Communication Technology and Democratic Participation*. New York: Praeger Publishers.
Lipow, A. (1996) *Political Parties and Democracy: Explorations in History and Theory*. London: Sage.
Lofgren, K. (2000) 'Danish political parties and new technology: interactive parties or new shop windows', in J. Hoff, I. Horrocks and P. Tops (eds), *Democratic Governance and New Technology*. London: Routledge.
Lowi, T.J. (1975) 'The political impact of information technology', in T. Forester (ed.), *The Microelectronic Revolution*. Oxford: Blackwell.
Lyon, D. (1988) *The Information Society: Issues and Illusions*. Cambridge: Polity Press.
McLean, I. (1989) *Democracy and New Technology*. Cambridge: Polity Press.
Michels, R. (1949) *Political Parties: A Sociological Study of the Oligarchical Tendencies of Modern Democracy*. New York: Free Press.
Mulgan, G. (1994) 'Lean democracy', *Demos Quarterly*, 3: 1–16.

Ostrogorski, Moisei (1908) *Democracy and the Organization of Political Parties.* Boulder, CO: Transaction Press.

Panebianco, A. (1988) *Political Parties: Organisation and Power.* Cambridge: Cambridge University Press.

Rubin, A.D. and Geer Jr., D.E. (1998) 'A survey of web security', *Computer,* September: 34–41.

Smith, C. (1998) 'British political parties: continuity and change in the information age', in J. Hoff, I. Horrocks and P. Tops (eds), *Democratic Governance and New Technology.* London: Routledge.

Statham, P. (1996) 'Berlusconi, the media and the New Right in Italy', *Harvard International Journal of Press/Politics,* 1 (1): 87–105.

Swaddle, K. (1989) 'Ancient and modern: innovations in electioneering at the constituency level', in I. Crewe and M. Harrop (eds), *Political Communications: the General Election Campaign of 1987.* Cambridge: Cambridge University Press.

Swaddle, K. (1990) *Coping with a Mass Electorate.* Unpublished PhD thesis, Oxford University.

Toffler, A. (1980) *The Third Wave.* New York: Bantam.

Tops, P. (1999) 'Political Websites during the 1998 parliamentary election in the Netherlands', in J. Hoff, I. Horrocks and P. Tops (eds), *Democratic Governance and New Technology.* London: Routledge.

Tsagarousianou, R., Tambini, D. and Bryan, C. (1998) *Cyberdemocracy: Technology, Cities and Civic Networks.* London: Routledge.

Varley, P. (1991) 'Electronic democracy', *Technology Review,* 94 (8): 43–51.

Varn, R.J. (1993) 'Electronic democracy: Jeffersonian boom or teraflop?', *Spectrum: the Journal of State Government,* 66 (2): 21–5.

Ward, R. and Gibson, R. (1998) *The First Internet Election? UK Political Parties and Campaigning in Cyberspace, Political Communications: Why Labour Won the General Election of 1997.* London: Frank Cass.

Wring, D. (1996) 'Political marketing and party development in Britain: a "secret" history', *European Journal of Marketing,* 30 (10/11): 92–103.

Wring, D. (1997) *Political Marketing and the Labour Party: Campaign Strategy and Intra-Organisational Power.* Unpublished PhD thesis, Cambridge University.

Wring, D. (1998a) 'The media and intra-party democracy: "New" Labour and the Clause Four debate', *Democratization,* 5 (2): 42–61.

Wring, D. (1998b) 'Guardian angel', *Tribune,* 4 December.

10 The Transformation of Political Modernity?

John Street

'This is not a protest . . .'

Recalling a Reclaim the Street demonstration she had taken part in, the author Naomi Klein told of the policeman standing nearby, who had said into his radio: 'This is not a protest. Over. This is some kind of artistic expression' (quoted in *Select*, April 2000: 75). In the same interview, Klein remarks that when political campaigners 'target a Starbucks or a Nike store, they're in the realm of pop culture. That has a lot more appeal for young people. It becomes *fun*' (*ibid.*: 74). Klein's observations suggest an intimate connection between political and cultural activity, one in which the distinction between the two has become so blurred as to be meaningless. This chapter explores this idea and its implications for our account of 'politics'.

Klein's comments refer to the link between culture and political/social movements. There is, it might be suggested, a fairly obvious homology between the cultural practice and movement politics. Certainly, it can be argued that the demonstrations against the World Trade Organization meeting in Seattle, like the 18 June 'Carnival Against Capital', worked by, among other things, 'aesthetizing politics' and drawing on the kind of cultural practices which emerged through rave culture (McKay, 1996, 1998; Scott and Street, forthcoming). Such changes are part of the 'transformations' that I am concerned with in this chapter, but my main focus is on what might be called 'mainstream politics' (i.e. that associated with liberal democratic political parties and presidential candidates) because, on the surface at least, they seem less likely to be a site for the reconfiguration of politics as popular culture. My interest is in the question of whether the political practices of the mainstream can be seen as a form of 'artistic expression' which aspires to make politics 'fun' (even if it fails in this ambition).

It is, of course, now a commonplace to observe how politicians and parties exploit the techniques and icons of popular culture to promote their ideas and images. Tony Blair famously invited the key figures of Britpop to 10 Downing Street, just as US presidential candidates solicit endorsement from Hollywood stars. We have seen Bill Clinton on MTV playing the saxophone and Neil Kinnock appearing in a pop video. We are equally familiar with the fact that pop, film and even sports stars should use their celebrity status to support political causes. At one end, this process translates into a film actor like Ronald Reagan or a basketball player like Bill Bradley running for president; at the other, it translates into the worthy causes taken up by rock performers like Bob Geldof (starvation), Sting (Amazonian rain forests), Bruce Springsteen (human rights), Bono (Third World debt).

And running parallel to this are many ways in which popular culture has been a vehicle for political ideas and arguments – whether as state propaganda (Leni Riefenstahl) or as anti-state protest (Woody Guthrie or John Lennon). But what I want to suggest is that these examples, and the way they are discussed, tends to leave the categories of 'politics' and 'popular culture' largely undisturbed. The relationship is viewed as an instrumental or opportunist one, in which parties *use* popular culture, or in which artists *inject* political ideas into popular culture. Put simply, the parties remain the same vote-winning machines as before, just as the political ideas or causes of pop stars are in no way different because they are promoted by rock singers or appear in movies. Traditionally, the only point at which there appears to be a genuine integration of politics and popular culture occurs within the idea and language of subcultures. Whether in reference to punk in the 1970s (Hebdige, 1979) or dance culture in the 1980s/1990s (McKay, 1996), the suggestion is that participation in these subcultures constitutes a form of political activity, that the symbols and lifestyles of the subcultures destabilize conventional ways of life. But while there is undoubtedly political significance to be extracted from such subcultural activity, this argument rests, as critics of subcultural analysis pointed out (see Gelder and Thornton, 1997), on claims about popular culture generally (Why punk and not glitter? Why The Sex Pistols and not The Bay City Rollers?), and upon interpretations of cultural activity that the participants might neither share nor recognize.

My concern here is not, however, with what might be called 'the politics of popular culture', with the ways in which politics can be 'read' into cultural activity. Rather my interest is with the ways in which self-conscious political activity can be understood *as popular culture*, which I take to be another way of examining Klein's suggestion that political activity might be characterized as 'artistic expression' and as the source of 'fun'. This idea draws upon the language and approaches of cultural studies, but it is directed towards a better understanding of political activity and the forces transforming it.

Modernizing politics

There is now a considerable literature on the claim that politics has been transformed to accommodate new media and forms of communication (Franklin, 1994; Jamieson, 1984; Kavanagh, 1995; Scammell, 1995). Although the explanation is not always couched in terms of accommodation or adaptation, much is made of the ways in which political parties have devised new methods for reaching voters and amassing popular support. Typically, these refer to the use of the skills and techniques of journalists, advertising executives and TV producers to manage media coverage of their activities. These developments are not confined, though, to the traditional struggle over the media agenda and the reporting of news, but extend into a shift in emphasis on to visual imagery (appearance, photo-opportunities) rather than textual exegesis, on sharply honed slogans (the soundbite) rather than elaborate discourse and on to branding strategies (the celebrity endorsement) rather than ideology.

In their international survey of such changes in party practice, Paolo Mancini and David Swanson (1996) argue that these innovations have to be understood as a process of modernization. The new communication techniques, though associated with 'Americanization', are essentially about managing social complexity, the key indicator of modernization. The transformation is not seen as a form of Americanized global culture in which everyone does politics the American way. Rather 'Americanization' is linked to a particular set of professionalized campaigning techniques. These techniques are addressed to two dimensions of social complexity. The first refers to structural transformations in old hierarchies, in the ways in which parties, together with systems of education and religion, played an integrative role. The second dimension of social complexity refers to the symbolic. 'Old aggregative anchors of identity and allegiance in traditional structures,' write Mancini and Swanson (1996: 8–9), 'are replaced by overlapping and constantly shifting identifications with microstructures that themselves are always entering into changing patterns of alliances with other structures in search of more effective ways of advancing interests.'

This general shift in the nature of modern politics, and the social circumstances that underlie this shift, account for the increasing personalization of politics. Parties can no longer afford to be anchored to one set of interests and identities, but must become 'catch-all' parties. Cohesiveness is no longer a matter of party structure and constitution, but rather of individual leaders who provide a focus for the diverse interests clustered around the party. It is this that results in the personalization of politics.

The impact of social change on party structure and character is but one element of the modernizing process. Another ingredient is the 'emergence of mass media as an autonomous power center' (Mancini and Swanson, 1996: 11). These mass media not only play a decisive role in communicating political ideas and setting political agenda, they also serve to reinforce the personalization of politics. This is not simply because they reflect and project the new party form; it is because 'the format of television favors personalization' (Mancini and Swanson, 1996: 13). It does so because television genres operate at the level of the individual rather than the collectivity, and these genres draw upon the conventions and demands of advertising which also operates at the level of the individual (particularly the individual as consumer).

The medium is not just important in personalizing politics; it also helps to constitute the audience. Viewers are constituted as spectators and politics as the spectacle (Mancini and Swanson, 1996: 16–17). This means that politics operates less as a rational process of cost–benefit analysis and of measurable policy consequences, and more as series of symbolic gestures to which we respond (as we do to soap operas and other forms of mass media). One sign of this is, as some observers have noted, the way in which election coverage focuses the battle of appearances (this photo-opportunity, that soundbite). The election became a contest between flickering images, rather than an elaboration of competing principles and policies (which, it is assumed, was once the case). The journalists were doing this for the best of reasons – bringing to their audience's attention the attempts at media management they were witnessing – but in doing so they were reinforcing the idea that this was all there was to elections: the struggle for a particular image.

Mancini and Swanson's overview provides a valuable framework from within which to explore the transformation of politics. What they give us is the thought that there are social, political and cultural trends which together create the conditions for personalizing politics. What is missing from this account is the question of how the political personality is itself constituted in this process.

Politicians as television personalities

If politics is personalized, then the issue becomes the form taken by these personalities. Joshua Meyrowitz (1985), for example, argues that there is a kind of technological determinism at work which, in general terms, brings politicians down to our level. By this he means that the medium of television has the effect of undermining the capacity for politicians to act as leaders in the traditional sense. They can no longer function as Roosevelt and Churchill once did. This is because television presents them as 'ordinary' and not 'great', and in so doing denies them the ability to inspire us to take risks and make sacrifices. Television, with the intimate gaze of the close-up and its focus on the small gestures of everyday conversation, makes ridiculous declamatory rhetoric and grand statements. For Meyrowitz, political communication is forced to take on the style of television's naturalism, and to adopt the codes and conventions that television demands. Meyrowitz's argument rest upon a claim about the general form of television, and as such it says more about what television cannot do and represent than about what it can offer. By focusing on the technical form of television, and besides the risk of technological determinism, Meyrowitz's account overlooks the details of genre that organize the coverage of politics.

Roderick Hart's *Seducing America*, while taking a similar line to Meyrowitz, is more sensitive to the power of generic convention, as opposed to the 'logic' of technical form. Hart (1999: 2) argues that television 'has changed how politics is conducted and how it is received', and to analyse this we need, says Hart (1999: 11), a 'new phenomenology of politics'. According to Hart (1999: 4), the forms of intimacy which television deploys serve to make the traditional public sphere of politics 'seem more private'. In this process, politics takes on the generic conventions of the medium – politics becomes melodrama through the recounting of personal anecdotes, interviews become therapeutic encounters (Hart, 1999: 25–9). But Hart goes beyond observing the representation of politics to comment on its *effects*. Drawing on Raymond Williams, Hart suggests that we have to understand how television, in representing politicians as personalities, structures feelings (Hart, 1999: 70). As television presents politics through the generic conventions of television, so politics is presented in 'television's most natural language'; this is the language of cynicism (Hart, 1999: 9). 'Television,' writes Hart (1999: 10, his emphasis), *'makes us feel good about feeling bad about politics.'* The suggestion is that the generic forms taken by television impose themselves on politics.

Such claims represent important components in the suggestion that politics has been transformed. But this move still leaves us short of important details. In particular it says little about the skills and techniques which politicians themselves bring to the medium. It is evident that some are better performers than others; or, less controversially, that they perform differently. The difference lies in the extent to which they manage to constitute themselves as 'popular', where this is not some absolute standard but rather is an ideal to which politicians aspire in their relations with voters. Politicians strive to find forms of address that give the appearance and effect of popularity. In traditional forms of political campaigning this is achieved in the role played by crowds (the kissing of babies and the shaking of hands) or mass meetings (the standing ovation). In mass media, though these images appear as part of everyday paraphernalia of photo-opportunities or soundbites, the real attention is upon the construction of a mass-media popularity, itself constituted within the conventions and techniques of popular culture.

Politicians as celebrities

In mass media, popularity is often, but not exclusively, linked to the notions of celebrity and fame. 'Popularity' is not some given fact of political effort and ability, but is culturally constituted, its constitution differing according to cultural and historical context (Braudy, 1997). The modern politician is required to seek popularity according to prevailing norms, and the current norm, argues David Marshall (1997), is that of 'celebrity', itself a direct product of the popular culture of film, television and pop music.

Marshall (1997: 203) suggests a strong parallel between a politician and an entertainer: 'In politics, a leader must somehow embody the sentiments of the party, the people, and the state. In the realm of entertainment, a celebrity must somehow embody the sentiments of an audience.' For Marshall, the two realms are connected through their mutual reliance on the rhetoric and devices of advertising: 'The product advertising campaign provides the underlying model for the political election campaign. Both instantiate the prominence of irrational appeal within a general legitimating discourse of rationality. Both are attempts to establish resonance with a massive number of people so that connections are drawn between the campaign's messages and interests of consumers/citizens' (Marshall, 1997: 205). Marshall (1997: 206) pursues this logic: 'The leader is re-constructed as a commodity', just as pop singers and film stars are constructed as commodities.

This is not just an elaboration of the economic model of democracy associated with Anthony Downs and Joseph Schumpeter, in which parties and politicians act as entrepreneurs act within the commercial market. For Downs and Schumpeter, politics is modelled on market exchanges, while Marshall is appealing to the idea of symbolic and cultural exchange. This is apparent in the way Marshall (1997: 226) draws a link between the public subjectivity of the film celebrity and that of the political leader. Just as film celebrities construct or are used to construct narratives, so too are political leaders – the narratives of national destiny and identity. This idea is perhaps most eloquently sketched in Michael Rogin's (1987) essay 'Ronald Reagan: the movie'.

What Marshall proposes is that political leadership be considered a generic form to be located within popular culture, and that we analyse and understand it as we understand other symbolic forms. But there is a danger in pursuing this similarity too far. We need to recognize that the film stars and politicians are not valued in the same currency. This is tellingly revealed in the way in which 'reputation' operates in politics.

Politicians and reputations

Celebrity in itself is insufficient to guarantee political popularity. When Jeffrey Archer was forced to resign as Conservative candidate for London mayor, because he was exposed as guilty of deception, his political career was ended; he has remained 'popular' as a writer, but not as a politician. Reputation matters in politics in different ways to that which it matters in other cultural forms, but it is a central component in the way which politics is enacted and understood. As Margaret Scammell (1999: 729, her emphasis) writes, 'Reputation . . . is the *only thing of substance* that a party can promote to potential voters.'

This line of argument emerges in John Thompson's (1997) analysis upon political scandal. He is not just content to note the way in which the media propagate scandal, but rather to draw attention to the role of the media in creating (and destroying) the key political resource of 'reputation'. A politician's ability to function as a politician depends on their ability to persuade and cajole, and their capacity to do this is crucially dependent on the trust in which they are held. 'Reputation' is a measure of this trust, and to lose it is to lose the power to act, to lose access to the political realm. As Thompson (1997: 58) writes: 'If we understand reputation as a kind of resource that individuals can accumulate and protect, then we can see why scandals often involve much more than the transgression of values or norms: they are also struggles over power and the sources of power.' In the UK, this loss of reputation and its political impact was brutally revealed in the careers of Neil Hamilton and Jonathan Aitken. Their loss of reputation was a result of how these politicians were represented through the popular rhetoric of 'sleaze', and the cultural iconography on which it draws.

In focusing on the place of reputation in politics, Thompson is not just drawing attention to the obsession with 'sleaze'. He is arguing that political power is forged through and with the elements that constitute 'reputation'. Thompson's argument, in refining the way in which we understand politics and political leadership, also advances the general claim that politics can be understood as a form of popular culture.

Politics as popular culture

So far I have tried to show how, according to a variety of different commentators, politics finds itself allied to popular culture. These writers have pointed to the ways in which conventional political organizations and actors have come to adopt, or be incorporated into, mass media and the generic conventions that operate within it. Politics has in this sense become coterminous with popular culture. The point is, however, that the story does not end here. We need to look more closely at the popular cultural forms within which politics is enveloped, if only because many of the observations about politics' alliance with popular culture are couched as criticisms. Politics is being, in the familiar phrase, 'dumbed down'. Now it is one thing to acknowledge changes in the form and character of political communication, it is quite another to pass judgement upon it. For the latter it is not enough just to assume that because politics communicates through the conventions of advertising it is automatically operating at a lower level. This is to make unwarranted claims about both how politics *was* communicated and about advertising. The critics may have a point, but for it to be made persuasively we need to look more closely at the objects of criticism. One way to do this is look in detail at particular examples where politics is articulated through the medium and conventions of popular culture. I have chosen two case studies. The first is a video (*Do It*) produced by the Labour Party in 1997, the second is an appearance by Tony Blair on *The Des O'Connor Show* in 1998.

Do It

In the run-up to the 1997 election, the Labour Party sent a video to the homes of young voters (Norris *et al.*, 1999: 37). This short video – the length of a standard pop single – had two obvious purposes. The first was to encourage people to vote, and the second was to get them to vote Labour. Neither of these purposes were immediately evident to any individual recipient. Along the side of the box was the slogan 'just play it', and on the front cover were the words 'do it' (and here there was a small clue: the 't' resembled a ballot paper 'X'). There was no mention of a political party or of politics of any kind.

Once the video starts, though, the first of its messages becomes clear quickly. The opening shot is of a red front door, and on the mat a newspaper front page, whose headline reveals that are three days to go before the general election. Then, through the letter box comes the mail, including a polling card (notifying the anonymous recipient of the details of their polling station). Pages ripped from a calendar mark the passing of the days to the election, and then the card is taken from a pin board and placed in the breast pocket of a blue denim shirt. The wearer turns out to be a casually dressed male – brown sneakers, cream trousers. We see nothing of his face, but as he walks through the streets to cast his vote he is greeted enthusiastically. An elderly man gives him the thumbs-up from a car; a young woman grabs flowers from a stall; another man hands out balloons; a lad having his hair dyed bright red leaps from his salon chair; the people rise from their tables at outdoor cafes to greet the passing figure. At the polling station, there are looks of admiration, even awe, from the polling staff. As our hero casts his vote, the crowd that has followed him vote too. Finally, as the previously anonymous figure casts his vote, he is revealed as Tony Blair, who smiles shyly to camera. The screen cuts to the handwritten slogan, 'do it', and Tony Blair's signature.

This entire story is cut to the sound of D:Ream's 1993 hit 'Things Can Only Get Better', the song that became Labour's theme tune. The video resembles a pop video – an anodyne version of Prodigy's 'Smack My Bitch Up', which chronicled a debauched night on the town by a figure whose identity, too, is only revealed at the end. But this aspect of the video also draws from other genres, most obviously the British TV quiz show *Question of Sport*, in which the teams have to guess the identity of a fellow sportsperson in a film clip in which, as with the Labour video, the full face is revealed only at the end. Besides pop video and TV formats, the video also draws heavily on advertising tropes. 'Just play it'/ 'Do it' echoes Nike's 'Just do it'. The pied piper effect (the crowd that follows Blair to the polling station) is also reminiscent of other advertise-ments in which people gather one-by-one to be seen together at the end. These familiar references points provide neat short-cuts and associations through which to reach the target audience. The video works to the extent that the codes are easily decoded. But the video carries other messages. Everyone is attractive, able-bodied, and mostly young. The streets are clean, the weather sunny, the people friendly.

Do It is a political pop video that is clearly intended to reach a particular audience. It is meant to be a bit of 'fun', but to deliver a serious message. Its reference points and style are those of popular culture, but to leave it here would be to overlook one crucial question: does it work, does it get the response it seeks? Whenever I have showed this video to groups of students, roughly the same age as the target audience, they have laughed mockingly. This laughter was a response to what they saw as the simple-minded nature of the video's message and the 'naffness' of the song. It may be that had the students seen the video on their own, their response would have been more muted, but seen in a group it failed in its ambition. So while *Do It* is a work of political popular culture, it is not a very good one. What *Do It* illustrates are the risks of using popular culture: the danger of not getting it right, not striking the right note according to the complex criteria by which popular culture is judged.

The Des O'Connor Show

A year after the general election of 1997, Tony Blair appeared on *The Des O'Connor Show*. Des O'Connor is a comedian and singer (although the latter skill is as often mocked as celebrated). His show is broadcast in a prime evening slot on ITV. In front of a studio audience, it mixes chat, songs and comedy. On the night Blair appeared, one of the other guests was Elton John. The show went out just as the World Cup was beginning, and the programme was dominated by football. The audience waved scarves printed with the names of the home nations; a children's choir ended the show with a World Cup song; and the guests, including Blair, were asked who they thought would win. O'Connor himself acted as an amiable, chummy host. The air of conviviality is, though, offset by his fixed, slightly nervous smile and exaggerated giggle.

This was Blair's second appearance on the show. His previous visit had been as Leader of the Opposition, when he had promised to return if Labour won the election. (He promised to return for a third time if England or Scotland won the World Cup, and to sing a duet with O'Connor. He was spared.) O'Connor introduced Blair as 'a politician who keeps his promises', and his entry from off-stage was accompanied by the theme tune to the film *Local Hero*. Both host and guest were in suit and tie, but Blair was the more formal of the two in his style and manner – he sat upright rather than sinking into the cushions on the sofa.

O'Connor's line of questioning seemed designed to get at the 'human'/ 'ordinary' side of the experience of being prime minister: what were the pleasures of the job ('meeting exciting people doing exciting things')?; what were the highlights (the Northern Ireland agreement – applause from the audience)?; what were the perks (he hadn't got tickets for the World Cup)? These led on to questions about his 'other life' – being a waiter in France, playing and watching football with 'the kids', trying his hand at tennis, renting a video, still strumming the guitar (a reference to the fact that Blair played in a group called Ugly Rumours when at Oxford). Then came several anecdotes, which included lines that might well have been pre-scripted. At a civic reception in France, his family were given a horse. 'I didn't know,' said Blair, 'whether to ride it or eat it.' Another, longer story was about his 'mother-in-law'. Was it true, asked O'Connor, that she acted as Blair's political advisor? This led into a story about how, at a visit to the home of the Spanish prime minister, when Blair was absent for the first three days because of the Northern Ireland talks, his mother-in-law sorted out the political business that Blair was meant to have dealt with. Though the 'mother-in-law' stereo-type framed the tale (O'Connor: Do you take her on holiday 'occasion-ally'? Blair: 'No, always, its obligatory'), it was also an opportunity to assert more formal notions of family closeness. He was quizzed about a tabloid story concerning 'Humphrey the Downing Street cat' – had he been put down? No he hadn't, but the story haunted him, and he was even asked about the cat by a visiting Italian politician (and Blair told the story using an Italian accent). A final anecdote recounted how he had to tell the Queen that he couldn't take her phone call (he was on a plane and had to switch off his mobile). The conversation ended back at football, and Blair's empathy for Glenn Hoddle, the England football coach – a tough job, taking tough decisions which will always be criticized.

O'Connor's treatment of Tony Blair was not significantly different from the way he treated his other main guest. Elton John was asked about being Chairman of Watford FC, rather than about his music; he was asked who would win the World Cup. Elton John was, though, a more relaxed interviewee, more attuned to the casual informalities of the chat-show, less worried about the possible repercussions of his utterances.

Blair's performance deployed the kind of devices that Hart (1999) characterizes as generically specific to television (the anecdote, the confession, etc.). These were used to develop a particular, pre-planned agenda. Television might configure the mode of address, but it did not set the political agenda. Blair, it seems, deliberately used the event to convey a number of messages, each intended to enhance or promote his political image, to 'brand' him. And it was about *him*, Tony Blair, rather than his party – Labour was not mentioned at all. One message was about his achievements, notably the Northern Ireland agreement, which appeared several times in different guises. Another was about the demands and importance of his job, revealed in his remarks about Glenn Hoddle and his anecdote about the Queen. A third message was about him as an ordinary, dutiful family man: doing regular things with his children, going on family holidays. And finally, there was a message about him as a personality. The jokes evoked an air of mild, carefully contained mischievousness, teasing ever so gently the conventions of proper behaviour or respectability (at least as they are thought to apply to the politically correct politician). These messages were not simply contained in the oral text but in the tones of voice, postures and facial expressions ('thanks' muttered through clenched teeth when O'Connor notes that he looks older after a year in office). Blair can, therefore, be seen to have used the opportunities provided by the chat-show to reinforces messages and images that are part of his political project.

At the same time, the format of the show, and the actions of the performers, sets in motion other meanings and images. The chat-show defines itself against other conversational televisual modes. It deliberately eschews the combative, confrontational mode of the standard political interview, which *de facto* allows politicians to deliver and defend their established theme or message, and in which the interviewer implicitly takes on the guise of the political opposition or the citizenry (Harris, 1991). The chat-show also defines itself against the confessional or revelatory mode of interview. In its political guise, this style seeks merely to explore, rather than challenge, the logic and implications of a given political position. In the UK, this interview mode was most closely associated with the ex-politician Brian Walden; in its non-political guise, it takes the form of psychotherapy (and one of its practitioners, Anthony Clare, is himself a psychiatrist). These are extended sessions of one-to-one interview in which particular themes or issues are explored at length. Each format defines itself against the other, and establishes particular roles and expectations for audience, interviewer and interviewee. The chat-show adopts the conventions of conversation, rather than interrogation or therapy; the interviewer takes on the role of a populist friend ('what everyone wants to know is . . .'), and provides a sympathetic and encouraging response to answers (at odds, say, with the scepticism of the political interviewer). The chat-show encourages informality, and in this sense seems more revealing. The audience is not addressed directly, but it looks, as it were, through the key-hole, eavesdropping on the conversation (Atkinson, 1984: 171). And the tone of voice, the trajectory of the discussion, is pitched to fit into a domestic setting.

There is, though, a further dimension to this exchange and the judgements it encourages. What is most distinctive about the chat-show (compared to most – but not all – political exchanges) is the presence of the audience. Their chorus-like commentary, although orchestrated from the studio floor, provides a set of reactions and responses which other forms of interview do not and which are only partially controlled by the two leading protagonists.

Blair's asides and jokes, his choice of accent and manner, all mediated partly by the studio audience's reaction, are also de-coded by the audience at home. As Paddy Scannell (1991: 3) has noted in his discussion of 'broadcast talk', 'the broadcasters, while they control the discourse, do not control the communicative event'. In front of a studio audience, however careful primed and presented, this element of control is further qualified. Where a politician is involved, continues Scannell (1991: 8), 'audiences make inferences about the character and competence of their elected representatives . . . on the basis of common-sense evaluations of their performances'. And, suggests Andrew Tolson (1991: 178), the chat-show, because it breaches the traditional protocols of the interview, 'presumes an increasing sophistication on the part of the television audience'. Where the politician is taking part in a chat show, the 'performance' is measured by different criteria, but it is assessed nonetheless. Blair's credibility as a 'lad' is tested by his knowledge of the 'appropriateness' of comparing the footballers Michael Owen and Teddy Sheringham, just as his remarks about family life are tested for their resonance with the daily routines of the audience. Blair's use of colloquial language, of joke-telling, of mimicry, all are part of the conventions of conversation. And as with any such conversation, the speaker is constructing an identity for themselves, in part deliberately, in part by default. However stage-managed, the chat-show format provides a different way of judging the politician, a way of measuring the extent to which they 'fit' into the home from which they are being watched. Does she seem like one of us? Does he *represent* us? Clearly, proper analysis of these revelations, or rather what is revealed, is beyond the scope of this chapter, and should, in any case, be addressed by empirical investigation. The point is that the chat show represents, like the Labour video, a form of political communication. But by the same token, the questions of whether this communication is justly to be identified as a sign of 'dumbing down' and whether it propagates Hart's cynicism cannot be answered by mere assertion. They too depend on closer scrutiny of the texts concerned and of the reactions they induce.

Conclusion

These two case studies represent particular examples of the claim with which this chapter has been concerned: the changing character of political communication, and the idea that politics be understood as a form of popular culture. The essence of this idea is that politics communicates through the techniques and rhetorics of mass media forms (pop videos, chat-shows, advertisements). My main concern has been to point to the kind of arguments that might be used to sustain the general thesis, and then to look at particular examples of popular cultural forms being incorporated into politics. It is not necessary to see the general claim as indicating a 'new politics'; arguably politics has always shared much with popular culture, but what is new is the explicit acknowledgement of mass mediated forms in political communication.

Drawing attention to politics as popular culture has important implication for the conduct of political analysis. Insofar as political thoughts and actions are symbolized and represented within popular culture, we need to draw upon literatures and approaches that have typically been found outside the formal bounds of political science. This, at least, is the implication of Naomi Klein's suggestion that politics can be seen as a form of 'artistic expression'. Her thought that it can also be 'fun' should lead us to think about the ways in which pleasure is constituted within popular culture. As Simon Frith (1996) has argued, the pleasures of popular culture are intimately connected to judgement of it. It is aesthetic judgement that underpins the value of popular culture. By the same token, if politics operates as a form of popular culture, it too has to be judged aesthetically (as well as in terms of political values, etc.). After all, the aesthetics of judgement are themselves ethical. Responses to Blair's performance on *The Des O'Connor Show* or to Labour's video entail judgements in which the aesthetic, the ethical and the political are entwined.

This means distinguishing between the popular cultural formats being employed, and between the skills of those who use them. 'Populism' is not a fact of popular culture, any more than it is of political rhetoric. Instead, the engagement with popular culture calls into play, for its audience (its citizens), the judgements that are always a product of engagement with popular culture, just as it tests the skills and imagination of the authors of the political communication. Caught in popular culture's embrace, political communication finds itself playing with one of popular culture's most practised modes – irony. The distancing effect of irony, the questions it poses for authenticity and integrity, creates new problems for politicians schooled in the conventions of democratic authenticity. The chat-show, as Tolson (1991: 178) observes, has an ambivalence inscribed in it: it is designed 'both to inform and to entertain; to appear serious and sincere, but also playful and even flippant'. These ambiguities, and the ironic reaction they evoke, can have negative political consequences – by making serious matters seem trivial – but it may also have positive democratic consequences.

References

Atkinson, M. (1984) *Our Masters' Voices*. London: Routledge.
Braudy, L. (1997) *The Frenzy of Renown: Fame and Its History*. New York: Vintage.
Franklin, B. (1994) *Packaging Politics: Political Communications in Britain's Media Democracy*. London: Edward Arnold.
Frith, S. (1996) *Performing Rites: on The Value of Popular Music*. Oxford: Oxford University Press.
Gelder, K. and Thornton, S. (eds) (1997) *The Subcultures Reader*. London: Routledge.
Harris, S. (1991) 'Evasive action: how politicians respond questions in political interviews', in P. Scannell (ed.), *Broadcast Talk*. London: Sage. pp. 76–99.
Hart, R. (1999) *Seducing America: How Television Charms the Modern Voter*. London: Sage.
Hebdige, D. (1979) *Subcultures*. London: Methuen.
Jamieson, K.H. (1984) *Packaging the Presidency*. Oxford: Oxford University Press.
Kavanagh, D. (1995) *Election Campaigning: The New Marketing of Politics*. Oxford: Blackwell.
McKay, G. (1996) *Senseless Acts of Beauty*. London: Verso.
McKay, G. (ed.) (1998) *DiY Culture: Party and Protest in Nineties Britain*. London: Verso.
Mancini, Paolo and Swanson, David (eds) (1996) *Politics, Media and Modern Democracy*. Westport, CT: Praeger.
Marshall, P. (1997) *Celebrity and Power: Fame in Contemporary Culture*. London: University of Minnesota Press.
Meyrowitz, J. (1985) *No Sense of Place*. Oxford: Oxford University Press.
Norris, P., Curtice, J., Sanders, D., Scammell, M. and Semetko, H. (1999) *On Message: Communicating the Campaign*. London: Sage.
Rogin, M. (1987) *Ronald Reagan: The Movie*. Berkeley, CA: University of California Press.
Scammell, M. (1995) *Designer Politics: How Elections are Won*. London: Macmillan.
Scammell, M. (1999) 'Political marketing: lessons for political science', *Political Studies*, XLVII: 718–39.
Scannell, P. (1991) 'Introduction: the relevance of talk', in P. Scannell (ed.), *Broadcast Talk*. London: Sage. pp. 1–13.
Scott, A. and Street, J. (forthcoming) 'New expressive gestures and old instrumental practices? The use of popular culture and new media in parties and social movements', *Information, Communication and Society*.
Thompson, J. (1997) 'Scandal and social theory', in J. Lull and S. Hinerman (eds), *Media Scandals*. Cambridge: Polity. pp. 34–64.
Tolson, A. (1991) 'Televised chat and the synthetic personality', in P. Scannell (ed.), *Broadcast Talk*. London: Sage. pp. 178–200.

Index